Risk Arbitrage

Introducing Wiley Investment Classics

There are certain books that have redefined the way we see the worlds of finance and investing—books that deserve a place on every investor's shelf. *Wiley Investment Classics* will introduce you to these memorable books, which are just as relevant and vital today as when they were first published. Open a *Wiley Investment Classic* and rediscover the proven strategies, market philosophies, and definitive techniques that continue to stand the test of time.

Books in the series include:

Risk Arbitrage

Guy P. Wyser-Pratte

WILEY

John Wiley & Sons, Inc.

Published by John Wiley & Sons, Inc., Hoboken, New Jersey.
Published simultaneously in Canada.

For general information on our other products and services or for technical support,
please contact our Customer Care Department within the United States at (800)
762-2974, outside the United States at (317) 572-3993 or fax (317) 572-4002.

Wiley also publishes its books in a variety of electronic formats. Some content that
appears in print may not be available in electronic books. For more information
about Wiley products, visit our web site at www.wiley.com.

Library of Congress Cataloging-in-Publication Data:

Wyser-Pratte, Guy P.
  Risk arbitrage / Guy Wyser-Pratte.
      p. cm. – (Wiley investment classics)
  Rev. ed. of: Risk arbitrage II. [c1982].
  Includes bibliographical references and index.
  ISBN 978-0-470-41571-9 (pbk.)
  1. Arbitrage.   2. Consolidation and merger of corporations.   3. Tender offers
(Securities)   I. Wyser-Pratte, Guy P. Risk arbitrage II.   II. Title.
  HG6041.W97 2009
  658.15'5–dc22

                                                            2008047000

Printed in the United States of America

10 9 8 7 6 5 4 3 2 1

Contents

v

Preface

R isk Arbitrage was originally the subject of the author's MBA Thesis at the Graduate School of Business Administration New York University in June, 1969. It was re-edited and published in The Bulletin of the Institute of Finance in May, 1971. It was republished by Salomon Brothers Center for the Study of Financial Institutions at the Graduate School of Business Administration New York University in 1982.

This updated version of Risk Arbitrage follows the development of the arbitrage community from the 1970s to the present time. A new chapter—"Active Arbitrage"—has been added to reflect the incipient melding of arbitrage and activism as a new art form.

The point of view of this work and its content reflects the author's practical experience as an arbitrageur/shareholder activist.

The author wishes to acknowledge the valuable assistance of the following people: his father, Eugene Wyser-Pratte, whose many years of arbitrage experience find their trace herein. He would also like to acknowledge the invaluable contribution of his two colleagues, Michael Kelly and Scott Principi who assisted in updating *Risk Arbitrage* to its present form. He also received valuable assistance from the administrative staff of Wyser-Pratte and Company in completing the work.

Chapter 1

Introduction

Derivation of Risk Arbitrage

The simple definition of "arbitrage"—buying an article in one
market and selling it in another—has undergone considerable re-
finement over the decades. Arbitrage had its origin in the late
Medieval period when Venetian merchants traded interchangeable
currencies in order to profit from price differentials. This "classic"
arbitrage, as it was and continues to be carried on, is a practically riskless venture in that the profit, or spread, is assured by the
convertibility of the instruments involved.

Communications, rudimentary as they were, assumed strategic
importance on the European financial scene. The notable London
merchant bank of Rothschild, as the story goes, staged an un-
precedented "coup de bourse" by use of carrier pigeons to receive
advance notice of Wellington's victory at Waterloo. Upon learn-
ing the news, Rothschild began, with much ado, selling various

securities, particularly British Government Bonds, on the London Stock Exchange. This was naturally interpreted as a Wellington defeat, thereby precipitating a panicky selling wave. The astute—and informed—Rothschild then began quietly purchasing, through stooges, all the Government Bonds that were for sale. When an earthbound messenger finally brought the news of an allied victory, Rothschild had a handsome profit.

As identical securities began to be traded on the different European exchanges, and as communications evolved from the pigeon to the wireless, simultaneous transactions in securities arbitrage gave way to "tendency" arbitrage. Thus, if for example one had good wire communications with London and Paris, where an identical security was being traded, one would try to detect a general market tendency in both markets. Should there prove to be sellers in London and buyers in Paris, an arbitrageur would sell into the buying in Paris, and try to cover his short position somewhat later when the selling tendency bottomed out in London; or vice versa. In any event, improved market liquidity and more advanced communications were providing the opportunity for "tendency" as well as "simultaneous" transactions.[1]

Riskless arbitrage found its way into the American securities market by way of instruments that are convertible into common stock (i.e., convertible bonds and convertible preferred stocks, rights, and warrants). This kind of arbitrage, according to Morgan Evans, ". . . is not a wild scramble of buying X common in New York, then selling it in San Francisco in a matter of moments, like the international arbitrageur who buys Shell Trading in Amsterdam and sells it in New York. Instead it is chiefly concerned with the buying of a security at one price and the selling of its equivalent (security) at a higher price, usually in the same market. . . . Convertibility of exchangeability lies solely in one direction. In this respect it differs from . . . two-way convertibility or exchangeability, which is associated with the foreign exchange markets."[2]

There were two distinct developments in the 1930s that had a profound influence on the evolution of arbitrage in the United States. First, many railroads in the late thirties were coming out of bankruptcy. In order to remove their heavy debt burdens and improve their capital structures, many of them were reorganized, (i.e., recapitalized). These reorganization plans, which had to be approved by the various classes of security holders, often required the issuance of new securities to be exchanged for the old debt and preferred issues. Arbitrageurs, finding that they could sell such new securities on a "when-issued" basis, would buy the shares being recapitalized at prices lower than, or below the parity of, these "when-issued" securities. These price discrepancies, or spreads, were available because of the inherent risk that the reorganization plan might not be consummated, thereby precluding the requisite one-way convertibility. The arbitrageur was able to take advantage of the spread and willing to incur the risk. Arbitrage was now moving, in fact, from riskless to risk operations.

The second and equally important development in this period was the 1935 Public Utility Holding Company Act, requiring many public utilities to divest themselves of their holdings of subsidiaries. As the parent companies formulated divestiture plans, "when-issued" markets developed not only in the shares of their subsidiaries, but also in the stock of the parent ex-distributions. Arbitrage was thus possible when the sum of the prices of these "when-issued" securities (i.e., the sum of the parts) was greater than the market price of the parent company (the whole) cum-distributions.

"The profits realized from these recapitalizations and reorganizations led the arbitrageur ultimately to exploit the stock price differentials, or spreads, available in mergers, liquidations, and tender offers."[3] The spreads were, however, only turned into profit when the necessary one-way convertibility of the riskless arbitrage became a legal fact through consummation.

The expansion of risk arbitrage on Wall Street is directly attributable to the great corporate merger wave of the 1960s when a surging supply of selling candidates was matched by an equally impressive list of buyers. The new notion of "synergy," that one plus one equals three, gained acceptability; inflated stock prices provided cheap financing in an ever-tightening money market; accounting for acquisitions on a "pooling of interests" basis permitted seductive proforma earnings calculations for acquisition-minded companies; and most important, a variety of tax savings was intensively exploited via a variety of security-exchange packages.

While this 1960s merger wave enabled the arbitrageur to develop expertise in the realm of risk arbitrage, the trade itself continued to generate new types of situations where the professional could apply a sharp pencil. In addition to mergers and recapitalizations, then, risk arbitrage, came to encompass stock tender offers, cash tender bids, stub situations, and spinoffs. As the number of synergistic mergers declines in weak securities and tight monetary markets, liquidity or necessitous mergers and un-merging activities are providing work for the enlarged arbitrage community.

The Arbitrage Community

"The big money makers of Wall Street often mask their expertise in mystery, and among them the most mysterious is a cliquish band of specialists known as arbitrageurs. On the Street, they are a peculiar group apart, noted for their ability to spot instantly tiny profits that can be jockeyed into big ones. 'It would take me an hour of paperwork to see that profit,' says one member of the New York Stock Exchange, 'and in that hour the chance would be gone.' Says another: 'I think of them as vague shadows with European backgrounds. I don't even know who they are.'"[4] Arbitrageurs love it that way.

The financial press has increasingly tried to explore the activities of the risk arbitrageurs over the past few years, yet has been unable to delve with any depth into their operations. Many arbitrageurs have been approached, but have been generally unhelpful, though congenial. "Arbitrageurs tend to keep their operations to themselves. 'Frankly, I'd prefer the average person didn't know how to accomplish arbitrage,' says one. 'Therefore, the less I say about it, the better.'"[5] Even Morgan Evans, whose *Arbitrage In Domestic Securities In The United States* surpasses anything yet published on the subjects of both riskless and risk arbitrage, falls short in explaining the modus operandi of these professionals.

The Arbitrage Community, then, consists of a dozen-plus Wall Street firms, who commit house capital as one of their primary functions, in the various forms of arbitrage. The list includes such outstanding firms as Lehman Brothers-Kuhn Loeb, Goldman Sachs, L.F. Rothschild, Morgan Stanley, and Salomon Brothers.

Many of the arbitrage firms will engage the capital of foreign banks in risk arbitrage situations. Most are reluctant to do so for domestic clients, as the latter are thought to be somewhat less discreet than their European counterparts. Some, in order to avoid conflicts of interest, will avoid arbitrage for client accounts altogether.

The Community is extremely cliquish. Each member of the club has his own particular set of friends within the Community with whom he will freely exchange ideas and information, often via direct private wires. Sometimes good friends will even work on a joint account for a particular deal. But to all others, both within and without the Community, the member will turn a cold shoulder.

Many Wall Street firms and many private investors have tried, at one time or another, to participate in risk arbitrage activity. Having neither (a) schooling or experience in the finer points of the trade, (b) the requisite expert staffs, or (c) membership in the Community, they tend to fall by the wayside. The cancellation of a few proposed mergers always singles out the amateurs and sends them scurrying back to the good old-fashioned business of investing in securities.

Any proper discussion of the Wall Street arbitrage community's changing dynamics over recent decades would be incomplete without some consideration of the context in which these professional traders were operating. For it has always been the talent of the skilled arbitrageur to distill from a complex and ever-changing marketplace, those opportunities that others fail to capture. As the most popular, or, as some might say, "notorious" community of arbs operated primarily in the field of mergers and acquisitions, a brief synopsis of the developments of the structure of the M&A business is essential for any student in assessing the challenges that confronted arbs as they adapted and thrived in the growing world of risk arbitrage. The mergers and acquisitions business as it existed in the late 1960s may seem like a foreign landscape to today's student of Wall Street practices. While each passing decade has brought new developments in the structure and pace of the deal market, the 1970s and 1980s were particularly formative years in laying the groundwork for the modern deal structure. Indeed, few developments in recent years match the pace of innovation seen during this critical period. The arbitrageur who ventured into these markets needed to be both agile and somewhat innovative in his own right. With the public face of the arbitrageurs, as well as the banker, and other participants, in the deal community becoming clearer, their activities gained a notoriety not seen before on Wall Street. The takeover battles of the 1970s assumed a "spectator sport" appeal to the rest of the financial and business community. Amid the growing deal frenzy, arbitrageurs grappled with an ever-changing terrain, formed by the ebb and flow of the economic, political, financial, and legislative conditions that were all refocused during this profound reshaping of corporate America.

A Changing Community from the 1970s to 2000

1970s

The 1970s saw the initial deal wave of the late sixties gather considerable momentum and, in the process, broaden the variety and the style of acquisition structure available to the corporate buyer. With mixed reactions from within the community, it also introduced the arbitrageur to the public. As could be expected, attention begets even greater attention and by the end of the decade the arbitrageur might be said to be swimming in a sea of deals . . . and arbitrageurs!

The 1970s could best be characterized as the years that propelled the M&A business toward increasingly novel and flexible deal structures. The unfolding techniques were more aggressive, the press more inquisitive, and the once congenial club of arbitrageurs who plied their expertise out of only a handful of firms found themselves in a market crowded by newer players.

One of the more significant developments, foreshadowed by the 1969 hostile takeover bid for BF Goodrich by Northwest Industries, was the first truly large-scale hostile cash tender offer. Launched in 1974 by Inco for ESB Corporation, the offer was significant not only for this new currency of the hostile offer, but also for what it represented: a bold new dimension in the world of deal making. The significance to the arb community was in the additional arrow it placed in the quiver of the would-be corporate buyer and, of course, the modification of the risk/reward considerations for those who assumed positions in such deals. Any expansion in the options available to bidder corporations expands in equal measure the profitable opportunities for the arbitrageur. In taking an offer directly to the shareholders, the debate over the appropriate balance between a board's fiduciary obligations, and shareholder's rights, began inching toward center stage—a position it would firmly occupy decades later. As "shareholder-friendly" generally equated to "arb-friendly," the new hostile tenders were, of course, greeted with open arms.

The decade was not finished with innovation, however, and the next change to come would involve the allocation of payment that the arbitrageur received. Typically, a tender offer for control is followed by a squeeze-out merger to bring the bidder to 100 percent control. Conventional expectations at this time were that an owner of stock acquired in a deal, whether hostile or friendly, would receive equal monetary consideration on both the front and back ends. The value of cash or non-cash consideration paid in the first stage tender offer would equal the consideration on the back end. The first significant departure from this assumption took place in the takeover fight for Pullman between McDermott and Wheelabrator Frye. McDermott offered a package that featured cash on the front end, with back-end securities that were markedly lower in value than the front. Ultimately, Pullman was acquired by Wheelabrator in a white knight rescue, but the "two-tiered" offer had arrived. It altered some of the financial constraints normally associated with the structure and financing of a bid, adding to the deal frenzy by allowing for more creatively structured deals and a reduced reliance on cash in a hostile approach.

The arbitrage community, while enjoying the increase in deal volume, was less excited by the new entrants it attracted to the business. The arb's return on investment is a direct function of the demand for that particular spread. With five or six arbs willing to trade a deal for no less than a 25 percent annualized return, the arrival of a new player who is willing to accept 20 percent compresses the profit available to the others. The new player will bid up the target's price while selling down the acquirer's price, leaving those who require a higher return outside or "away" from the market. This new crowding of the arb market can best be described in the words of the arbs themselves during this period as printed in a story run by Barron's.

"By the seventies . . . the arbitrage community was having difficulty hiding its role in the mounting volume of corporate takeovers. In 1975, Ivan Boesky, lawyer, accountant, and securities analyst, established what probably was the first large limited partnership specializing in risk arbitrage. Boesky, to attract capital and much to the disgust of the rest of the community, stomped all over the unwritten rule proscribing publicity. "Boesky was the first of the queens to come out of the closet," says Alan Slifka, a partner in L.F. Rothschild Unterberg Towbin's arbitrage division. In 1977, Boesky was spread across two pages of *Fortune*, wreathed in smiles over the $30 million he and a handful of other arbitrageurs had picked up in the takeover of Babcock & Wilcox by United Technologies. The jig was up!

Money poured into risk arbitrage. Merrill Lynch and Morgan Stanley quickly set up arbitrage departments. Many experienced arbitrageurs formed their own limited partnerships, and a whole slate of smaller firms joined the act.

With quality firms selling for bargain-basement multiples, it had become cheaper for a company to acquire another than to make a capital investment itself. But the flat equity markets also meant that takeover stocks became "the only game in town"—a game in which hungry registered representatives were eager to interest equity-shy clients. At least two large brokerages, Oppenheimer & Co. and Bear Stearns, launched an organized assault publishing research for retail and institutional clients. No figures are available, but the guesstimate is that as much as half the arbitrage activity in some deals was "non-professional."

"A shakeout is the best thing that could happen in this business," says John Monk, an arbitrageur at Cohn, Delaire and Kaufman. Chief among Monk's beefs is the narrowed spreads brought about by too many players jockeying for a piece of the same action. "The single greatest complaint I hear these days is the spreads," Monk says. "A few years ago, if $25 was bid for a company, you might see it open up at $19 or $20. Everybody was reasonable. Today, spreads are nothing."

Disorderly markets are another problem. "There are 33,000 registered reps out there," continues Monk, "and they can cause severe dislocation in the market. The non-professionals tend to get out at the first sign of trouble, dumping all their stock back into the market."

Complains Steve Hahn of Easton & Co.: "There never used to be any problem of getting as much stock as you wanted. Now I find sometimes I'll go after 5,000 shares of something and only be able to get, say, 3,000." But arbitrageurs used to dealing in blocks ten or a hundred times larger scoff at such squawks. Their sanguine philosophy is that "when the going gets tough, the tough get going." Says one whose firm is believed to put some $100 million at the disposal of its arbitrage department: "Markets have a magnificent way of correcting themselves. For example, if you take a situation like we saw with Marathon, where the stock was quickly run up to $90 after the Mobil bid of $85, you'll find that most of that was non-professional or inexperienced money. Not till the stock came down again to the low eighties did you find the arb money coming in a significant way."

Certainly, the year was trying for professionals and non-professionals alike. Stratospheric interest rates dampened most investment sectors. High rates cut two ways in arbitrage. On the one hand, the carrying costs must be factored into the spreads on any given deal, although one arbitrageur declares: "If the difference between 15 percent and 20 percent interest rates is the deciding factor in whether you do a deal, you probably shouldn't be even considering it in the first place."

It is the author's contention that the private as well as the institutional investor should be more conversant with risk arbitrage, for it often appears as though one-half of the list on the New York Stock Exchange would like to swallow the other half. Thus, stocks involved in mergers and other forms of risk arbitrage will often perform in accordance with other than their fundamental or technical characteristics. In addition, the average investor should know how to evaluate a particular package of securities offered in exchange for those securities that he is holding. The answers to some of these problems will enable the investor to make an important investment decision: whether to hold his position in the security, or dispose of it. It is thus the author's intention to explain and describe these market reactions by discussing the various activities in which the arbitrageur gets involved.

Whereas in the first edition of *Risk Arbitrage* there was extensive coverage of merger arbitrage reflecting the emphasis of the 1960s, cash tender offers became much more important in the 1970s and 1980s and are given greater coverage in later sections. Indeed, cash tenders became the favorite vehicle for effecting what were called "Saturday Night Specials," or hostile tender offers. It will be shown in the examples that follow that participation in these cash tender offers was far more profitable for the arbitrage community than participation in mergers, in that the former usually forced the target brides to seek competitive bids.

1980s

The eighties brought the arbitrage business to new heights on the back of the largest takeover boom to date. Propelling the expansion in deals was the introduction of high-yield-bond or "junk" financing for hostile takeovers. The concept of purchasing a corporation using its own assets as the collateral had been long pondered but not put to significant use with public companies. This decade brought such action and did so on a scale never before imagined. The prowess of Michael Milken's junk bond desk at Drexel Burnham Lambert was such that, at times, it seemed that no deal was too big or too bold to be launched. The unbridled success, or some may say, excess of Drexel financing and those who profited from it would ultimately end in the indictment of arbitrageur Ivan Boesky, and later Milken, in a widespread insider trading scandal. Alongside these developments came the beginnings of the collapse of the junk bond market and Drexel itself. But not before this financing machine and the man who ran it left an indelible mark on both M&A and the arbitrage business.

What Milken created was a market for corporate raider debt obligations. Milken's new debt instruments stood on their own, requiring no convertibility to equity. They allowed the corporate raider to, among other things, finance a bid entirely in cash and work around the Mill's Bill, which had disallowed the deduction of interest on takeover debt linked to equity. A raider needed only a "highly confident" letter from Drexel that it could raise the necessary financing and it could be assured that its intentions would be taken seriously by the Street and a target's board.

The eighties also brought an increase in the frequency of "white knight" rescues. Among some notable examples were DuPont's 1981 winning bid for Conoco following an initial bid from Seagrams and Occidental Petroleum's 1982 rescue of Cities Service from T. Boone Pickens' Mesa Petroleum. That year also brought a new term to the deal lexicon: PacMan defense—used to describe a defensive tactic where the target of a hostile offer bids for its suitor. Bendix found itself the victim of such a defense by Martin-Marietta after it had launched its own hostile bid for the latter. In the end, Bendix was acquired in a white knight rescue by Allied Corporation. All of these situations meant one thing for the arbitrageur: opportunity. The frequency of bidding wars was obviously a boon to the community. As the decade progressed both the risk arbitrage and M&A businesses would be shaped by the opposing forces of the Drexel money machine and, on the legislative side, the counterweight of antitakeover legislation.

One of the more onerous developments of the 1980s was the widespread adoption of the "poison pill" takeover defense. In upholding the pill, the Delaware Superior Court essentially sanctioned a device that would for years impair the rights of shareholders to receive a fair price from a suitor deemed unfriendly by a sitting management. The obvious conflict between this new antitakeover defense and the basic rights of shareholders was, and is to this day, inexplicably lost on the Delaware courts. Adopted by a simple board resolution, the poison pill had the effect of a charter amendment without shareholder approval. The basic concept behind a poison pill was to dilute the voting power of a hostile shareholder by disallowing its shareholder's equal participation in a discount stock issue that would be triggered by the raider crossing a stated percentage shareholding threshold. In the 1985 case of Moran vs. Household International the Delaware Supreme Court rejected a request by Moran to strike down Household's poison pill. This historic decision solidified the presence of an antidemocratic takeover device that, regrettably, continues to undermine shareholder rights.

The stock market crash of 1987 was the defining event of the decade and brought the first major macroeconomic shock to the arb community. Since, at the time, most of the high-profile announced deals were for cash consideration, the arbitrageur lacked the short side which, when moving in tandem with the long, insulates a position from day-to-day market movements. Spreads widened so sharply on that historic day that the entire arb community suffered significant losses. The question in the immediate aftermath of the crash was: What's next? Opinions varied on the future of the risk arbitrage business as the financing of mergers and acquisitions business itself hinges on investors' appetite for risk. Some firms elected to close their arbitrage operations entirely, while others, seeing a quick end to what they believed was simply an index arbitrage meltdown, elected to extend additional credit lines to their arb desks. The idea was to capitalize on the drastically oversold market conditions and mispriced spreads brought on by the panic selling. Those firms that withstood the panic profited handsomely, as the market stabilized under the watchful eye of the Federal Reserve, spreads narrowed, and the naysayers were proven wrong. Only one year late in fact, KKR, armed with Drexel's war chest, won a bidding war and acquired RJR for $25 billion in the largest LBO to date.

A two-year respite from the 1987 turmoil was shattered in 1989 with the catastrophic collapse of the $300-per-share, union-led buyout of UAL. If the 1987 crash was the seminal event of the decade for the larger financial community, the UAL deal collapse was its counterpart to the arbitrageurs. Referred to in gallows humor as "United Arbitrage Liquidation" the UAL deal made tragically clear the meaning of "risk" in the risk arbitrage game. The one-day plunge in UAL's share price and the collateral damage from arb desks dumping positions to raise capital for margin calls sent the DJIA down a then-significant 190 points. UAL was a shining example of one of the many perils of an overheated market: the phenomenon of confidence overtaking caution, a time-tested recipe for disaster. With the benefit of hindsight, many an arb looked longingly at the prices of the out-of-the-money put options on UAL common stock just prior to the collapse. A simple married put strategy would have insulated every arb from the damage to their long positions. Instead, some arbs found themselves setting up their own shops as their benefactors shied away from the risk arb business entirely. The UAL deal, while a calamity in its own right, was also a symptom of a larger problem. The overleveraging and general excess that had for the better part of the decade consumed Wall Street was finally coming home to roost.

The decade that had brought so much innovation to the arbitrage community and M&A business, as well as to corporate America, was ending on a decidedly sour note. Suspicions that the junk bond market was beginning to live up to its name were exerting enormous pressure on Drexel's ability to sell new debt. The firm was suddenly rudderless without the presence of Michael Milken, who in 1988 had been indicted on 98 counts of fraud and racketeering. Drexel itself was busy fending off its own indictment from then New York Attorney General Rudy Giuliani, and the earlier insider-trading scandals involving Ivan Boesky, Dennis Levine, and John Mulheren had begun to shape a somewhat villainous image of the arbitrageur. The predictions at the time were dire. Risk arbitrage itself appeared to be imperiled by the tribulations of its host, the M&A business and, with a slowing economy raising fears of a recession, lighthearted Wall Street discussions of bidding wars gave way to more somber discussions of defaults and bankruptcies.

1990s

The early part of the next decade was a quiet period for the risk arbitrage business. The country was experiencing its first recession since 1982 and the job cuts and retrenchment within corporate America had all but extinguished the heady feel of the "go-go" eighties. Drexel Burnham in 1990 officially ended its reign as the premiere bond house on Wall Street when a series of credit rating downgrades forced it from the commercial paper market and into bankruptcy proceedings. The speed with which the junk bond powerhouse had risen to prominence and then vanished was stunning. The rest of corporate America was coping with the debt hangover of the eighties and the junk bond market, which once dominated conversation on Wall Street, was in ruins.

With the absence of an active deal market, spreads on announced deals suffered. The thinning of the arbitrage community had been more than offset by the scarcity of deals. This left the remaining arbs chasing few opportunities and doing so for lower returns. What followed was a movement by some firms into distressed arbitrage. In an attempt to capitalize on the rash of defaults and bankruptcies, some arbitrage departments turned their attention to valuing the outstanding debt of those companies that were facing restructuring. The idea was to then position their firm's capital in the debt of those companies in the hope of recovering a larger payout than a panicky bond market was anticipating. While this business was popular with some in the community, many arbs stood their ground, concerned by the lack of liquidity in some of the debt issues, and viewing the heavy component of bankruptcy law as well as the new structure of analysis as an imprudent stretch from their classical training. As the economy recovered, the risk arb business was again given life by the new catch phrases of corporate America: scale and global positioning. Corporations were finding that the needs for scale within industries and indeed across continents were again pushing them toward the consolidation game.

After the drought the arbs were ready. The mid and late nineties saw a wave of consolidation amid a tech boom that transformed the productivity of corporations on a scale not seen since the industrial revolution. It appeared that American CEOs had concluded that it was simply easier to purchase market share than to grow it organically, and they had at their disposal the perfect currency: their own stock. The rise in equity prices throughout the nineties was the same boon to stock deals as the availability of junk bond financing was to the cash deals of the eighties. As in most economic rebounds, CEOs were finding that out of the wreckage of recession they and their competitors were emerging with leaner balance sheets and attractive stock valuations. The newly expanding economy provided the impetus to adjust to a more aggressive growth focus and the deal machine was once again in high gear.

One of the notable developments of the decade involved the resilience of the poison pill and its ability to shelter boards using the "just say no" defense. The development was the increasing objection to the device by shareholders. The targets of two closely followed hostile deals faced a new element ... organized shareholder resistance. In 1995 Moore Corp launched a hostile offer for Wallace Computer. Wallace adopted the standard "just say no" defense and relied on its poison pill for protection. Moore Corp petitioned the Delaware Federal court to strike down Wallace's antitakeover defenses, namely the pill. Moore withdrew its offer after its petition failed and the pill was upheld, but not before Wallace found itself the target of a shareholder proposal to amend the company's bylaws so that its takeover defenses would terminate

90 days after a qualified offer had been received by the company. This event was one step in what became a turning point in the attitudes of shareholders toward recalcitrant boards. The "just say no" defense was now being reconsidered as an acceptable measure. What had been sanctioned by the Delaware courts was now coming under fire by popular revolt. The issue was again in focus in 1997 when the board of Pennzoil rejected a cash and stock offer from UPR. While the board consistently argued that the offer was too low, the real impediment was the company's poison pill and the prospect of costly litigation that it promised. After failing to bring Pennzoil's board to the negotiating table, UPR did in fact withdraw its offer, citing a deterioration in the value of Pennzoil's assets. To the arb it appeared more likely that the poison pill was the real culprit. While victorious in the end, Pennzoil, too, found itself the target of a shareholder revolt in the form of a proposal to elect a dissident director to the board and a demand for sweeping changes to the company's governance of change of control situations. It was becoming clear that by the late nineties, shareholders were no longer willing to accept a board's refusal to allow them to judge the fairness of an offer. Shareholders wanted their say as owners and their relationship to a board of directors was changing forever.

The arbitrage business continued to feel the influx of new players as it was being seen by increasing numbers of people as an attractive use of capital. The compression of spreads continued but by the late nineties the proliferation of derivatives was bringing pressure from a new direction. Spreads were being compressed not only by the volume of players but also by the margin that they employed. Arbitrage positions were now being taken by way of simple collateral deposits on derivative contracts, rather than through the actual purchase of common stock. The result was an amount of leverage that allowed arbs who were using these methods to profitably play spreads that appeared too thin for a profitable return. This action further squeezed the profit that was available by playing the deals through the common stock and began to raise the issue of whether the "risk" in risk arbitrage was being mis-priced.

2000

The current decade began in a manner reminiscent of some of the difficulties faced in the early nineties. In this instance, the aftermath of a speculative boom in Internet and technology stocks that had distorted both the traditional risk/reward expectations of investors, as well as the historical price to earnings multiples of entire sectors of the market, had utterly poisoned market sentiment. It was a period marked by the brutal and seemingly endless destruction of wealth that had been created in the dotcom boom of the late nineties. A new distrust of corporate management, sown by the accounting scandals at Enron and Worldcom, as well as by the complete collapse of the Internet stocks, was now deeply rooted in both Wall and Main streets. CEOs were now being required, for the first time, to certify their company's financial reports in writing. The performance of the equity markets reflected a nation of investors disenchanted by corporate malfeasance. The revelations were beginning to make the explosive equity returns of the nineties look, in hindsight, like nothing more than a shell game. Gone were the days when a technology company's CEO could entice the shareholders of a target company with the implied promise of two- or three-fold gains in the combined company's stock price. The folly of Internet stocks was being driven home even at staid, blue chip corporations like Time Warner which, in one of the most glaring examples of poor judgment in corporate history, had accepted AOL common stock in the two companies' much touted 2001 merger. The arbitrageur in these days was wise to maintain a full hedge, for while the deals were still being churned out by optimistic investment bankers, the risk of a collapse in an acquirer's stock price could have been lethal. What has defined the current decade more than any development in the arbitrage or investment banking field, are the changes in the relationship of shareholders to their fiduciaries at publicly traded corporations.

What in the 1970s and 1980s might have been described as a "rogue shareholder," was now operating under the label "activist." What started in the nineties as revolts against entrenched managements that had ignored their shareholders in rejecting high premium offers from unwanted suitors, was now an institution. Funds designed specifically for the purpose of engaging managements to enhance shareholder value were raising capital at an astonishing pace. The new idea was to establish a position in shares of an underperforming company and then present a solution, in the form of a new business plan, to management. In prior years, resistance had been common; the old "just say no" defense was still prevalent in boardrooms and the spirit of it had been used successfully against shareholders who wished to voice their concerns. The current decade brought a widespread change to attitudes regarding a shareholder's voice. Perhaps the distrust of managements had given way to a new willingness to demand, publicly, better performance from management. Activists, although still not genuinely welcome in the boardroom, were now warmly greeted by both the press and the investment community. Hedge funds, unencumbered by the investment banking ties of their larger competitors, were free to voice their opinions without the fear of a backlash from a parent company or an investment banking division fearful of losing its next underwriting fee. Activist funds were, in increasing numbers, succeeding in gaining board seats, and pushing agendas that ranged from changes to administrative governance frameworks, to more aggressive plans such as restructurings and even mergers. The age of the activist had clearly arrived. Once the low-hanging fruit at poorly managed U.S. corporations had been picked, activists turned their attention to Continental Europe. European companies were, by comparison, decades behind their western counterparts in the area of corporate governance. Equally archaic, however, were their attitudes toward shareholder's rights. The specter of a fund manager challenging a board of directors at a shareholder meeting was appalling to European managements and even to some of their large shareholders. The activist needed to plan a careful approach to avoid losing a public relations battle before his ideas were even on the table. As the decade progressed, even European managements began to adopt a more shareholder-friendly posture. European CEOs were recognizing that without reforms, their markets might be viewed as less efficient and therefore less competitive. Without efficiency, they might fail to attract capital from the international community. While the European business community has begun to change its attitudes toward active shareholders, the political establishment, particularly in Germany and France, continues to object to the participation of these funds in the management of public companies, on the grounds that they have no long-term interest in the companies themselves, or in the economies of the countries in which they invest. During the recent political season in Germany, for example, activists were labeled as "locusts" in an attempt to paint them, for political purposes of course, as the enemy of the German worker. The absurdity of this argument has not been lost on business leaders, and many have publicly cautioned their elected officials about the economic perils of appearing unwilling to embrace a more modern management philosophy that is inclusive of all ideas to enhance value. The activist battles between shareholders and managements in both the United States and Europe will undoubtedly continue for years to come. Any movement within the business community that has as its purpose the efficient management of a corporation's assets is unlikely to be derailed. Surely there will be mistakes and periods of backlash against aggressive shareholders, but the essential elements of the activist movement are here to stay.

One can examine the field of active value investing in terms that are quite familiar to the arbitrageur. It is possible to identify what is, in a sense, the spread in these situations. For each activist target there is a current market price, which can be seen as reflecting the performance of the current management. A research department may then analyze the potential values of the corporation's assets under an array of restructuring scenarios and arrive at a target price which, to a classically trained arbitrageur, might be the activist equivalent of a bid price under a traditional takeover scenario. The difference between the current market price and the anticipated values under each restructuring scenario can be considered "the spread." The spread could be captured in the event that the restructuring succeeds. An arbitrageur who commits capital to such a situation is taking both the risk that the proposal is accepted and that the proposal is sound. The time frame is of course considerably longer than the traditional risk arbitrage scenario, as it may require a full meeting cycle or longer for even the successful activist to implement a new agenda. What might be called "active arbitrage" is a demanding endeavor. Some investors from the arbitrage community elect to participate silently in the projects of other activists, while others are using their expertise in valuing corporations under restructuring scenarios, as well as their extensive knowledge of change-of-control scenarios and the attendant tactics associated with them, to initiate activist agendas themselves. Few professional investors, in fact, are better qualified to navigate the unique obstacles of corporate activism than the classically trained risk arbitrageur. The still-developing field of activism may hold great promise for those who honed their skills during the takeover wars of past decades.

Chapter 2

Merger Arbitrage

General

An arbitrageur is not an investor in the formal sense of the word: (i.e., he is not normally buying or selling securities because of their investment value). He is, however, committing capital to the "deal" (the merger, tender offer, recapitalization, etc.) rather than to the particular security. He must thus take a position in the deal in such a way that he is at the risk of the deal, and not at the risk of the market. He accomplishes this by taking a short position in the securities which are being offered, as part of the deal, in exchange for the securities which he purchases. So, in a merger of Company X into Company Y, the arbitrageur's investment is one of X long and Y short, or, the merger of X into Y. Once he has taken his hedged position, then the arbitrageur is no longer concerned with the vagaries of the marketplace—so long as the deal goes through. "If you're caught when a merger falls through, then you become . . . an investor."[1]

There is a definite and fairly common sequence to the arbitrageur's financial analysis that allows him to arrive at his investment decision. He (a) gathers information about the particular deal, (b) calculates the value of the securities offered, (c) determines the length of time he can expect his capital to be tied up in the deal, (d) calculates his expected per annum return on invested capital, (e) determines and weighs all the possible risks and problem areas that might preclude consummation of the transaction, (f) assesses the various tax implications and establishes his tax strategy, (g) determines the amount of stock available for borrowing in order to be able to sell short, and (h) determines the amount of capital to be committed to the deal based on a careful balancing of (a) through (g) above.

In this chapter, the author is concerned primarily with this sequence. In analyzying it, he will adopt the viewpoint of the arbitrageur who is with a member firm of the New York Stock Exchange. The author will digress from this viewpoint at times in order to compare it with that of the private or institutional investor.

Gathering Information

The arbitrageur's task begins with the announcement of a proposed merger, which will appear in the financial press, usually the *Wall Street Journal*, or perhaps the Dow Jones or Bloomberg, or other newswire. The arbitrageur's first question will be: "Is this a good deal?" The question pertains not so much to the potential profitability for the arbitrageur's firm, but rather to the business logic of the merger, the quality of the two partners proposing the marriage, their record of successful marriages, the fairness of the financial terms of the merger to the shareholders of the "Bride," and a post-merger proforma evaluation of the "Groom." The essential question here is: "Will the deal go through?"

The answers to many of the above questions may be obtained by an analysis of the annual reports of the companies, plus the write-ups in either Moody's or Standard and Poor's stock records. The business logic of the merger may require deeper analysis, particularly an assessment of industry trends together with an evaluation of the financial and competitive postures of both companies within their respective industries. It is often best to hear from the companies themselves the purported reasons for their proposed merger. It is at this point that the curtain rises on one of the great comic operas of Wall Street: obtaining information from the involved companies about their proposed merger. It is indeed comic because the companies will always present a rosy prognosis for the successful consummation of their proposed marriage, while the Arbitrage Community, always suspicious, will, in their conversations with the companies, try to draw out the hard and cold facts about the real state of affairs: the actual stage of the negotiations as well as the matter of business logic. Because of SEC police actions in the securities industry during the 1970s, getting answers from the companies, much less straight ones, has become habitually difficult. Even when companies do answer, the arbitrageur must carefully read between the lines, as the companies are aware that their answers may influence an arbitrageur to buy or sell their respective securities, and managements are extremely sensitive to market price fluctuations.

Approaching companies to gather information is thus ticklish for the arbitrageur. He must tailor his approach depending on whether he is interrogating the Bride or the Groom. The Bride is normally totally cooperative, realizing that the arbitrageur can, by purchasing her stock, accumulate votes that will naturally be cast in favor of the merger. So, to the Bride, the arbitrageur can candidly state his business. The Groom is an entirely different matter. He will not be pleased that his stock may become the subject of constant short selling by arbitrageurs; he is thus often elusive in his responses. To counteract this, the arbitrageur must often become the "wolf in sheep's clothing" by assuming the role of investment banker who seems to be desirous of assisting the Groom with his acquisition program—both the present proposed merger and future plans. In this manner the arbitrageur ingratiates himself with the host in order to ask those delicate questions about the pending merger negotiations. The arbitrageur may also don the grab of the institutional salesman who is attempting to place with institutional investors the new securities that may be offered to the Bride. If he is to sell those securities effectively, he must know the details of the merger, particularly the date when these securities will be issued, which will coincide roughly with the closing of the merger transaction. Not surprisingly, most Grooms with active acquisition programs are well aware of the guises of the arbitrageur. Some cooperate, others don't. Those whose stocks will least be affected by short selling seem to cooperate most.

The information that is sought from the companies is hardly of an "inside" nature—a fact most companies do not realize—but rather has to do with the information set and related decisions which will have to be made to consummate the merger, and the current status of the information. The arbitrageur's questions therefore, deal basically with the following:

a. The accounting treatment (purchase versus pooling)
b. The type of reorganization under the IRS Code: Statutory merger, sale of assets, etc.[2]
c. Whether a preliminary agreement has been reached, or whether the negotiations consist only of a handshake
d. If a definitive agreement has been reached, and if not, when
e. Conditions under which the definitive agreement may be terminated by either party
f. Whether a formal tax ruling will be required from the IRS, or whether parties will proceed on advice of counsel
g. The approximate date the application will be made for the tax ruling
h. The approximate date that the proxy material will be filed with the SEC
i. The date the proxy material is expected to clear the SEC and be mailed to the shareholders

j. The dates for the respective shareholder meetings
k. Where the major blocks of the companies' stock are held
l. The other rulings that may be required—FCC, CAB, Maritime Board, Federal Reserve Board, ICC, Justice Department, Federal Trade Commission (see paragraph on antitrust considerations)
m. The probable closing date

Once the arbitrageur has established the answers to some or all of the above, he will seek to verify anything either of the companies tells him or others. He will, for example, check with the SEC to determine that the proxy material has really been filed, with the IRS to ascertain that the tax ruling application has been filed, etc. As the seriousness of the companies' intent to merge is corroborated by activities meeting the various requirements, the arbitrageur will become increasingly interested in either taking a position or adding to it. That the companies are serious is evidenced by the extent of the paperwork carried out.

But further evidence of the merits of the merger proposal is required. It is necessary to analyze the financial terms from both parties' points of view, to see, first, if the terms are likely to be favorably voted upon. For the Bride, this entails among other things a comparison of: its market price with the market value of the securities to be received; the current dividend rate with the rate to be received on the package of the Groom's securities; the current earnings with the earnings represented by the securities offered by the Groom; and a comparison of the growth of those earnings. Brides often find these days that they are giving up future earnings for current market value.

The Groom requires a pro-forma evaluation. Whether or not the Groom will experience dilution now or in the future depends on the respective earnings growth rates translated through the proposed payment to be made for the Bride. Too much initial dilution is someting which would cause immediate concern to the arbitrageur, as would the danger of this in the future. For example, the proposed merger of C.I.T. Financial Corporation and Xerox never reached the altar due to the drag that C.I.T. was expected to cause on Xerox's future earnings.

Figuring of Parities

Hardly a day passes without the announcement of at least one or two new merger or exchange offers. As each particular deal is promulgated, an arbitrageur may or may not immediately decide to take a position. In any case, he must be able, with relative agility, to figure out what each package of securities is worth, for he is in the precarious position of having to commit his firm's capital to a high-risk situation. The total, or "work-out," value of a particular package is commonly referred to as the "parity."

Packages of securities offered in all types of reorganizations are becoming increasingly difficult to calculate because of the use of warrants, debentures, sliding ratios, etc. The moral of the story is: A deal, more often than not, is worth neither what the newspapers nor what the merger parties say it is worth. It is generally worth much less. So investor beware!

Taking a simple illustration, Canteen Corporation was to be merged into ITT on the basis of 0.2686 ITT common shares and 0.1930 Series K Convertible Preferred for each share of Canteen. With ITT common selling at $52.75 and the K preferred at $98.75, the parity calculation would be

$$0.2686 \times \$52.75 + 0.1930 \times \$98.75 = \$14.17 + \$19.06$$
$$= \$33.23$$

In Appendix A, the author has calculated parities in a diverse selection of corporate reorganizations. These, together with the 12 merger cases examined in Chapter 3 and the cash tender cases in Chapter 4, portray almost every instrument and technical mechanism employed to finance reorganizations. Those elements chosen for presentation in Chapter 5 are of a different nature, and require separate analysis. Yet they also involve a determination of the value, or parity, of a given situation.

Determination of the Time Element

An accurate determination of how long it will take to consummate a particular arbitrage transaction is of the utmost importance to the arbitrageur, for it represents one of the key elements determining the potential return on invested capital. Determination of the probable period of time the funds will be tied up is by no means an easy task, for there are many variables involved in each of the requisite steps to complete a merger, any one of which may involve incalculable delays postponing the legal closing of the deal.

One begins, then, by ascertaining the various approvals that are required to consummate a particular transaction. We review here the various steps involved in a merger proposal, as it is normally the lengthiest type of transaction. Other arbitrage situations, which require only some of the approvals to be covered in this section, will usually have a shorter timetable, calculable along lines similar to those utilized below.

The following steps or approvals are usually required to consummate a merger: (1) a preliminary agreement, which stipulates the exchange ratios and broadly outlines the main conditions of the merger and designates an executive committee from each company's board of directors to formulate and execute a definitive agreement; (2) the definitive agreement, which specifies the exact conditions of the merger, as well as the conditions under which either party may terminate the agreement; (3) an audit of the Bride to verify her purported dowry; (4) a formal tax ruling from the Internal Revenue Service as to the various tax aspects of the merger for both parties; (5) SEC clearance of the proxy statements soliciting shareholder approval of the merger proposal; (6) shareholder approval at a formal shareholders' meeting; (7) approval of any one of a number of governmental regulatory agencies, other than the SEC under whose jurisdiction the merger may fall, relative to the type of merger involved (airline mergers are subject to CAB; transportation mergers to the ICC; gas companies to the F.P.C., etc.); and then there is always the Justice Department and the FTC who by their respective injunctive powers may preclude consummation; (8) the legal closing.

The probable timetable in the average merger situation (one not requiring governmental clearance other than by the SEC and the IRS) is best indicated by the signing of the definitive agreement. The steps that ensue are fairly systematic, and with a little experience, can be gauged and estimated with a remarkable degree of accuracy. Once the definitive contract is signed, the audit has already been completed, and there is normally a simultaneous request to the IRS for the tax ruling and a filing under the Hart-Scott-Rodino Antitrust Improvements Act (see the section on "Antitrust Considerations" on page 45). The proxy material, which has been in the process of preparation concomitantly with the definitive contract, is dispatched to the SEC within three to four weeks. One can anticipate a period of four to six weeks before SEC clearance of the proxy material is obtained, assuming that there are no major deficiencies to be corrected. Upon SEC clearance, the proxy material is printed in the final form and, with little delay, sent to shareholders. The date of shareholders' meetings will then be set—usually three weeks ahead—to abide by the respective corporate charter, which stipulates the requisite advance notice that shareholders must be accorded prior to the meeting.

Once shareholder approval is obtained, there remains, in our normal merger situation, only the legal closing, except for one small factor: the receipt of a favorable tax ruling from the IRS. This often turns out to be the deciding element in the timetable because it is usually an unwaivable condition that a favorable ruling be received prior to closing. When the ruling can be expected to be received (and the merger thus consummated) will be dictated by (a) the date of application to the IRS, (b) the complexity of the ruling, and (c) the backlog at the IRS. The arbitrageur, as part of the information gathering process discussed above, is romancing the merging companies to determine the exact date of application to the IRS. The complexity of the ruling depends on the nature of the package of securities offered in exchange, the presence of options, possible insider tax problems, etc. The simplest ruling would be one involving an exchange of solely common voting stock of the Groom for the common stock of the Bride (a simple "A" or "C" reorganization), with no option or insider problems. Depending on the current backlog situation at the IRS, a simple ruling might take 90 to 100 days, while the more complicated ruling would take 100 to 120 days. A few years ago, a complex ruling could be expected in 90 days. But when merger fever began to run high, the backlog and thus the delays became correspondingly longer.

In situations requiring the approval of government agencies such as the FPC, ICC, Federal Reserve Board, Comptroller of the Currency, CAB, Federal Maritime Commission, SEC (under the Public Utility Holding Company Act, etc.), then the determination of the time element hinges on a knowledge of the procedural functioning of the particular agency involved. Generally speaking, the ruling of these agencies requires many months—in the case of the ICC, many years.

Return on Investment

With the calculation of the expected dollar profit, plus an estimate of the amount of time his capital will be employed in the particular transaction, an arbitrageur can estimate the (annualized) return on investment.

Chapter 3 (Merger Arbitrage: Practical Applications) goes into elaborate detail in calculating returns on merger situations that fall basically into two time periods: when the monograph was first published in 1971, and for the situations covering the late 1970s through the current period. We will not digress at this particular juncture by going into the "how to" aspect of figuring returns on investment but leave it to Chapter 3 in all its resplendency.

The Risks

Prior to establishing a position in an arbitrage situation, the arbi-trageur must carefully weigh the various potential risks involved.

Any one of a number of elements can result in an enormous loss
if the deal is not consummated, or may sharply reduce the return
on investment if it is not completed according to schedule. The
following are considered to be the normal risks involved during
the course of merger negotiations.

a. *Double Price Risk.* Premiums, ranging generally from 10 percent to even 50 percent—exceptionally even 100 percent—may be
offered for acquisition targets. An arbitrageur, when he takes his
long position, is thereby assuming a great part of this premium in
the price he pays. Should the deal be sabotaged for some reason,
the down-side price slide can be rather large. So one must carefully
calculate the downside risk.[3] In addition, there is a price risk in
the stock of the Groom, which has been sold short. If there is a
lack of liquidity in this stock, there may be an equally large loss on
covering the short sale. When a merger proposal is terminated, all
arbitrageurs try to cover their short sales at the same time, causing
an artificially higher price for the Groom.[4] (If the short sales had
artificially depressed the price of the Groom during the period the
Groom was subject to arbitraging, one can assume that upon covering the short, the Groom will return whence it came, *pari passu*).
In any case, the arbitrage position is a double-edged sword if the
merger breaks.

b. *Alteration of the Terms.* If the exchange ratio is changed after
a position has been taken, the change is likely to alter the projected
profit. For example, if there was an exchange of Y common for
X common, and more Y common was subsequently offered for
X, it would mean greater profit. However, if in place of Y common it was decided to give Y debentures plus Y warrants, then the
arbitrageur would be short Y common, which would have to be
covered, possibly eliminating the profit. Naturally, less Y common
for X would also result in the arbitrageur being short Y common (or short X), with an accompanying reduction in projected
profit.

c. *A Sharp Increase in the Market Price of the Groom.* This will
often cause the Groom to feel he is perhaps paying too much for the

Bride and if he tries to renegotiate a cheaper price for her, she may decide not to accept the lower offer. In any case, a sharp run-up in the Groom's price causes great discomfiture to the arbitrageur, who is forced to pay a greater premium for the Bride—over her investment value—as the parity, which corresponds to the price of the Groom, increases. If the arbitrageur has taken his full hedge position before this run-up, then the threat of a broken deal looms ever more ominous.

   d. *A Sharp Decrease in the Groom's Market Price.* The reverse of (c) with the Bride becoming disenchanted over the diminishing value (parity) of the offer, with an eventual attempt at renegotiation.

   e. *Competing Bids.* It is a nice feeling to be long the stock that is the subject of a bidding contest. However, when one has taken the full arbitrage position, long and short, the necessity to cover the short in the face of another's bid may prove disastrous.

   f. *Shareholder Dissent.* Certain shareholders of the Bride may feel they are selling out too cheaply or those of the Groom may feel that they are paying too much. These feelings may lead to what are termed "nuisance suits," usually resulting in delays in the timetable.

   Shareholder dissent may present a real threat when, by state law, shareholders are accorded appraisal rights on their securities. Managements of both companies will normally have set a limit on the number of shares that can request appraisal and payment of cash in lieu of the securities of the Groom. If the limit is substantially surpassed there is a high probability of termination of the merger agreement. This sometimes stems from the fact that the tax-free status of the merger may be endangered by the payment of too much cash.

   g. *Substantiation of Financial Warranties.* The financial warranties promulgated in the definitive agreement are subject to auditing reviews. One of the usual termination clauses stipulates that there will have been no material changes in the business or financial status of Company X between the date of the execution of the contract and the date of the legal closing. There is thus the need for the accountant's "Cold Comfort Letter" to cover this interim period.

A deterioration in earnings picture of the Bride may sufficiently discomfort the Groom so that negotiations are terminated.

h. *Tax Problems.* There is always the chance—albeit a small one—that the IRS will render an unfavorable ruling as to the tax-free status of the merger.[5] In addition, there are often insider tax problems which may not be obvious, but which may nevertheless sufficiently dishearten an insider about the deal, so that his vote is cast against it.

i. *Governmental Intervention.* If applicable, the strongest threat is that of the Department of Justice. When the latter decides to prevent a merger, it usually gets its way. The risk is especially great because, as standard practice, the Department of Justice must request a temporary injunction to prevent the legal closing; and unfortunately for arbitrageurs, it usually chooses to do so at the "11th hour." The granting of the injunction is the death knell for the deal, as both parties are normally unwilling to fight lengthy and expensive court battles. The arbitrageur is indifferent to the fact that a merger may be attacked after its legal consummation. In fact, the eventuality of a court decision against a completed merger may provide him with additional business in the form of a divestiture, which may then become a spinoff.

The Federal Trade Commission is another intervenor which has become more aggressive by virtue of being authorized on 1/4/75 to represent themselves in court. In addition FTC complaints often result in consent decrees, which are essentially out-of-court settlements.

j. *Unusual Delays.* There is always the chance that negotiations may become hopelessly bogged down, or that inexperienced officials may be handling the enormous quantities of paperwork involved, resulting in errors, legal tieups, and extended periods of SEC scrutiny.

k. *Personalities.* Personality clashes are always a possibility when two sets of officers, each accustomed to its own modus operandi, begin to realize that things may be done differently after the merger. Officers of the Bride in particular have to be treated with just the

right amount of respect, in order that they not be left with the
feeling that they "had" to merge. Such respect is represented by
proper jobs, appropriate titles, financial compensation, options, and
so on.
   1. *"Freeze-in" Risk.* See Chapter 6.

Average Expected Returns

Both a subjective and an objective element combine to formulate what to the arbitrageur is a satisfactory return, or, an average
expected or required return in any given arbitrage situation.

   The subjective element involves discounting the specific risks
inherent in the deal. Those risks to which the arbitrageur as-
cribes the greatest importance are the price risk—both long and
short—and the antitrust risk. The arbitrageur's discount for these
two risks—and thus the required return—will be directly propor-
tioned to his evaluation of the seriousness of said risks.

   The objective element is the aggregate of the alternative risk
arbitrage situations. Experience has shown that at a time when
there is a great variety of situations in which to commit their risk
capital, arbitrageurs are afforded the luxury of choosing amongst
the available spreads, as there is less competition in the Arbitrage
Community for a specific spread. Also, the amount of capital available to arbitrageurs as a group is fairly fixed in size over a given
time span. Thus, where there are fewer attractive arbitrage deals,
the same fixed capital is chasing the fewer spreads, often leading to
a phenomenon referred to as "spread squeezing." This is an important factor to keep in mind, as popular brokerage clichés such as
"the normal discount"—i.e., spread—considered to be roughly 10
percent will not be appropriate when referring to merger spreads
in a risk arbitrage market characterized by a supply curve that has
shifted upward.

   Combining both the subjective and the objective element,
then, what is a normal or average required rate of return?

In establishing his requirements, an arbitrageur will calculate, for a quick point of reference, the return on investment rather than on capital. The latter is normally determined only after the transaction has been consummated (see the calculations of return on capital in Chapter 3). Assuming, then that we have a typical merger arbitrage transaction involving a standard set of risks, and furthermore that there is an ample number of attractive spreads available, the arbitrageur will require and will aim to take the long and short positions at prices that will yield a return on investment of 40 percent per annum. In the final analysis, however, he is usually willing to settle for 30 percent as he will inevitably encounter unexpected delays in either the consummation of the merger or in the physical exchange of securities. Therefore, as a "rule of thumb" one aims at 40 percent but settles for 30 percent per annum. This does not necessarily imply that an arbitrageur will forego a return of 20 percent. The 40 percent rate is after all only an average, and if he can obtain a rate of return of 20 percent in a transaction in which he visualizes very little risk, then he will take a position so long as his financing cost is exceeded. It is, in fact, safe to say that when a spread is well below the normal rate of return for a "risk" arbitrage situation that the arbitrageurs, by collectivity taking their positions, view it closer to the "riskless" variety. On the other hand, a return of 60 percent per annum may not warrant a position if it is thought the Justice Department is lurking around the corner with an injunction request in hand, or if a stock selling at $40 is worth only $10 per share without the deal.

What if the spread or discount in a particular arbitrage does not meet the arbitrageur's requirement? The answer is simply that he does not participate in it. So, in effect, if the collective body of opinion—the discount applied by the market—is not shared by the arbitrageur, he retreats to the sidelines and either waits for his desired spread to appear, or he goes off to greener pastures. Often there may be non-arbitrage elements that effect the size of the spread—e.g., speculation by private investors—which keep arbitrageurs looking on somewhat forlornly from the sidelines. In such cases, a well-placed rumor—regarding the possibility of the merger's cancellation—may result in yet another phenomenon, known as "inducing the required rate of return."

Taking a Position

Having (a) studied the merger, (b) calculated the profit potential, (c) weighed the possible risks, and (d) compared these calculations with other arbitrage situations, an arbitrageur may decide to take a position in the subject deal. Let us assume X is merging into Y, and that each X will get one Y in the exchange of securities, with X selling at $35 and Y at $40, and neither company will pay dividends prior to consummation. It is estimated that the merger will close four months hence, yielding a potential gross return on investment of 42.9 percent per annum before taxes, at the current prices.

$$\frac{\$40 - \$35}{\$35} \times 3 \text{ (four-month periods per year)}$$

$$= \frac{\$5}{\$35} \times 3 = 42.9 \text{ percent per annum}$$

The size of the position that may now be taken will depend on (1) availability of capital, (2) degree of risk, (3) supply of X, (4) demand for Y, and (5) the availability of Y to be borrowed for delivery against the short sales of Y. With the Stock Exchange attentive to the "fail to deliver" problem, the ability to borrow stock has attained unparalleled importance, and often restricts the size of the position which may be taken when the Street supply is thin, or when Y has a small capitalization.

Selling Y short in merger arbitrage is an integral part of the position. In buying X at $35, one is also creating Y at $35, assuming the merger is consummated. So, for all intents and purposes, one is long Y at $35 by virtue of the purchase of X. The actual price of Y—$40—is the price that must prevail at the closing of the transaction if the arbitrageur is to realize his projected profit. The only way to assure this profit is to sell Y short, thereby removing exposure to the vagaries of the marketplace. As a result of this short sale, the arbitrageur is strictly at risk of the deal, and not at the risk of the market.

"Another reason for selling short prior to the closing date of the merger is that it will spare the arbitrageurs the frustration of simultaneously trying to find buyers for the new securities that they can expect to receive in exchange for their old securities. This is significant since the arbitrageurs, cumulatively investing large sums of money, may become entitled to an unusually large number of new shares in the acquiring company. This enormous quantity of stock would be very difficult to dispose of if it were offered for sale immediately after the closing date of the merger. If an earlier short sale had not been established, then the combined selling pressure of arbitrageurs would, no doubt, tend to push down the price of the acquiring company's shares...,"[6] resulting in virtual elimination of the originally contemplated spread. (It must be emphasized that the arbitrageur is not an investor in securities, but an investor in deals. Should he stay long Y by virtue of a long position in X, he becomes an investor in Y, rather than in the merger of X into Y).

A further reason for selling Y short is to realize potential tax benefits, which result in the creation of long-term capital gains, and also possibly short-term capital losses which can offset short-term gains. This matter will be considered later in the chapter.

In actually taking a position in X long and Y short, one must carefully gauge the general market atmosphere as well as the liquidity of both X and Y. For example, if X is thin and there is a good demand for Y, it would be unwise to short Y prior to establishing the long position in X, particularly in a strong market. Similarly, in a weak market one would presumably have difficulty in shorting Y due to a need of an uptick, so that it would probably be better to short Y prior to going long X. As a general "rule of thumb," it is better to short Y before buying X in a falling market, and better to buy X before shorting Y in a rising one. In a static market, the short sale should also precede the purchase.

Positioning small lots—300 to 500 shares at a time—is also a wiser course than attempting 3,000 to 5,000. The latter involves substantial market risk, unless the corresponding blocks of the "mate" are immediately available for positioning. To short 5,000 Y with only 300 X available at the desired spread would be sheer folly. And vice versa.

Turning a Position

Let us again assume a share for share exchange of X for Y, with X at $30 and Y at $40. The merger is scheduled to be closed four months hence. An arbitrageur decides to take a position with this roughly ten-point spread, and let us say that one month later the spread has narrowed to four points. Having an unrealized profit of six points or 20 percent in one month, an arbitrageur will often turn his position, i.e., close it out, rather than maintain it in order to make the remaining 13 percent, which would necessitate holding it for an additional three months.

A more delicate and precarious impetus for turning a position may develop when an arbitrageur has reason to believe that a deal will not be consummated, or that it may be delayed for a considerable period of time due to legal or antitrust complications. The arbitrageur, if he wishes to obtain the optimum prices for his long and short positions, must try to liquidate them in an unobtrusive manner. This often involves the use of "stooges," for were the arbitrage firm's name revealed on the floor of the Stock Exchange, it could well cause panic, price deterioration on the long position that is to be liquidated, and the disappearance of sellers in the case of the short position that must be covered. Bailing out of a listed stock simply involves utilizing a friendly "Two-Dollar Broker" to execute the order. The latter is not obliged to give up the name of his sponsor until after the expiration of the day's trading, which is normally sufficient time to liquidate a major portion of the position. In a non-listed stock, one must try to find a friendly Over-the-Counter firm who, for a commission, will try to liquidate his sponsor's position amongst the brethren of the Arbitrage Community. Every arbitrage firm has its established "stooge" to whom it can turn in such an emergency. This points out the very dangerous nature of risk arbitrage, for bad positions are often graciously turned over to one's competitors, who are presumably not aware of the problems in the deal until it is too late to do anything about it. Arbitrageurs cheerfully contend that this is all a part of their code: that all is fair in love, war . . . and arbitrage.

Consummation

As mentioned above, in the normal course of events, after shareholder approval has been obtained, the only remaining requirement for the legal closing to occur is the receipt of a favorable tax ruling from the Internal Revenue Service. Once this has been received, the New York Stock Exchange will usually declare a "short exempt ruling" on the security that has previously been the object of short sales.[7] This indicates that the Stock Exchange is itself satisfied that all conditions for merger between X and Y have been met and that there is practically no chance that any further complications will arise to prevent the merger. This "short exempt ruling" allows those investors who are long X and who wish to dispose of the shares, to do so either as X, or if they prefer, in the form of Y, even though in the strict legal sense X is not yet equal to Y. This ruling also permits the sale to be effected without the normally required uptick, and, for private investors, without a 50 percent "good faith" margin deposit. Those individual investors who henceforth buy X and simultaneously sell Y can hold both positions on margin of only 10 percent of the long position. Thus, from the time the ruling is rendered, the simultaneous purchase of X and sale of Y is recognized by the Stock Exchange as a "bona fide" arbitrage situation. For a member firm of the Exchange, long and short positions taken henceforth can be held in a "special arbitrage account" with a zero charge to the firm's capital.[8] In addition, the long X and short Y positions in the investment accounts no longer require a 30 percent capital charge once the "short exempt ruling" is delivered.

The "short exempt ruling" is a key factor of which few investors are aware. For if they wish to sell their X, they would often fare far better if they sell it as Y, as the X can only be sold to the discount (from parity) bid of the arbitrageur. The interesting fact is that the discount is somewhat greater than the normal commission that would be charged plus the carrying costs to be incurred pending exchange of securities. In fact, arbitrageurs do a huge volume of business after the closing of a merger by bidding Over-the-Counter (OTC) for a newly de-listed stock of the "just married" Bride. The arbitrageur, by purchasing the public's X and immediately selling it as Y, cashes in on the public's indolence or ignorance.

The "short exempt ruling" has the additional effect of causing sudden pressure to be brought to bear on Y, as all sales of Y by arbitrageurs no longer require the uptick. Thus often just as a merger is completed, there is an appreciable price erosion in Y. This pressure is strictly technical and usually abates once all the floating X is taken out of circulation. This artificial pressure is something which predictably coincides with merger closings, and may provide excellent buying opportunities for the shrewd investor.

Value Line has in the past drawn attention to this type of market activity:

New securities coming out of mergers and tenders are frequently under severe pressure when a merger exchange or tender offer becomes effective. Due to technical circumstances, the market price of the new and complicated issues often are depressed temporarily by supply and demand factors.

Many participants in merger arbitrage are short-term holders with no intention of maintaining positions in the securities. Where possible, the securities involved in a merger or equivalent securities are sold "when-issued." When a sizable arbitrage situation exists, arbitrageurs and other aggressive investors will find it expedient to sell off exchanged securities promptly in order to nail down profits and to deploy their funds into another situation. The idea is to generate small but sure profits on quick turnovers.

Investors who are aware that an arbitrage situation is creating temporary selling pressure can obtain convertible and other securities at bargain prices. Frequently, the newly issued securities settle at higher price levels as soon as the sell-off by arbitrageurs subsides.[9]

That statement was essentially the first publicized recognition of this post-merger phenomenon.

Tax Strategy

As mentioned in the section "Average Expected Returns," an important reason for selling Y short is to derive certain tax benefits. The short sale gives the arbitrageur some strategic options in the qualitative, i.e., after-tax, returns of not only this department but of his firm as well. This potential benefit arises from the fact that the shares of two companies—X and Y—planning to merge are, as a rule of thumb, considered to be not substantially identical for tax purposes until the shareholders actually vote favorably on the merger proposal. Thus, if X and Y are respectively bought and sold in separate investment accounts prior to shareholder approvals, they are considered to be not substantially identical.

Between the date of the shareholders' meeting and the day when New York Stock Exchange will declare Y "short exempt" (which signifies that there is no longer any risk involved and that a holder of X may, if he wishes, sell X in form of Y without the uptick and related margin requirements), there may exist a gray area as to whether or not securities are substantially identical. The Treasury Regulations say that this is to be judged on the basis of "the facts and circumstances in each case" and suggest as guidelines "the relative values, price changes, and other circumstances." Even though shareholders have approved a merger, such approval does not necessarily render the securities substantially identical, especially where there is still opposition to the merger by dissenting shareholders or government authority. Thus, if one wishes to continue building the position in X long and Y short, it should be done in a separate, or "number 2" investment account. Then, should the IRS take the position that X and Y were substantially identical during the latter period, it could be argued that the "number 2" account functioned as an "arbitrage account."

In the normal course of events, when there is little likelihood of further problems after shareholder approval has been obtained, so that X and Y are most assuredly substantially identical, any further positions should be placed in a "Special Arbitrage Account" so as not to endanger the positions in the investment accounts of X and Y. Any gains or losses resulting from the "Special Arbitrage Accounts" are naturally short-term. There exists the danger, however, that purchases in the "Special Arbitrage Account" may contaminate short sales of Y in the investment account. This danger can be minimized by closing the positions in the "Special Arbitrage Accounts" prior to closing those in the investment accounts. Also, care should be taken to leave no net short position in the arbitrage account at the close of any business day.

A long-term capital gain can be created in the X and Y investment accounts simply by establishing the requisite one-year holding period. When the merger is consummated, X is exchanged for securities of Y, so that the resulting positions in the two investment accounts are Y long and Y short. When the requisite holding period is attained, the arbitrageur is in the highly desirous position of having two alternatives. First, if Y is higher than $40 (recalling that we sold Y at that price)—let us say $45—then he can, on succeeding days, buy Y and sell Y until his Y long and Y short positions are completely closed out. In this manner, the Y long (formerly X) is sold for a long-term capital gain greater than the initial five-point spread. The covering of the Y short position results in the recognition of a short-term capital loss which can be utilized to offset short-term capital gains of the arbitrage department, and also for the firm. The net economic gain is still the initial five-point spread per share, but the character of the gain and loss is significantly different.

Secondly, if after the requisite holding period, Y is below $40, so that it would not be advantageous to reverse the positions as above (indeed, reversing would produce a long-term capital loss and a short-term capital gain), then the arbitrageur can record a long-term capital gain simply by pairing-off his Y long and Y short positions with a journal entry.

The same general procedure as outlined above would be employed if, let us say, instead of an exchange of Y for X there would be a new issue of Y convertible preferred offered in exchange for X. In this case, the arbitrageur would, before the shareholders' meetings, go long X and short the amount of Y common represented by Y convertible preferred, so as to hedge the market risk in the new issue. After consummation and the exchange of securities, the accounts would show Y convertible preferred long and Y common short. The position is then held open for the requisite period, after which the arbitrageur simply converts and pairs-off the positions or reverses them depending on market price relationships.

The closing out of positions in the marketplace for tax purposes thus produces increased activity in the securities for the former Groom. Many arbitrage firms may be doing this during approximately the same time span as their respective positions attain long-term maturity. Their aggregate interaction in such cases will lend additional liquidity to the marketplace, particularly in a taxable year in which there are large arbitrage short-term gains to offset.

Treatment of New Convertible Securities

Messrs. Alan Slifka and Richard Baer, in discussing convertible securities issued through corporate reorganizations, stated some time ago that—

> ... the arbitrageur has to make an educated guess, perhaps as far as three months in advance, as to what the institutional investors will pay for those securities when they can be traded. Besides taking the "normal" arbitrage risks, the arbitrageur takes the risk of the stock market and the money market, a risk which underwriters would never take. [10]

As a practical matter, the arbitrageur is not in so unenviable a position, for he will generally be able to hedge against market risks in the new convertible by selling short the common stock underlying the new convertible security.

When a new convertible is issued, there are two ways of calculating the parity; either on straight conversion or with a premium on the new convertible. The calculation of premium is based on the current market price, the interest rate structure, and the yields and premiums on comparable securities. Since it is difficult to assign a premium and yield basis some months in the future, the premium is not counted in the initial determination of return on investment. The parity on total conversion serves as a basis for investment decision, and should a premium develop when trading in the security develops, it is a bonus. Taking the example of the merger of Chubb and First National City Corp. (1969), with the later trading at $74, the parity for Chubb was figured by adding the 0.4 common portion to an additional 0.6 common represented by the new convertible preferred. Thus, by selling the sum of these two portions short, one could establish a parity of $74. With Chubb at $65, there was ample room. If, when the merger was to be consummated, the common of First National City had risen to a point where the yield basis on its conversion parity did not command a premium over conversion value, the arbitrageur would have converted the preferred into common, thereby covering that portion of his initial short sale. If, on the other hand, First National City common had remained at the current level, or had fallen, so that the preferred did command a premium, then—and this is a key point—the arbitrageur would have covered that portion of his short sale in the marketplace and likewise would have sold the new preferred that he had received by virtue of the merger. In this way, the arbitrageur would have realized an additional profit on the transaction. Rarely will the arbitrageur have exposed himself to the market risk by not hedging with the preferred's underlying equity.

This technique of reversing positions to take advantage of a premium on a newly issued convertible security engenders an additional phenomenon in the marketplace. Once SEC clearance or the proxy or prospectus is obtained, it is legally permitted to make an OTC market in the new convertible security on a "when-issued" basis. Should there be a premium on the "when-issued" convertible security, the arbitrageur will attempt to effect a swap with an institutional investor. The arbitrageur will have accumulated a large inventory of the new issue, but will correspondingly have sold short the underlying equity in order to hedge market risks. Meanwhile, the institutional investor who is long a block of the common stock—which the arbitrageur is short—may desire to replace the common with the new preferred—which the arbitrageur is long. He may wish to do so because of the interest yield on the new convertible vis-a-vis the common yield. In any event, whatever the reason, he has an added incentive in that by purchasing the new security OTC, he can deal on a "net" (no commission) basis with the arbitrageur, who also offers liquidity. In addition, because many arbitrageurs will be trying to do exactly the same thing, the premium will probably be less than that which may be expected to appear once the new convertible is listed on an exchange.

In these "swap" arrangements, the premium is negotiated between buyer and seller. When the premium is fixed, the common stock is "crossed" (a trade arranged with the specialist, who assures the same price for buyer and seller), normally in a single block, at the prevailing market price. Then the arbitrageur sells to the institution the convertible at the stipulated premium, on a "net" basis, in the OTC market.

With the great number of convertibles issued through mergers, there has been a great deal of this type of activity in the marketplace. It is, therefore, not unusual to see large blocks of the Groom—representing just such a "swap" being traded soon after the consummation of a merger.

Those firms who either do not have tax shelters, or who are simply not interested in maintaining positions for long-term capital gains, will effect many "swaps." Those who do concentrate on the long-term aspect will hold the new securities.

Antitrust Considerations

Either the Department of Justice or the Federal Trade Commission
can threaten a deal with its legal authority to seek a divestiture
or an injunction. Either agency has legal authority to challenge
a merger as violative of Section 7 of the Clayton Act. Section 7
makes mergers unlawful if they substantially lessen competition in
any line of commerce in any area of the country. Private persons
and corporations, with the Bride in an unfriendly tender offer the
most likely plaintiff, also have legal standing to apply for injunctive
relief in federal court.

The granting of a preliminary injunction is usually the death
knell for the deal, as both parties are normally unwilling to fight
lengthy and expensive court battles. A way around an injunction is
a hold-separate order issued by the court, which permits the tender
offer or merger to proceed. The arbitrageur is indifferent to the
fact that a merger may be attacked after it is legally consummated.
In fact, a court decision against a completed merger may provide
him with additional business in the form of a spinoff.

The Justice Department and the FTC decide during the prenotification period preceding the deal which of them will study its
legality. Prenotification filings, with both companies detailing information about their business and markets, have been required
since 1978 under the Hart-Scott-Rodino Act. Prenotification is
also needed for an acquisition of $15 million or 15 percent of a
company's stock. The filings of forms must await an agreement in
principle or the public announcement of a tender cannot be sub-
mitted beforehand. After filing, the companies must wait 30 days
for a merger and 15 days in the case of a tender before the deal
can be consummated. The Justice Department or the FTC, but
only one of them, can request additional information. If additional
information is requested, the waiting period is extended 20 days in
the case of a merger and 10 days for a tender. Additional extensions
can only be made by a Federal District Court by formal application. If either the FTC or Justice Department finds a substantial

anticompetitive effect from the combination of a particular area plant or division, an agreement to divert the problem is sometimes reached, but usually at the "11th hour" of the second request.

The guidelines that suggest a substantial lessening of competition have not changed since 1968, although different administrations have been more or less tolerant within the same guidelines. The guidelines suggest that a concentrated industry is one in which the top five companies control 50 percent of the business. A merger bid from one of these five would not likely succeed. Often the relevant geographic markets are appropriately smaller than the nation as a whole, however, and state and regions become the focus, perhaps preventing an otherwise allowable deal based on nationwide market shares.

New guidelines, expected to be more lenient to horizontal mergers than those dating from 1968, include an index derived by squaring the market share of each producer in an industry and adding them up. A deal that leaves the industry with an index of 1000 or less, including the market share of the combined entities squared, will likely be considered legal. At 1400 on the index the deal has potential problems, while over 1600 the combination is suspect, at best. (See Appendix B.)

Summary

This chapter has explained the various steps comprising the arbitrageur's financial analysis of "merger" arbitrage. However, risk arbitrage, as we shall see, has other manifestations and forms. The strictly financial analyses required for these other forms is very similar to that previously delineated, but in view of their different market characteristics, these deserve separate attention, which they are accorded in Chapter 5. The modus operandi for merger arbitrage previously outlined has one central aim: to assist the arbitrageur in determining whether or not the subject transaction is a "good deal."

Chapter 3

Merger Arbitrage: Practical Applications

C hapter 2 provided an analytical background for merger arbitrage. In this chapter we test the usefulness of this approach by applying it to various merger arbitrage situations that occurred first during the pre-1971 period of the first edition of *Risk Arbitrage* and then to subsequent and more recent merger situations. In each case the author will explain how he has arrived at the parity and then follow through to see what the actual return (or loss) on capital would have been if positions had actually been taken at the quoted prices.

Mergers Prior to 1971

In this section we will go through a "how to" exercise in calculating the return on investment for the arbitrageur who was in the employ of a New York Stock Exchange member firm in the pre-1971 era, and then go to a calculation of return for a private or institutional investor who was subject to much greater capital requirements. The returns will be figured on a net basis disregarding income taxes and transfer taxes.

Generic Calculation of Co. B. Being Acquired by Co. A (Co. B/Co. A)

As our example, let us assume that Company A, whose common stock is trading at $50, will offer one of its common for each common of Company B, trading currently at $45. Let us further assume that the 90-day Treasury Bill yield, or the "call" rate, is 7 percent, and that A and B will have a dividend record date prior to the consummation of the merger, with A paying a dividend of $0.50 and B, $1. The merger is expected to be consummated three months hence. Prior to the merger announcement, the common stock of B had been selling at $35.

The arbitrageur will take his position by buying one share of B at $45 and selling short one of A at $50. The cost of carrying the long position for the required three months is $\frac{1}{4}$ of 7 percent times $45 = $0.79 per share. Since the arbitrageur is long B and short A, there will be a receipt of $1 as a long dividend and a loss of $0.50. Subtracting this from the carrying cost, we are left with a new carrying cost of $0.29. This is added to our cost price for B, boosting it to $45.29. With the parity at $50, the resulting spread is $4.71.

With this figure in hand, we wish to determine the per annum return, first on total investment, and then on invested capital. The former is fairly straightforward. Since the funds will be employed for three months, $4.71 × 4/$45.29 = 41.6 percent on total investment. When it comes to establishing the return on capital, we discover that one of the fundamental advantages of the New York Stock Exchange member firm in doing arbitrage for its own account is the relatively small amount of capital required to finance the arbitrage position. There is basically a "haircut" (capital charge)[1] of 30 percent on the long position. In addition, in order to borrow funds for this position, the member firm must adhere to the 15-to-1 liabilities-to-capital ratio, amounting to roughly 4.38 percent of capital.[2] Thus, the total capital requirement on the total of the long and short position is approximately 34.38 percent, as there is no requirement on the short sale. In the above situation, the per annum return on capital becomes

$$\$4.71 \times 4/\$45 \div 0.3438 = 122 \text{ percent}$$

The private or institutional investor didn't fare nearly as well. Federal Regulation "T" requires (as of 1971) a nonmember of the Exchange to deposit 80 percent, in form of capital (not borrowed funds) against both a long and a short position. Thus, while there is the same carrying cost of $0.29 on the long position, there is also an opportunity cost (assume 7 percent per annum) on the 80 percent required to support the short position. In the actual case, 80 percent of $50 equals $40 and 7 percent of that figure—for three months—amounts to $0.70. The cost of carrying both positions thereby becomes $0.99 for the non-New York Stock Exchange member. When you add to this cost the brokerage commissions on executing the long and short positions, or $0.86, the net spread is whittled down to $2.73, which is in sharp contrast to the $4.71 above. The private investor's return on capital, then, becomes

$$4 \times \$2.73/\$76 \text{ total capital } = 14.36 \text{ percent}$$

Let us now compare risk/reward ratios based on these calculations. Recalling that the price of a share of B prior to the merger announcement was $35, we can presume that B would return to that price (at best)[3] should the merger for some reason be abandoned. This would represent a loss of $10 per share. Let us assume that there is a potential additional loss of $2.00 per share on the covering of the short position, and thus a total loss of $12.00 per share. For the NYSE member firms, the risk/reward is $12/$4.71 = 2.5 and for the nonmember $12/$2.73 = 4.4.

When you also figure that the 2.5 risk ratio may yield 122 percent on capital for the NYSE member and that the 4.4 risk ratio may only yield 14.36 percent, then it may be said that it is 8.5 times more advantageous—from a viewpoint of return on capital—for a NYSE member than for a private investor. Let us now examine some 1969–1970 mergers, to be followed by some more recent examples.

Scientific Data Systems/Xerox

A. Parity Calculation
Terms: 1 Scientific Data Systems ($115) = ½ Xerox ($249)
Parity: $1/x \times \$249 - \$124.50$
Gross Spread: $124.50 − $115 = $9.50

B. Practical Application
  (1) Position taken: 100 Scientific Data (long) at $115; 50 Xerox (short) at $249
  (2) Date position taken: April 11, 1969
  (3) Merger consummated: May 16, 1969
  (4) Exchange of securities effective: July 28, 1969
  (5) Total time involvement [(4) − (2)] = 108 days
  (6) Theoretical Gross Spread (from above): $950 per 100 Scientific Data
  (7) Realized Gross Spread: Also $950, since there are no new securities involved
  (8) Net Spread:

$950.00	Gross Spread
(271.40)	Interest Cost @ 8 Percent for 108 Days on $11,500[4]
—0—	Long Dividends
(22.50)	Short Dividends
$656.10	Net Spread

  (9) Annualized return on capital: According to NYSE Rule #325, the capital requirements will vary for the NYSE member firm depending on the status of the merger. Until the merger is consummated (or when the Exchange renders a "Short Exempt" ruling), there is a 30 percent "haircut" on the long position. After this time, there is only the 15-to-1 requirement against "Aggregate Indebtedness." Accordingly, the following two conditions will exist:

(a) Average Statement of Financial Condition —
April 11–May 16, 1969
Assets
    100 Scientific Data (long) $11,500.00

Liabilities and Capital

50 Xerox		
(short)	$12,450	
Less 50 Xerox		
(borrowed)	(12,450) ...	—0—
Bank Borrowings	....	7,547
Capital		
30 Percent "Haircut"	$3,450	
15-to-1 Ratio	503	3,953
		$11,500

(b) Average Statement of Financial Condition —
17 May–28 July, 1969
Assets
    100 Scientific Data Systems $11,500

Liabilities and Capital

Bank Borrowings	.... $10,781
Capital	
15-to-1 Ratio	 719
	$11,500

Average Capital Employed:

$$\frac{36 \text{ days}}{365 \text{ days}} \times \$3,953 + \frac{72 \text{ days}}{365 \text{ days}} \times 719 = \$532$$

$$\frac{\text{Net Spread}}{\text{Average Capital}} = \text{Return on Capital}$$

$$\frac{\$656.10}{\$532.00} = 123.3 \text{ Percent per Annum (pre-tax)}$$

Hartford Fire Insurance/ITT

A. Parity Calculation

Terms: 1 Hartford Fire (65\frac{1}{4}$) = 1 new ITT Series "N" $2.25
Preferred convertible into 1.25 shares of ITT common (58\frac{5}{8}$).

Parity: There are two ways of viewing a new issue of a convertible
security:

(1) On straight conversion—this means that we calculate the
value of the common stock underlying the preferred. This
is its minimum value, for one could always convert the
preferred and sell the underlying equity. In this case,

$$1.25 \times \$58\tfrac{5}{8} = \$73.28$$

(2) With a premium on conversion—in this way we try to
assign a value (premium) over the conversion value which
would be attributable to

(a) a more senior claim on assets (than the common stock)
in case of liquidation of the company.

(b) the greater dividend yield.

(c) a priority on dividends paid over the common.

(d) the conversion feature.

Since there is a long list of ITT convertible preferreds
already traded on the NYSE, the task should not be
too difficult. Within a certain yield range, the new
preferred can be expected to sell at a premium to its
conversion parity.

(a) Assumed Market Price of New Preferred	(b) Current Yield on New Preferred	(c) Percent Over Conversion Value[5]	(d) Current Yield on Common	(c) (b)-(d) Payback Period[6]
$73.28	3.07%	—0—	1.8%	—0—yrs.
75.00	3.00	2.34	1.8	1.9
76.00	2.96	3.70	1.8	3.2
77.00	2.92	5.08	1.8	4.5
78.00	2.89	6.44	1.8	5.9
79.00	2.85	7.81	1.8	7.5
80.00	2.81	9.20	1.8	9.0

A glance at the three existing convertible preferreds of ITT will reveal the following:

	Market Price	Current Yield	Percent Premium Conversion Value	Payback Period
$4.50 "I" Pfd convertible @ $61	$104³⁄₄	4.30	9%	3.9 yrs.
$4.00 "J" Pfd convertible @ $61¹⁄₂	100	4.00	4.9	2.2
$4.00 "K" Pfd convertible @ $64	96³⁄₄	4.13	5.6	2.4

It would appear from our table that at current yields of 3 percent and below, there would be little chance of a premium on the new preferred. At a yield of 4 percent or better, it seems reasonable to expect a slight premium, which would afford a payback period of 1 to 2 years, or let us say a premium roughly 2 percent. For this to occur, therefore, the price of ITT would have to drop to around $45.

The above analysis would naturally require a very fundamental investigation of the combined interest/preferred dividend coverage.

Gross Spread:
  (1) On straight conversion: $73.28 − $65¹⁄₄ = $8.03.
  (2) With a premium on conversion: Since at the current yield, there would probably be no premium, the gross spread is also $8.03.

B. Practical Application
  (1) Position taken: 100 Hartford Fire (long) at $65¹⁄₄; 125 ITT (short) at $58⁵⁄₈.
  (2) Date position taken: November 14, 1969.
  (3) Exchange offer consummated: June 15, 1970.
  (4) Exchange of securities effective: 1 July 1970.
  (5) Total time involvement [(4) − (2)]: 230 days.

(6) Theoretical Gross Spread: $803.00 per 100 Hartford Fire

(7) Realized Gross Spread: While no premium over conversion parity was expected on the new ITT $2.25 "N" Preferred at yields which one would have encountered on the Preferred—2.81 percent to 3 percent—at the then prevailing price for ITT, the latter's price had dropped substantially by the time the reorganization was consummated, so that on June 19, 1970, with ITT common at $38, the Preferred was selling at $48.25 with a current yield of 4.6 percent. This amounted to a premium of

$$48.25 - (1.25 \times 38) = \$0.75$$
$$\text{or a premium of } 1.58 \text{ percent}$$

Thus, one would sell 100 Preferred at $48.25, and simultaneously cover the short sale of 125 ITT common at $38, accruing an additional profit of $75 per 100 Hartford Fire. Accordingly, the realized gross spread became

$803	Original Profit
+75	Premium Profit
$878	Realized Gross Spread

(8) Net Spread:

$878.00	Gross Spread
$(328.88)	Interest Cost for 230 Days on $6,524 @ 8 Percent
70.00	Long Dividends
(52.50)	Short Dividends
$566.62	Net Spread

(9) Annualized return on Capital:

   (a) Average Statement of Financial Condition
      November 14, 1969–June 15, 1970

     Assets
      100 Hartford Fire (long) $6,525

Liabilities and Capital
125 ITT

(short) $7,328

Less 125 ITT

(borrowed)   (7,328)   ... $—0—

Bank Borrowings $4,282

Capital
30 Percent "Haircut" $1,958

15-to-1 Ratio   285 2,243

$6,525

(b) Average Statement of Financial Condition
June 15–July 1, 1970

Assets
100 Hartford Fire (long) $6,525

Liabilities and Capital
Bank Borrowings $6,117

Capital
15-to-1 Ratio 408

$6,525

Average Capital Employed:

$$\frac{214}{365} \times \$2,243 + \frac{16}{365} \times \$408 = \$1,333$$

$$\frac{\text{Net Spread}}{\text{Average Capital}} = \text{Return on Capital}$$

$$\frac{\$567}{\$1,333} = 42.5 \text{ Percent per Annum}$$

Canada Dry/McCall's/Hunt Foods

A. Parity Calculation

Terms: 1 Canada Dry ($36) = 0.6875 new Norton Simon common
plus 0.3125 of a new $1.60 preferred which is immediately
convertible into 0.875 of the new common.

1 McCall's ($37) = 0.6875 new Norton Simon common + 0.3125 of the new $1.60 convertible preferred

1 Hunt Foods ($58) = 1.25 new Norton common + 0.3125 of the new $1.60 convertible preferred

In addition, there was to be a 5 percent stock dividend to Hunt Foods shareholders before the merger.

Parity: Since the terms are the same for each Canada Dry and McCall's, one could actually buy 1 Canada Dry and sell 1 McCall's short, and deliver the new securities against the short position. In view of the prevailing prices one could make one point on the transaction; which is hardly the way to view this particular situation.

The 5 percent stock dividend to holders of Hunt means that each 1.05 shares of Hunt would receive the package originally intended for 1 full share of Hunt, since there was to be no adjustment for the dilution. Thus 1 Hunt Foods = 1.25/1.05 = 1.19 Norton Simon common + 0.297 new preferred. Now, since all three companies will receive common shares of new Norton Simon common, and using the same procedure outlined in (c) in Appendix A, we can establish a ratio expressing either Canada Dry or McCall's in terms of Hunt Foods common stock. Thus, forgetting for a moment the new preferred stock:

$$1 \text{ Canada Dry } = \frac{0.6875}{1.19 \text{ Hunt Foods}} = 0.578 \text{ Hunt Foods}$$

However, one should only sell short as much Hunt Foods as will yield a net short position of 0.587 Hunt per Canada Dry after the stock dividend of 5 percent is lost on the short position. Therefore, one could only count on the proceeds of 0.55 Hunt Foods per Canada Dry.

As regards the distribution of new preferred per Canada Dry, since one is short 0.578 Hunt Foods after the stock dividend, one would also lose

$$0.578 \text{ Hunt } \times 0.297^7 \text{ new preferred}$$
$$= 0.1717 \text{ new preferred}$$

Accordingly, since each Canada Dry is due to receive 0.3125 new preferred, each Canada Dry will be left with

$$0.3125 - 0.1717 = 0.1408$$

new Norton Simon preferred

Thus, if one purchased a single Canada Dry at $35 and sold 0.55 Hunt Foods at $58, the 0.1408 preferred will have cost

$$\$36 - (0.55 \times \$58) = \$4.10$$

If 0.1408 preferred costs $4.10, one full share costs (is created at)

$$\frac{\$4.10}{0.1408} = \$29.12$$

The new preferred, based on calculations similar to those utilized in (2) above, was valued to sell at around $40.00 per share.

Gross Spread: $40 − $29.12 = $10.88 per Norton Simon preferred

or

$$(\$58 \times .55) + (0.1408 \times \$40) - \$36$$
$$= \$1.53 \, \text{per Canada Dry}$$

B. Practical Application

(1) Position taken: 100 Canada Dry (long) at $36; 55 Hunt Foods (short) at $58

(2) Date position taken: May 17, 1968.

(3) Merger consummated: July 16, 1968.

(4) Exchange of securities effective: September 17, 1968.

(5) Total time involvement [(4) − (2)]: 123 days.

(6) Theoretical Gross Spread: $153 per Canada Dry.

(7) Realized Gross Spread: On July 12, 1968, 14.33[8] of new Norton Simon preferred were sold at $39½, so that 55 Hunt Foods × $58 + $14.33 new preferred × 39½ − $3,600 = $156 realized.

(8) Net Spread:

$156.00	Gross Spread
(79.00)	Interest Cost for 123 Days on $3,600 @ 6½ Percent
12.73	Long Dividends
(12.50)	Short Dividends
$77.23	Net Spread

(9) Annualized Return on Capital:

    (a) Average Statement of Financial Condition
    May 17, 1968–July 16, 1968

    Assets
      100 Canada Dry (long) $3,600

    Liabilities and Capital
      578 Hunt Foods

(short)	$3,190	
Less 578 Hunt Foods		
(borrowed)	(3,190)	...$—0—
Bank Borrowings	....	2,362
Capital		
30 Percent "Haircut"	$1,080	
15-to-1 Ratio	158	 1,238
		$3,600

    (b) Average Statement of Financial Condition
    July 16–September 17, 1968

    Assets
      100 Canada Dry (long) $3,600

    Liabilities and Capital
      Bank Borrowings $3,375
      Capital
        15-to-1 Ratio 225
                         $3,600

Average Capital Employed:

$$\frac{60}{365} \times \$1{,}238 + \frac{63}{365} \times \$225 = \$242.34$$

$$\frac{\text{Net Spread}}{\text{Average Capital}} = \text{Return on Capital}$$

$$\frac{\$77.23}{\$242.34} = 31.8 \text{ Percent per Annum}$$

Eversharp / Warner Lambert Pharmaceutical

A. Parity Calculation

Terms: 1 Eversharp ($29.25) = some combination of a pro-rata share of 1.1 million Warner Lambert ($72⅝) + a pro-rata share of 1,319,514 new common shares in Frawley Enterprises (no market). This reorganization involved Warner Lambert's purchasing Eversharp's wet-shave business in exchange for Warner Lambert common shares, leaving Eversharp with the assets of its non–wet-shave business. These assets had to be distributed to Eversharp's shareholders in order to qualify the entire transaction as a reorganization to both companies, and be nontaxable to Eversharp shareholders. Accordingly, Eversharp transferred the non–wet-shave assets to a controlled corporation, Frawley Enterprises, whose shares it planned to distribute to Eversharp shareholders by means of an offer to exchange their Eversharp shares for shares in Frawley Enterprises, on the basis of

3 Frawley Enterprises for each 1 Eversharp tendered

Any Eversharp shares so exchanged would not receive any Warner Lambert common, thereby shrinking the pool of common stock and common stock equivalents of Eversharp which would be entitled to receive the Warner Lambert. An oversubscription for the Frawley was to be pro-rated. Finally, any shares of Frawley not subscribed to were to be distributed on a pro-rata basis to those Eversharp shareholders who hadn't

subscribed and who were in any case entitled to receive the
Warner Lambert common.

Parity: Three elements must be ascertained in order to arrive at an
approximate value for the total package:

(1) The total pool of common stock and common stock equivalents entitled either to subscribe for the Frawley Enterprises
or to receive the Warner Lambert common shares:

Eversharp Common—		2,254,227 shares outstanding
300,000 Eversharp		
$0.50 Preferred	=	105,769 common
259,506 Eversharp		
$1.00 Preferred	=	230,672 common
Unexercised stock options	=	39,965 common
Total pool	=	2,630,633

(2) A probable market value for the new shares of Frawley Enterprises:

The non-wet-shave business of Eversharp to be transferred to Frawley included the manufacture of ballpoint
pens, the operation of hospital and alcohol addiction treatment facilities, the manufacture of medical instruments,
and drug research. Also, Eversharp would transfer shares in
Schick Investment and Technicolor having a combined market value of approximately $9.9 million. Proforma deficits
on the above businesses had increased from $0.04 in 1965 to
$1.38 in 1969, so that a capitalization rate approach would
not be feasible.

A possible valuation could be established, however, on
the basis of net asset values. Stockholders' equity amounted
to approximately $17 million, taking stock investments at
market value. This would yield a book value per share of

$$\$17 \text{ million}/1,319,514 = \$12.90 \text{ per share}$$

Taking only the liquid assets—cash and marketable
securities—less total liabilities, there would be a value of
$12.5 million, or $9.50 per share. Assuming that the marketplace would take an extremely dismal view of this

company and value it at only $\frac{1}{3}$ of its liquid book value, then the Frawley Shares could be expected to sell in a range of $2.50–$3.50.

(3) The amount of Frawley which might possibly be subscribed for:

Mr. Patrick Frawley, chairman of the board of both Eversharp and Frawley, was the beneficial owner of 296,500 Eversharp. It was very likely that he would exchange a good part of his shares for Frawley Enterprises, as he presumably would want to control as much as posible of a company bearing his name—and in essence continue to own the business (Hartley Pen Company) from which he built his fortune. Other than Mr. Frawley, himself, it was highly unlikely that others would subscribe to the Frawley stock because the probable market value of three shares of Frawley—3 × $3.50—was significantly less than the market value of the Eversharp ($29.25) that would be surrendered in exchange.

The following is a tabulation of the possible parities per share of Eversharp based on the possible range of subscriptions for Frawley Enterprises.

A	B	C		D
Eversharp Common Pool	Total Frawley Available for Exchange	Subscriptions for Frawley Percent	Shares	Equivalent Eversharp ($\frac{1}{3}$C)
2,643,056	1,319,514	—0—	—0—	—0—
2,643,056	1,319,514	10	131,951	43,984
2,643,056	1,319,514	20	263,902	87,967
2,643,056	1,319,514	30	395,853	131,951
2,643,056	1,319,514	40	527,804	175,935
2,643,056	1,319,514	50	659,757	219,919
2,643,056	1,319,514	60	791,706	263,902
2,643,056	1,319,514	70	923,660	307,887
2,643,056	1,319,514	80	1,055,608	351,869
2,643,056	1,319,514	90	1,187,563	395,854
2,643,056	1,319,514	100	1,319,514	

E Balance of Frawley (B-C)	F Balance of Eversharp (A-D)	G Distribution Warner Lambert per Eversharp (1.1 mil./F)	H Distribution Balance of Frawley per Eversharp (E-F)
1,319,514	2,630,633	0.4162	0.5016
1,187,514	2,586,649	0.4232	0.4591
1,055,608	2,542,666	0.4305	0.4151
923,660	2,498,682	0.4381	0.3697
791,706	2,454,698	0.4459	0.3225
659,757	2,410,714	0.4540	0.2737
527,804	2,366,731	0.4623	0.2230
395,853	2,322,746	0.4711	0.1704
263,902	2,278,764	0.4801	0.1158
131,951	2,234,779	0.4895	0.0590
—0—	2,190,795	0.4993	—0—

I Market Value in Warner Lambert (G × $72⅝)	J Market Value in Frawley (H × $2.50)	K Parity per Eversharp (I + J)
$30.23	$1.25	$31.48
30.73	1.15	31.88
31.27	1.04	32.31
31.82	0.92	32.74
32.38	0.81	33.19
32.97	0.68	33.65
33.57	0.56	34.13
34.21	0.43	34.64
34.87	0.29	35.16
35.55	0.15	35.70
36.26	—0—	36.26

It is fairly apparent from the above table that the higher the subscriptions for Frawley Enterprises, the greater will be the total market value to which the nonsubscribing shareholders of Eversharp will be entitled. This relationship would exist (at the quoted price of $72⅝ for Warner Lambert) for any price for the new Frawley shares up to $12.08, calculated as follows:

$$\frac{\$36.26^9 - \$30.23^{10}}{0.5016\,\text{Frawley}^{11}} = \$12.02$$

Above the "break-even" price of $12.02 for the new Frawley shares, then a lesser degree of subscriptions would benefit the nonsubscribing Eversharp shareholders by enhancing the market value of distributions. The author has, however, selected and utilized the price of $2.50 for the new Frawley shares for reasons cited above, so that the table would be useful in the computation of the parity.

Gross Spread: In arbitrage, one must always be on the side of conservatism. Accordingly, from the table we should assume that the worst would happen; that no one would subscribe for the Frawley. Accordingly, the spread would be:

$$\$31.48 - \$29.25 = \$2.23$$

However, for reasons cited above, the author would expect Mr. Frawley to tender approximately 20 percent to 30 percent of his Eversharp in exchange for Frawley, and that a few other stockholders would—oblivious to market value—likewise tender, so that there would be an acceptance of roughly 30 percent of Frawley. In this case, the gross spread would have been:

$$\$32.74 - \$29.25 = \$3.49$$

B. Practical Application

(1) Position taken: 100 Eversharp (long) at $29.25; 42 Warner Lambert (short) at $72\frac{5}{8}$.

(2) Date position taken: January 15, 1970.

(3) Merger consummated: May 15, 1970.

(4) Exchange of securities effective: June 29, 1970.

(5) Total time involvement [(4) − (2)]: 165 days.

(6) Theoretical Gross Spread (from above): It was anticipated that roughly 30 percent of Frawley would be subscribed for and that the new shares of Frawley would sell at a minimum

of $2.50 per share, yielding a gross spread of approximately
$3.49.

(7) Realized Gross Spread: Mr. Frawley did tender, as outlined
in the prospectus dated March 26, 1969, for 360,000 Frawley, amounting to 27.282 percent of Frawley. The prospectus
also stipulated that if no one else accepted the tender, that
Mr. Frawley could exchange his Eversharp for an additional
7.79 percent. On May 15, it was determined that the distributions to the nonsubscribing holders of Eversharp would
be

$$0.4419 \text{ Warner Lambert} + 0.3362 \text{ Frawley}$$

This meant that 35 percent of Frawley was subscribed for
(see table on pages 61 and 62). This happens to coincide
exactly with the total to which Mr. Frawley would have
been eligible according to the prospectus. In other words
no one else tendered for Frawley.

On May 15, 1970, when the distributions were set,
33.62 Frawley could be sold at $27\frac{7}{8}$, and an additional
2.19 Warner Lambert could be sold at $49\frac{1}{4}$ (since 42 had
been sold short instead of 44.19).

Thus total proceeds amounted to

$42 \times \$72\frac{5}{8}$	=	$3,050.25
$33.62 \times 2\frac{7}{8}$	=	96.66
$2.19 \times 59\frac{1}{4}$	=	129.76
Total Proceeds		$3,276.67
less cost of 100 Eversharp		2,925.00
Realized Gross Spread		$351.67

(8) Net Spread:

$351,67	Realized Gross Spread
(105.78)	Interest Cost for 165 Days @ 8 Percent on $2,925
—0—	Long Dividends
(25.20)	Short Dividends
$220.69	Net Spread

(9) Annualized Return on Capital:

   (a) Average statement of Financial Condition
      January 15–May 15, 1970

      Assets

100 Eversharp (long)		$2,925

      Liabilities and Capital

42 Warner Lambert (short)	$3,050	
Less 42 Warner Lambert (borrowed)	(3,050)	...—0—
Bank Borrowings		$1,919
Capital		
30 Percent "Haircut"	$878	
15-to-1 Ratio	128	 1,006
		$2,925

   (b) Average Statement of Financial Condition
      May 15–June 29, 1970

      Assets

100 Eversharp (long)		$2,925

      Liabilities and Capital

Bank Borrowings		$2,742
Capital		
15-to-1 Ratio		183
		$2,925

Average Capital Employed:

$$\frac{120}{365} \times \$1{,}006 + \frac{45}{365} \times \$183 = \$353.30$$

$$\frac{\text{Net Spread}}{\text{Average Capital}} = \text{Return on Capital}$$

$$\frac{\$220.69}{\$353.30} = 62.47 \text{ Percent per Annum}$$

Alloys Unlimited/Plessey, Ltd.

A. Parity Calculation

Terms: 1 Alloys Unlimited, Inc. $(19^{1}/_{2}) = 6^{1}/_{2}$ new American Depository Receipt (ADR) dollar shares of Plessey, Limited. The new ADR dollar shares would be identical in every respect to sterling shares of Plessey Limited traded on the London Stock Exchange with the exception that

(1) The payment of dividends on the dollar shares would be made in U.S. dollar shares.

(2) Only subsequent to June 30, 1975—approximately five years hence—would the ADR dollar shares be convertible on a share-for-share basis into the sterling shares, in order to comply with Bank of England regulations.

The new shares were due to be listed on the New York Stock Exchange upon consummation of the merger. Purchase of these ADRs would be exempt from the Interest Equalization Tax, whereas the sterling shares traded in London would be subject to the tax.

Parity: The London price for the sterling shares of Plessey was $4^{7}/_{8}$ in U.S. dollars.[12] In addition, there was an over-the-counter (OTC) market in the United States for the existing ADR shares of Plessey Limited, which are immediately convertible into the sterling shares. These ADR's were simultaneously bid at $4^{3}/_{4}$. There were thus three securities to consider in establishing a parity:

(1) The sterling shares trading in London.

(2) The ADRs already traded in New York.

(3) The new ADR dollar shares, which could not be converted into the sterling shares for five years.

With a small discount normally existing between the existing ADRs—which are immediately convertible—and the sterling shares, the question becomes one of determining how large a discount would be attributable to the delayed conversion privilege between the new ADR dollar shares and the sterling shares.

Since Alloys unlimited was a British company, it would be fair to assume that the major interest in the new shares would come from British investors. In order for a British private or institutional investor to buy the new ADR dollar shares, rather than the sterling shares (which he can do through a London broker with much less problem and less time involvement), there must be at least enough of a discount to offset the currency premium which the Britisher would lose upon reconversion of dollars—which he initially brought for purchase of the ADRs—into pound sterling (recall that this analysis refers to 1970).

There are two exchange rates that a British investor must be concerned with:

(a) The free rate, which is generally around the fixed parity of $2.40 for the pound sterling.

(b) The security sterling rate, which has generally ranged from premiums of 25 percent to 50 percent over the official rate, depending on the amount of demand for securities outside the Commonwealth, and also the British balance of payments.

British exchange control regulations require that for a British subject to buy foreign currency for the purchase of foreign securities, he must pay the premium rate of 100 percent of the amount of pound sterling involved. When he later resells the foreign security, he can, with the proceeds, repurchase only 75 percent of the equivalent pound sterling at the premium rate, the balance having to be applied against the free rate of exchange. This means that the British investor would lose—with absolute certainty—whatever premium existed at the time of purchase on 25 percent of the money involved, or

$$\text{Exchange loss} = 25\,\text{percent} \times 25\,\text{percent premium} = 6.2\,\text{percent}$$

This is his minimum "premium" risk. There is simultaneously the risk that on the other 75 percent the premium itself could fluctuate between purchase and sale. It would be favorable to our British investor if the premium increased, and unfavorable if it decreased. Once again, conservation must prevail, and he must face the possibility that the entire premium could disappear[13] by the time that he sold his ADRs and wishes to repurchase pound sterling, or

$$\text{Additional exchange loss} = 75 \text{ percent} \times 25 \text{ percent premium}$$
$$= 18.8 \text{ percent}$$

Thus, in order to buy the new ADR dollar shares in favor of the sterling shares, a British investor would already require a discount equal to the exchange loss on 100 percent of the money involved, which is in this case 25 percent. To this one would add an additional 5 percent for the normal foreign exchange risk (in this case a possible devaluation of the dollar during the time that the new shares are not convertible) and for the "nuisance factor."

Therefore, with a security sterling premium of 25 percent, a total discount of 30 percent could be normally expected to exist between the bid prices of the new ADRs and the sterling shares. With a sterling premium of 30 percent, a discount of 35 percent would exist; and so on.

Gross Spread: 70 percent $\times$ $4\frac{7}{8} \times 6.5 - \$19\frac{1}{2} = \$22.18 - \$19.50$
$= \$2.68$

B. Practical Application

(1) Position taken:
100 Alloys Unlimited (long) at $19\frac{1}{2}$.
650 Plessey Ltd. ADRs (short) at $4\frac{3}{4}$.

(2) Date position taken: April 23, 1970.

(3) Merger consummated: July 17, 1970.

(4) Exchange of securities effective: August 25, 1970.

(5) Total time involvement [(4) − (2)]: 124 days.

(6) Theoretical Gross Spread (from above): $267 per 100 Alloys Unlimited, based on a discount of 30 percent for the new ADRs against the London price for Plessey common.

(7) Realized Gross Spread: On June 30, 1970, after shareholder approvals were obtained, a "when-issued" OTC market

began in the new ADR dollar shares. On this date, the following bid prices existed:

Regular ADR Shares	—	$3.50
Sterling Shares	—	$3.60
New ADR Dollar Shares	—	$2.50

In other words, there was a discount of $28\frac{1}{2}$ percent—and not 30 percent as had been estimated—on the new ADR dollar shares.[14] Now since we had taken a short position of 650 regular ADRs, they had to be covered, since the new ADRs could not be delivered against them. Also the new ADRs had to be sold out. Accordingly,

Original Sale of 650 Regular ADRs @ $4.75	=	$3,087.50
Repurchase of 650 Regular ADRs @ $3.55	=	(2,307.50)
Sale of 650 New ADRs @ $2.50	=	1,625.00
Original Purchase of 100 Alloys @ $19\frac{1}{2}$	=	(1,950.00)
Realized Gross Spread	=	$455.00

(8) Net Spread:

$455.00	Realized Gross Spread
(53.00)	Interest Cost for 124 Days @ 8 Percent on $1,950
10.00	Long Dividends
(26.65)	Short Dividends
$385.35	Net Spread

(9) Annualized Return on Capital:
   (a) Average Statement of Financial Condition
        April 23–July 17, 1970

   Assets
        100 Alloys Unltd. (long) $1,950.00

Liabilities and Capital
   650 Plessey Ltd.
   ADRs (short) $3,087.50
   Less 650 Plessey Ltd.
   ADRs (borrowed)   (3,087.50) ....—0—
   Bank Borrowings 1,277.00
   Capital
      30 Percent "Haircut" $585.00
      15-to-1 Ratio   88.00 ....   673.00
                                    $1,950.00

(b) Average Statement of Financial Condition
   July 18–August 25, 1970
   Assets
      100 Alloys Unltd (long) $1,950.00
   Liabilities and Capital
      Bank Borrowings $1,828.00
      Capital
         15-to-1 Ratio 122.00
                                    $1,950.00

Average Capital Employed:

$$\frac{85}{365} \times \$673 + \frac{39}{365} \times \$122 = \$169$$

$$\frac{\text{Net Spread}}{\text{Average Capital}} = \quad \text{Return on Capital}$$

$$\frac{\$385.35}{\$169} = 228 \text{ Percent per Annum}$$

Chubb Corp./First National City Corp.

A. Parity Calculation
Terms: 1 Chubb Corporation ($65) = 0.4 FNC Corp. ($74) + $\frac{1}{2}$ new $4.24 preferred convertible into .12 common.

Parity:
   (1) On straight conversion into common:

$$0.4 + (0.5 \times 1.2) = 1 \times 74 = \$74$$

   (2) With a premium on the preferred
      At this point, it would be useful to introduce the concept of "creating" a new convertible security. If one buys a security and, through an exchange of securities obtains a new convertible security, one buys, or "creates" the latter through the former. In the actual case, by buying Chubb at $65 and selling 0.4 FNC common at $74, one is creating $\frac{1}{2}$ of a new $4.24 preferred at: $65 - 0.4 \times \$74 = \$65 - \$29.60 = \$35.40$. Since $\frac{1}{2}$ of a preferred is created at this price, one entire preferred is created at twice the latter, or $70.80. In this manner, one is able to determine the current yield basis upon which the new security is created. In this case $4.24/\$70.80 = 5.9$ percent. In fashion similar to that utilized in case #2, an attempt is made to ascribe a premium and proper yield for the new preferred. In so doing, the author arrived at a probable yield of 4.4 percent, and a 10 percent premium over the conversion parity of $88.80, which is translated to a price of $96.

Gross Spread:
   (1) On straight conversion:
      $74 - \$65 = \$9.00$
   (2) With a premium on conversion:
      $77.60 - \$65 = \$12.60$; or $96 -
      $70.80 = \$25.20$ per new preferred

B. Practical Application
   (1) Position taken:
         100 Chubb (long) at $65;
         100 First National City Corp. (short) at $74.
   (2) Date position taken: Febrauary 20, 1969.
   (3) Merger plan cancelled: June 16, 1969.
   (4) Positions reversed: June 18, 1969.
   (5) Total time involvement: (4) − (2): 118 days.

(6) Theoretical Gross Spread: $900 per 100 Chubb, taking the more conservative approach.

(7) Realized loss: Sell 100 Chubb at $42½; cover 100 First National City at $64½.

Result:

$6,500	Cost of Chubb
−4,250	Proceeds of Chubb sale
($2,250)	Loss on Chubb
$7,400	Proceeds on First Natl. City sale
−6,450	Cost of repurchase
$950	Profit on First Natl. City.

The realized loss per 100 Chubb is therefore $1,900 before expenses.

(8) Net Loss:

($1,900)	Realized Loss
(168)	Interest Cost for 118 Days @ 8 Percent on $6,500
63	Long Dividends
(56)	Short Dividends
($2,061)	Net Loss

(9) Annualized Rate of Loss on Capital:

Average Statement of Financial Condition

February 20–June 18, 1969

Assets

100 Chubb (long) $6,500

Liabilities and Capital

Less 100 First Natl. City (short)

Less 100 First Natl. City (borrowed) .. $—0—

Bank Borrowings 4,264

Capital

30 Percent "Haircut"	$1,950	
15-to-1 Ratio	286	.... $2,236
		$6,500

Average Capital Employed:

$$\frac{118}{365} \times \$2,236 = \$720$$

$$\frac{\text{Net Realized Loss}}{\text{Average Capital}} = \text{Loss on Capital}$$

$$\frac{\$2,061}{\$720} = 286 \text{ Percent per Annum Loss}$$

Mergers from 1971 to the Present

New England Nuclear Corp. with Dupont DeNemours Inc.

For Broker/Dealer Operating under the Alternative Net Capital Requirement

A. Parity Calculation
Terms: 1 New England Nuclear (\$43) = 1.3 Dupont (\$37)
Parity: 1.3 × \$37 − \$48.10
Gross Spread: \$48.10 − 43 = \$5.10

B. Practical Application
(1) Position taken: 100 New England Nuclear (long) @ \$43; 130 Dupont (short) @ \$37
(2) Date position taken: December 5, 1980
(3) Merger consummated: March 9, 1981[15]
(4) Exchange of securities effective: April 9, 1981[16]
(5) Total time involvement: [(4) − (2)] = 126 days
(6) Theoretical Gross Spread: \$510 per 100 New England Nuclear
(7) Realized Gross Spread: \$510 (no new securities)
(8) Net Spread:

\$510.00	Gross Spread
(278.32)	Interest Cost (18.9 Percent[17] for 125 Days on 4,300)
7.5	Long Dividends[18]
(60.0)	Short Dividends[19]
\$179.18	Net Spread

(9) Annualized Rate on Capital

(a) Average Statement of Financial Position
December 5, 1980–March 9, 1981
Assets
100 New England Nuclear (long)....$4,300
Liabilities and Capital
130 Dupont (short) $4,810
130 Dupont (borrowed)   ($4,810)   —0—
Bank Borrowings 2,857
Capital
30 Percent "Haircut"[20]

(b) Average Statement of Financial Position
March 9, 1981–April 9, 1981[21]
Assets
100 New England Nuclear (long) .. $4,300
Liabilities and Capital
Bank Borrowings $4,300

Average Capital Employed:

$$\frac{94 \text{ days}}{365 \text{ days}} \times \$1443 = \$371.62$$

$$\frac{\text{Net Spread}}{\text{Average Capital}} = \text{Return on Capital}$$

$$\frac{\$179.18}{\$371.62} \times 100 = 49 \text{ Percent}$$

For Broker/Dealer Operating under the Aggregate Indebtedness Net Capital Requirement. The calculations remain the same as (1) through (8).

(9) Annualized Return on Capital

(a) Average Statement of Financial Position
December 5, 1980–March 9, 1981
Assets
100 New England Nuclear (long) .. $4,300

Liabilities and Capital
    130 Dupont (short)   4,810
    Less 130 Dupont (borrowed) (4,810) —0—
    Bank Borrowings $2,678
    Capital
        30 Percent "Haircut"[22] 1,443
        15-to-1 Ratio[23] 179
                                     $4,300

(b) Average Statement of Financial Position
     March 9, 1981–April 9, 1981

    Assets
        100 NEN (long) $4,300
    Liabilities and Capital
        Bank Borrowings $4,031
        15-to-1 Ratio 269
                                       $4,300

Average Capital Employed:

$$\frac{94\ days}{365\ days} \times 1622 + \frac{31\ days}{365\ days} \times 269 = \$440.56$$

$$\text{Return on Capital} = \frac{179.18}{440.56} \times 100 = 40.7\ \text{Percent}$$

For an Individual. Again, the calculations are the same from (1) through (7).

(8) Net Spread

$510	Gross Spread
(300.40)	Interest Cost (20.4 Percent[24] for 125 Days on 4,300)
7.50	Long Dividends
(60.0)	Short Dividends
157.1	Net Spread

(9) Annualized Return on Capital

  (a) Average statement of Financial Position
    December 5, 1980–March 9, 1981
    Assets
      100 New England Nuclear (long) .. $4,300
    Liabilities and Capital

130 Dupont (short)	$4,810	
Less 130 Dupont (borrowed)	(4,810)	.... $—0—
Capital required—Federal[25]	4,555	
Capital required—house[26]	—0—	
	4,555	

  (b) Average Statement of Financial Position
    March 9, 1981–April 9, 1981
    Assets
      100 NEN (long) $4,300
    Liabilities and Capital
      Bank Borrowings $3,870
      Capital Requirement[27] 430
                                $4,300

Average Capital Employed:

$$\frac{94}{365}(4555) + \frac{31}{365}(430) = \$1,209.59$$

$$\text{Return on Capital} = \frac{\text{Net Spread}}{\text{Average Capital}}$$

$$= \frac{157.1}{1210}$$

$$= 13 \text{ Percent}$$

Reliance Electric/Exxon

Parity Calculation
Terms: 1 Reliance Electric ($61) = $72
Gross Spread: $72 − 61 = $11

Practical Application
(1) Position taken: 100 Reliance Electric (long) at $61
(2) Date position taken: May 25, 1979
(3) Shares tendered: July 11, 1971
(4) July 11, 1979
(5) Total time involvement $[(4) - (2)] = 123$ days
(6) Net Spread

$11.	Gross Spread
(2.34)	Interest Cost (11.4 Percent on $61.00 for 123 Days)
(.40)	Dividends (Exchange Date July 10)
$8.26	Net Spread

(7) Annualized Return on Capital
  (a) Average Statement of Financial Condition
     May 25, 1979–September 25, 1979[28]

Assets
    100 Reliance Electric (long) $6,100

Liabilities and Capital
    Bank Borrowings $5,185
    15 Percent "Haircut" 915
                            $6,100

  (b) Average Statement of Financial Condition
     July 11, 1979–September 25, 1979

Assets
    100 Reliance Electric Corp $6,100
Liabilities
    Bank Borrowings 5,185
    "Haircut" 915
                            $6,100

Average Capital Employed:

$$\frac{(123 \text{ days})}{(365 \text{ days})}(915) = \$308$$

$$\text{Return on Capital} = \frac{826}{308}$$

$$= 267 \text{ Percent}$$

CIT Financial/RCA

Parity Calculation
Terms: 1 CIT Financial (\$56) = \$65 up to 49 percent of stock
  1 CIT Financial = 1 RCA regular 3.65 preferred (\$32) plus
  1 RCA 2.125 convertible preferred (\$21) for remaining 51 percent
  1 RCA convertible preferred − 0.7143 RCA common stock

Gross Spread:

On tender = .62 (65 − 56) = \$5.58
On stock = .38 ($32\frac{1}{8}$ + $22\frac{1}{2}$ − 56) = (0.20)
Gross Spread = 5.38

Practical Application
(1) Position taken: 100 CIT Financial (long) at \$56.
(2) Date position taken: August 22, 1979
(3) Date tendered: November 8, 1979
(4) Proration factor announcement made: November 26, 1979
(5) Cash received for 62 shares on: December 4, 1979.
(6) Position Taken: 38 shares 3.65 RCA preferred W/I at $32\frac{1}{8}$
    38 shares 2.125 RCA preferred W/I at $22\frac{1}{2}$
(7) Date short position taken: December 11, 1979
(8) Merger consummated: January 31, 1980
(9) Exchange of securities effective: February 7, 1980

(10) Net Spread

$538	Gross Spread
(225)	Interest Cost (14.1 Percent on $5,600 from August 22, 1979–December 4, 1979)
(55)	Interest Cost (15.3 Percent on $2,128 from December 4, 1979–February 7, 1980)
98	Dividends on Long Position[29]
$356	Net Spread

(11) Annualized Return on Capital

   (a) Average Statement of Financial Condition
   August 22, 1979–November 26, 1979

   Assets

      100 CIT Financial (long) $5,600

   Liabilities and Capital

      Bank Borrowings $4,760
      15 Percent "Haircut"   840
                                                 $5,600

   (b) Average Statement of Financial Condition
   November 26, 1979–December 11, 1979

   Assets

      38 CIT Financial (long) $2,128

   Liabilities and Capital

      Bank Borrowings $1,809
      15 Percent "Haircut"   319
                                                 $2,128

   (c) Average Statement of Financial Condition
   December 11, 1979–January 31, 1980

   Assets

      38 CIT Financial (long) $2,128

Liabilities and Capital

38 3.65 RCA Preferred W/I	1,220.75	
38 2.125 RCA Preferred W/I	855.00	—0—
Less 38 3.65 RCA Preferred		
(borrowed)	(1,220.75)	
Less 38 2.125 RCA Preferred		
(borrowed)	(855.00)	—0—
Bank Borrowings		$1,490
30 Percent "Haircut"		638
		$2,128

(d) Average Statement of Financial Condition
January 31, 1980–February 7, 1980
Assets

38 CIT Financial (long)	$2,128

Liabilities and Capital

38 3.65 RCA Preferred W/I	1,220.75	
38 2.125 RCA Preferred W/I	855.00	
Less 38 3.65 RCA Preferred		
(borrowed)	(1,220.75)	
Less 38 2.125 RCA Preferred		
(borrowed)	(855.00)	—0—
Bank Borrowings		$2,128
"Haircut" (short exempt)		—0—
		$2,128

Average Capital Employed:

$$\frac{96\,\text{days}}{365\,\text{days}}(\$840) + \frac{15}{365}(\$319) = \frac{51}{365}(638) = \$323$$

$$\frac{\text{Net Spread}}{\text{Average Capital}} = \text{Return on Capital}$$

$$\frac{\$356}{\$323} = 110\,\text{Percent per Annum (pre-tax)}$$

Richardson-Merrell/Dow Chemical

Parity Calculation

Terms:

 1 Share Richardson-Merrell ($39) = 1 share Richardson-Vicks (31\frac{1}{2}$) (distribution) March 6, 1981
 1 Share Richardson-Merrell ($39) = 0.3458 shares of Dow Chemical (35\frac{1}{2}$)^{30}

Gross Spread: (35\frac{1}{2}$) (.31158) = 31$\frac{1}{2}$ − $39 = $3.56.

Practical Application

(1) Position taken: 100 Richardson Merrell at $39
(2) Date position taken: January 14, 1981.
(3) Position taken: 31 Dow Chemical (short) at 35$\frac{1}{2}$
(4) Date position taken: February 10, 1981
(5) Position taken: Vicks when issued (short) at 31$\frac{1}{2}$
(6) Date position taken: May 9, 1981
(7) Merger consummated and effective: March 10, 1981
(8) Total time involvement: 65 Days
(9) Net Spread

$356	Gross Spread
(128)	Interest Cost (18.4 Percent for 65 Days on $3,900)
33	Dividends Long
—0—	Dividends Short
$261	Net Spread

(10) Annualized Return on Capital
 (a) Statement of Financial Condition
  January 14, 1981–February 10, 1981
  Assets
  100 Richardson Merrell (long) $3,900
  Liabilities and Capital
  Bank Borrowings $3,315
  15 Percent "Haircut" 585
                $3,900

(b) Statement of Financial Condition
February 10, 1981–March 9, 1981
Assets
    100 Richardson Merrell (long) $3,900
Liabilities and Capital
    31 Dow (short) $1,100.50
    −31 Dow (borrowed)   ($1,100.50)   —0—
    Bank Borrowings $3,160
    "Haircut"[31]   740
                                              $3,900

(c) Statement of Financial Condition
March 9, 1981–March 10, 1981
Assets
    100 Richardson Merrell (long) $3,900
Liabilities and Capital
    31 Dow Chemical short $1,100.50
    Less 31 Dow (borrowed)   (1,100.50) .... —0—
    100 Vics W/I   3,150.00
    100 Vics W/I (borrowed)   (3,150.00) .... —0—
    Bank Borrowings 2,625
        30 Percent "Haircut" 1,275
                                              $3,900

Average Capital Employed:

$$\frac{27 \text{ days}}{365 \text{ days}}(\$585) + \frac{27}{365}(\$740) = \frac{(1)}{(365)}(\$1{,}275) = \$101$$

$$\text{Return on Capital} = \frac{\$261}{\$101}$$

$$= 258 \text{ Percent}$$

Twentieth Century Fox Film Corp.

Parity Calculation

Terms: 1 Twentieth Century Fox Film ($62) = $60 plus 1 United Television Inc. (UTV) ($7^3/_4$)
Gross Spread: $60 + 7^3/_4 - 62 = \$5.75$

Practical Application

(1) Position taken: 100 Twentieth Century Fox (long) at $62

(2) Date position taken: February 24, 1981

(3) Position taken: 100 UTV W/I (short) at $7\frac{3}{4}$

(4) Date position taken: May 19, 1981.

(5) Merger effective: June 12, 1981 (consummated June 10, 1981)

(6) Proceeds received: June 12, 1981

(7) Total time involvement: 107 days

(8) Net Spread

$575	Gross Spread
(325)	Interest Cost (17.9 Percent on $6,200 for 107 Days)
45	Dividends (.45 Stock Record 3/10)
$295	

(9) Annualized Return on Capital

   (a) Average Statement of Financial Condition

      February 24, 1981–May 19, 1981

      Assets

         100 Twentieth Century Fox Film ... $6,200

      Liabilities and Capital

         Bank Borrowings $5,270

         15 Percent "Haircut" 930

                       $6,200

   (b) Average Statement of Financial Condition

      May 19, 1981–June 10, 1981

      Assets

         100 Twentieth Century Fox Film ... $6,200

      Liabilities and Capital

         100 UTV (short) $775

         Less 100 UTV (borrowed) (775) —0—

         Bank Borrowings $5,270

         15 Percent "Haircut" 930

                       $6,200

Average Capital Employed:

$$\$930\frac{(105)}{(365)} = \$267$$

$$\text{Return on Capital} = \frac{\$295}{\$267}$$

$$= 110 \text{ Percent per Annum}$$

Use of Options in Merger Arbitrage

Utah International/General Electric (without Options)

Parity Calculation
Terms: 1 Utah International ($53) = 1.3 General Electric ($54\frac{1}{8}$)
Gross Spread: ($54\frac{1}{8} \times 1.3$) − 53 = $17.36

Practical Application
  (1) Position taken: 100 Utah International (long) at 53
                  130 General Electric short at $54\frac{1}{8}$
  (2) Date position taken: March 24, 1976
  (3) Merger consummated: December 15, 1976
  (4) Exchange effective: December 21, 1976
  (5) Total time involvement: 272 days
  (6) Net Spread:

$1,736	Gross Spread
(237)	Interest Cost (5.5 Percent Interest on $5,300 for 272 Days)
90	Dividends (Long)
(125)	Dividends (Short)
$1,464	Net Spread

  (7) Annualized Return on Investment
     Average Statement of Financial Condition
     March 24, 1976–December 15, 1976
     Assets
       100 Utah International (long) $5,300

Liabilities and Capital
    130 GE (short) $7,036
    Less 130 GE (borrowed)   (7,036) . . . . . —0—
    Bank Borrowings $3,190
        30 Percent "Haircut" (on short) 2,110
                                       $5,300

Average Capital Employed:

$$(\$2,110)\frac{(266\ \text{days})}{(365\ \text{days})} = \$1,538$$

$$\text{Return on Capital} = \frac{\$1,464}{\$1,538}$$

$$= 95\ \text{Percent per Annum}$$

Utah International/General Electric (with Options)

A. Possible Combinations

B. Parity Calculation

    Terms: 1 Utah International ($53) = 1.3 General Electric (52)
    Gross Spread: 7.25 from option sale

$$\frac{+(1.3)(50) - (2)(1.3) - (53)}{\$16.65}$$

C. Practical Application

  (1) Position taken:
      Buy 100 Utah International at $53
      Sell 1.3 Oct 50 GE options at $7\frac{1}{4}$ ($54\frac{1}{8}$)
  (2) Date position taken: March 24, 1976
  (3) Oct 50 GE options exercised, sell short at 52
  (4) Date exercised: October 22, 1976
  (5) Merger consummated: December 15, 1976
  (6) Exchange effective: December 21, 1976
  (7) Total time involvement: 272 days

(8) Net Spread:

      $1,665   Gross Spread
       (237)   Interest Cost (6.0 Percent on $5,300
                for 272 Days)
         90   Dividends (Long)
        (45)   Dividends (Short)
      $1,473

(9) Annualized Return on Investment
  (a) Average Statement of Financial Condition
     March 24, 1976-October 27, 1976

     Assets
       100 Utah International $5,300
     Liabilities and Capital
       Bank Borrowings $3,502
       Capital employed:

"Haircut"[32]	$2,111	
Less Market Value of Option	(725)	
Plus In the Money Amount	412	1,798
		$5,300

  (b) Average Statement of Financial Condition
     October 22, 1976–December 15, 1976

     Assets
       100 Utah International $5,300
     Liabilities and Capital

130 GE (short)	$6,760	
Less 130 GE (borrowed)	(6,760)	—0—
Bank Borrowings		3,272
"Haircut"		2,028
		$5,300

Average Capital Employed:

$$(\$1,798)\frac{212\,\text{days}}{365\,\text{days}} + (\$2,208)\frac{(60)}{(365)} = \$1,378$$

$$\text{Return on Capital} = \frac{\$1,473}{\$1,378}$$

$$= 107\ \text{Percent per Annum}$$

Whether examples of the period of the late 1960s or late 1970s and 1980s are used, and whether the low carry costs of the earlier period or the higher rates of the later period are considered, it is clear that the arbitrage game offers a substantial return for the professional (see Table 3.1). And while losses can occur (and at a high loss rate—see Chubb/First National City Corp. results), it is clear that we have here the classic high-return, high-risk game that professionals play.

Table 3.1 Summary of Returns for Arbitrage Professionals: 1968–1981

	Pre-tax Annualized Return on Capital (in percent)
Early Period	
Scientific Data System/Xerox	123
Hartford Fire Insurance/ITT	43
Canada Dry/McCalls/Hunt Food	32
Eversharp/Warner Lambert	63
Alloys Unlimited/Plessey Limited	228
Chubb Corp./First National City Corp.	(286) Loss
Later Period	
New England Nuclear/DuPont	49
Reliance Electric/Exxon	267
CIT Financial/RCA	110
Richardson Merrill/Dow Chemical	258
20th Century Fox/Marvin Davis	110
Utah International/GE	95
Utah International/GE with options	107

Source: Chapter 3

It is instructive, finally, to recall that in the New England Nuclear/Dupont case, in which the results are worked out for an individual arbitrageur as well as for a professional, the individual would have achieved a 13 percent rate of return. That return is not much more that a quarter of the rate of return (49 percent) achieved by the pros.

Chapter 4

Cash Tender Offers

Situations Prior to 1971

Arbitrage activity in the realm of cash tender bids was strictly the private preserve of the Arbitrage Community prior to the adoption of the SEC's "Short Tendering Rule" in May 1968.[1] This Rule severely curtailed the Community's participation in what had been the most profitable and undoubtedly the most exciting of all arbitrage situations. It is important to comprehend how the arbitrageurs functioned in this activity before the Rule was adopted, and after its adoption, because the difference manifests itself not only in arbitrageurs' profit and loss statements, but more importantly, in the marketplace as well.

What the Rule did, among other things, was to prohibit "short tendering," a practice that involved tendering, or offering securities which an arbitrageur had not actually purchased. In short tendering, the arbitrageur would not be "long"—in the legal sense of

89

the word—some or all of the securities that he was tendering in acceptance of a particular cash tender offer. "Short tendering" assumed strategic importance in any offer for cash which was for less than all of a company's outstanding common stock. The ability to tender short was the hedge that the arbitrageur needed in order to safeguard his profit and reduce his price risk, very much in the same way as he was accomplished through a short sale in a merger arbitrage. Tendering short could be accomplished in two different ways. First, if physical securities were not needed to accompany the required Letter of Transmittal, the arbitrageur could sign a "pledge tender" as provided on the Letter of Transmittal. This was the arbitrageur's guarantee to the bidding company that he would make physical delivery of the pro-rated number of securities that he had tendered, not later than a stipulated number of business days after the Groom called for their delivery. Secondly, if the physical securities had to accompany the Letter of Transmittal, then the arbitrageur could borrow securities and tender same.

Let us assume that Y is bidding $90 each for 300,000 shares of X, of which there are one million outstanding. Before the announcement of the offer, X was trading at $60 per share, but after the announcement arbitrageurs bid the stock up to $85 (a fairly typical occurrence). If a person were to buy X at $85 and tender them to Y in order to receive $90, and all 900,000 of the outstanding X were tendered, then only 33 percent of his tender, on a pro-rata basis, would receive $90, and the remaining 66 percent could be sold in the marketplace, presumably for a price comparable to the pre-announcement price, let us say $60. The result of this transaction would be a gain of $5 per share on 33 shares, and a loss of $15 per share on 66 shares, with a net loss $8.25 per share.

The arbitrageur, in the same situation, would buy 100 X at $85 but would tender 300 X to Company Y, with the result that the arbitrageur's real long position in X would be accepted in its entirety. Thus, by tendering short—or over-tendering—200 shares, the arbitrageur could net a $5 gain per share. The fact that he could do this permitted him to pay the $85 for X. The fact that today, he can no longer "short tender" induces him to pay considerably less for X.

The calculation that induced the arbitrageur to short tender a particular number of shares in a cash offer similar to the one described above was often both difficult and delicate. Referring once again to the case cited above, he would have to determine the following elements:

1. Blocks of major insider and institutional holdings that might not necessarily comply with the offer.
2. Blocks already held by Y.
3. Amount of X bought by the Arbitrage Community since the inception of the offer.
4. The amount of stock held by the public.
5. The percentage of the public's stock that would be tendered.
6. The actual total number of shares that the bidder would accept under the terms of the offer.
7. The amount of stock that the Arbitrage Community would short tender.

Each of the above could be considered variables that were constantly—even up to the last minute of the offer—liable to change. Yet, an arbitrageur as part of his job approximates each of the above. Let us take the elements in the above sequence.

First, the "stationary" blocks could often be ascertained by contacting the major blocks and inquiring whether or not the owners intended to accept the offer.[2] Second, Y would normally reveal its accumulated position, and would rarely increase same after the offer was promulgated. Third, the Arbitrage Community's position was roughly the total of all daily volumes in X since the announcement of the offer. After all, only arbitrageurs could afford to pay the high market price (which they then could hedge). Fourth, the amount of stock held by the public at the moment could be calculated in the following way:

Total shares outstanding − stationary blocks − block already held by Y − amount bought by Arbitrage Community

Fifth, an approximation of the amount that would be tendered by the public could be calculated by canvassing the large brokerage houses for the percentage of total customer positions which were accepting the offer. The various percentages would then be averaged. Sixth, determining the number of shares that would actually be accepted under the offer by Y was a matter of a basic faith in human nature, one eye on the cost of money, and the other on its availability. The problem usually was that the Groom was asking for tenders for a specific number of shares yet usually leaving itself open to the possibility that it could take more than that amount if such were to be tendered. Thus, an arbitrageur had to assume that based on the company's actual cash position and lines of credit, and the cost of money, that either Y would accept the specified amount, or that it would accept more than that amount. If the general feeling was that more than the minimum would be accepted, then, in order to obtain a rough idea of the additional quantity, the arbitrageur would have to rely on his contacts in the banking world. Seventh, the members of the Arbitrage Community would notify each other of their own individual short-tendering plans, so that the arbitrage intelligence network could piece together the consensus.

Let us assume in the actual case the arbitrageur is able to determine that: (1) the public holds 700,000 shares and (2) will tender 600,000, (3) that the Arbitrage Community has bought 500,000 shares and (4) plans collectively to short-tender an additional 150,000 shares, and (5) that Y will only accept 300,000 shares. Thus, with a total of 900,000 shares tendered, there will be a pro-ration of $33\frac{1}{3}$ percent. If the arbitrageur in question has himself purchased 5,000 shares, he would arrange to tender a total of 15,000 shares.

The classic example of what can go wrong in a similar situation was the cash offer made by the Banque de Paris et des Pays-Bas (Geneva) for Columbia Pictures in August 1966. The offer was at $33.50 per share for 350,000 of the 1,966,000 shares outstanding at that time. The stock of Columbia Pictures had been trading in the lower twenties prior to the offer.

As the expiration of the tender offer approached, the following information was available in the Arbitrage Community:

- Stationary blocks amounted to 733,000 shares.
- The Arbitrage Community had purchased roughly 300,000 shares.
- The public held 933,000 shares, of which 25 percent would be tendered, or 230,000 shares.
- The Arbitrage Community was planning to short-tender 200,000 shares.

Thus, if the Banque de Paris were only going to accept 350,000 shares on a pro-rated basis, it was easy to figure that roughly 730,000 shares would be tendered, and that there would be a pro-rata acceptance of 47 percent. Yet at the eleventh hour, rumors began to reach Wall Street that the Banque de Paris might take considerably more than the stipulated 350,000 shares, which actually threw the delicate calculation into jeopardy. At this very crucial juncture, the local representative and tender agent for the Banque de Paris issued a written statement to the effect that there was absolutely no possibility that more than 350,000 shares would be accepted under the offer.

The aftermath is a bit of history that arbitrageurs wish to forget. There were 650,000 shares tendered, and all 650,000 shares were accepted! The arbitrageurs were thus short the 200,000 shares which they had effectively short-tendered. Therefore, what they bought in the range of $29–31, plus what they short-tendered was accepted for $33.50; but the short positions had to be covered in the range of $38 to $40.

It was during the actual tender period of Ling-Temco-Vought's bid for 63 percent of Jones & Laughlin Steel that the SEC adopted its "Short Tendering Rule." The offer was $85 per share.[3] Jones & Laughlin had been trading in the $50s prior to the offer. After the announcement, the stock quickly made its way to the $78 level, as arbitrageurs began their intricate short-tender calculations. When during the course of trading, it was announced over the Dow Jones

News Service that the "Rule" had effectively been adopted, there was a mild shock in the Community, with Jones & Laughlin retreating to $74–$75. Arbitrageurs were forced to quickly find a new way to hedge their long positions in this cash offer, or else face severe losses. Some resorted to buying put options for the number of shares they previously had counted on being able to short-tender. Others tried selling short the equivalent of their short-tender position, but the SEC ruled that only net long positions could be tendered. Those who thus could not buy put options—and there was only a limited supply of puts in J&L—had to rely on the aftermarket in J&L, which was very risky. However, fortunately in this situation, 7,024,000 shares were tendered, resulting in a pro-rata acceptance of 71.3 percent which was rather on the high side. The balance of the Arbitrage Community's position—that which was not accepted under the offer—was placed on the market. Here again, the Community was fortunate in that the stock reopened at $62, held up by rumors of a fairly imminent stock deal with LTV for the remaining shares of J&L. Thus, an arbitrageur who paid $75 for his stock had 71.3 percent of his position accepted at $85, and sold the balance at $62 after the expiration of the offer, enabling him to register an overall profit of $3.40 per share.

The fact that arbitrageurs are now forced to throw themselves on the mercy of the after-market vagaries explains why the spreads are now considerably wider in pro-rated cash tender offers. The SEC was undoubtedly trying to protect the public through the "Short Tendering Rule" but in retrospect it may have done more harm than good by eliminating the practice. Previously, a private investor or institution had the option of selling his or its entire position at the Arbitrage Community's high bid in the marketplace, rather than risk having to face the after-market for the non-accepted portion of a tender. Now, however, the Arbitrage bid is proportionately lower, and a good deal less liquid.

Nevertheless, one is not defenseless in protecting one's position during a pro-rated cash tender offer. While Rule 10b-4 is subject to constantly changing interpretations by the SEC as to the meaning of a "net long position," it seems to be currently accepted by the staff of the SEC that an investor may choose one of the following alternatives or any combination thereof:

- Sell shares short of the target company which he will have been able to borrow after having made an irrevocable tender of his long position. This is exceedingly difficult because most of the outstanding shares are usually tendered and very few people are willing to lend shares for such purposes. This option is severely limited due to the unavailability of shares to sell short.
- One may write (sell) call options either before or after he tenders his shares. The writing (selling) of such contracts will not reduce the amount of shares that may be tendered in computing whether holders are "net long" of the target company shares. However, an irrevocable tender will result in the uncovering of a previously covered writing position. Accordingly, option writers may be required to satisfy assignment notices either through the delivery of other shares held long, borrowed, or through open market purchases at the current market price.
- In addition to selling a call option, one can buy a put option in order to try to protect against the aforementioned after-market vagaries of the target company's shares.

No matter what combination of the above one utilizes in protecting a position, the choice comes down to a question of what kind of insurance is available and at what price. Experience in these matters is such that just as one looks for the premium on an insurance policy, one finds that premiums on options to protect an investment position can also be quite costly.

Cash Tender Wave of the Late 1970s and Early 1980s

Introduction

Whereas one would occasionally see a cash offer in the takeover period of the 1960s, most of these were either cash merger offers or a tender offer proposed on a friendly basis.

A new era was spawned in July, 1974, however, when Inco made a surprise offer to purchase the ESB Corporation (the old

Electronic Storage Battery Company). This concept, to be called the "Saturday Night Special," was largely designed at the investment banking firm of Morgan Stanley and was meant to circumvent recalcitrant directors by proceeding to make an offer directly to shareholders. It was construed in such a way that the target Bride's shareholders would have to respond quickly to such an offer in the hope that the attacking Groom would quickly make off with a controlling interest in the Bride's share. Thus was born the "hostile tender offer." United Technologies finally emerged as a rival bidder along with Inco, but the latter flexed its financial muscle to the limit and finally won the favor of the now not-so-reluctant Bride with a preemptive offer.

A variation to this hostile tender offer was what became known as the "bear hug" strategy. Often a target company would not reveal the fact that it had received an offer from a prospective groom and would simply stifle it through non-action. Here again, Morgan Stanley, most notably in the offer of Anderson Clayton for Gerber Baby Foods, decided to force the issue by announcing the offer publicly and stating that it wished to negotiate a friendly offer, thereby forcing Gerber's management to react. Unfortunately for Gerber shareholders, this offer never came to fruition as it was tied up in the courts and by state takeover statutes for a long period of time (see the section "Corporate Freeze-Ins").

The examples cited below were the direct result of these "Saturday Night Specials" and eventually each one of them resulted in provoking the necessary assistance and eventual salvation by a "white knight."

Babcock & Wilcox/McDermott/United Technologies—Merger Chronology (All information is from prospectus and joint proxy statement issued February 22, 1978)

3/28/77 — United Technologies Corp. ("United") proposal of $42/share for any and all

4/4/77 — B&W rejects United proposal

4/6/77 — McDermott purchases 1,205,600 B&W shares in
5/13/77   open market transactions (at 39.75 to $45.125/share)
8/5/77 — United amends offer to $48/share
8/10/77 — McDermott proposes $55/share for 4,300,000 shares
8/14/77 — B&W recommends McDermott offer to
          stockholders
8/18/77 — United amends offer to $55/share
8/19/77 — McDermott increases offer to $60/share
8/23/77 — United increases offer to $58.50
          McDermott increases offer to $62.50
8/25/77 — McDermott amends offer to provide $2.50 special
          dividend/share declared by B&W to be payable to
          tendering stockholders and increases number of
          shares it will purchase to 4,800,000
8/25/77 — United terminates its offer
9/16/77 — McDermott owns 49 percent of B&W outstanding
          stock
12/2/77 — McDermott issues press release concerning United's
          interest in acquiring McDermott
12/8/77 — Terms of B&W–McDermott merger announced
3/30/78 — Stockholders approve merger effective 3/31/78 with
          $23^{3}/_{4}$ close

A. Parity Calculation

Terms: 1 Babcock and Wilcox (34.5) = $62.50 for 4,800,000 common B&W shares (39 percent) and 1 $2.20 convertible preferred stock plus 1 $2.60 preferred stock for remainder

Gross Spread:

On tender: (.52)(62.5 − 34.5)

On sale: $\dfrac{(.48)(56 - 34.5)}{\$24.88}$

B. Practical application

(1) Position taken: 100 B&W long at $34^{1}/_{2}$
(2) Date position taken: March 29, 1977
(3) Tendered shares purchased: September 16, 1977

(4) Cash received for 52 shares: September 26, 1977
(5) 48 Shares sold: September 16, 1977
(6) Merger consummated: March 30, 1981
(7) Exchange of securities effective: March 31, 1981
(8) Net Spread:

$2,488	Gross Spread			
(95)	Interest Cost (5.9 Percent Interest on 3,450 for 171 Days)			
(2)	Interest Cost (6.5 Percent Interest on 1,176 for 10 Days)			
325	Dividends on Long Position	$.375	Exchange	6/6
$2,716	Net Spread	.375	Date:	6/9
		2.5		6/9

(9) Annualized Return on Capital

(a) Average Statement of Financial Condition
March 29, 1977–September 16, 1977

Assets

100 B&W (long) $3,450

Liabilities and Capital

Bank Borrowings $3,083
15 Percent "Haircut" 367
$3,450

(b) Average Statement of Financial Condition
September 16, 1977–September 26, 1977

Assets

52 B&W tendered $1,794

Liabilities and Capital

Bank Borrowings $1,794

Average Capital Employed:

$$\frac{(171 \text{ days})}{(365 \text{ days})}(\$3,083) = \frac{(10)}{(365)}(\$1,794) = \$1,493$$

$$\text{Return on Capital} = \frac{\$2,716}{\$1,493}$$

$$= 182 \text{ Percent per Annum (pre-tax)}$$

Carborundum / Kennecott Eaton Offer of $47/Share

11/16/77 — Kennecott Copper Corp. offers $66/share ($567M value). Eaton drops out of bidding

11/17/77 — Directors of Kennecott and Carborundum approve cash offer

11/25/77 — Kennecott served with stockholders suit

12/6/77 — Holders motion for preliminary injuction denied

12/19/77 — NY appeals panel clears cash offer

Carborundum/Kennecott Copper Corp.

A. Parity Calculation
Terms: 1 Carborundum ($62\frac{1}{2}$) = $66 any and all
Gross Spread: $3.5

B. Practical Application:
   (1) Position taken: 100 Carborundum long at $62\frac{1}{2}$

   (2) Date position taken: November 17, 1977

   (3) Shares tendered: December 12, 1977

   (4) Payment received: December 28, 1977

   (5) Total time involvement: 41 Days

   (6) Net Spread

       $3.50 Gross Spread

        .51 Interest Cost (7.25 Percent for 41 Days on $6,250)

      —0— Dividends

      $2.99 Net Spread

   (7) Return on Capital

      (a) Average Statement of Financial Condition
November 17, 1977–December 28, 1977

Assets

100 Carborundum (long)	$6,250

Liabilities and Capital

Bank Borrowings	$5,312
15 Percent "Haircut"[4]	938
	$6,250

Average Capital Employed:

$$\frac{(41 \text{ days})}{(365 \text{ days})} (\$938) = \$105$$

$$\text{Return on Capital} = \frac{299}{105}$$

$$= 284 \text{ Percent per Annum (pre-tax)}$$

Rosario/Amax

10/23/79 — Amax Inc. and Rosario Resources Corp. agree in principle on acquisition tender offer $55/share for 49 percent

11/8/79 — Terms changed to $55/share for 20 percent of outstanding stock, remainder for .55 share of $9.30 convertible preferred

11/29/79 — Definitive agreement signed

12/24/79 — FTC requests additional information—20-day delay from when information supplied

1/11/80 — Hudson Bay Mining & Smelting will offer $65/share for any and all; value of $403M vs $341M Amax offer. Must initiate tender offer or withdraw it by 1/16/80, deadline which had been recently enacted by new provision of the Securities and Exchange Act

1/18/80 — Amax accord terminated by Rosario. Rosario's stock price up to $71/share vs. $65/share offered by Hudson Bay

2/4/80 — Amax announces it purchased 37 percent of Rosario's stock outstanding

2/5/80 — Amax & Rosario sign new agreement valued at $465M

2/8/80 — Amax board of directors ratify agreement 1 share Rosario = 1.37615 Amax

A. Parity Calculation

Terms: 1 Rosario Resources ($47) sold at $57

1 Rosario Resources ($56) = 1.37615 Amax ($43)

Gross Spread: $(57 - 47) + [(1.37615)(43) - (56)]$

B. Practical Application
(1) Position taken: 100 Rosario Resources at $47
(2) Date position taken: October 23, 1979
(3) Shares sold at 57
(4) Date sold: January 10, 1980
(5) Position taken: 100 Rosario Resources at 47
             137.6 Amax short at 43
(6) Date position taken: March 22, 1980
(7) Merger consummated and exchange effective: April 10, 1980
(8) Total time involvement $= [(4)-(2)] + [(6)-(5)] = 98$ days
(9) Net Spread

$1,317	Gross Spread
(158)	Interest Cost (15.5 Percent for 79 Days on $4700)
(55)	Interest Cost (18.7 Percent for 19 Days on $5600)
45	Dividends
$1,149	Net Spread

(10) Annualized Return on Capital
  (a) Average Statement of Financial Condition
    October 23, 1979–January 10, 1980
    Assets
    100 Rosario Resources (long) $4,700
    Liabilities and Capital
    Bank Borrowings $3,995
    15 Percent "Haircut" 705
                        $4,700

  (b) Average Statement of Financial Condition
    March 22, 1980–April 10, 1980
    Assets
    100 Rosario Resources (long) $4,700

Liabilities and Capital

137.6 Amax short	$5,917	
Less 137.6 Amax (borrowed)	($5,917)...	—0—
Bank Borrowings		$2,925
30 Percent "Haircut"		1,775
		$4,700

Average Capital Required:

$$\frac{79 \text{ days}}{365 \text{ days}}(\$705) = \frac{19}{365}(\$1775) = \$245$$

$$\text{Return on Capital} = \frac{\$1149}{\$245}$$

$$= 469 \text{ Percent}$$

Warner Swasey / Bendix / Dominion Bridge

10/23/79 — Dominion Bridge Co. plans a $57 share offer to Warner Swasey Co.—value $200M

10/24/79 — Offer filed today (10/24/79)

11/9/79 — FTC requests additional information

11/13/79 — Bendix plans $70/share offer for 56 percent of outstanding shares—2 shares of convertible preferred for each share of remaining Warner & Swasey common

12/17/79 — Dominion Bridge increases cash bid to $75/share 12/14/79. 5 hours later Bendix increases bid to $83/share and raises liquidation value of preferred from $35 to $41.50/share

12/28/79 — FTC requests additional information from Bendix

1/22/80 — Bendix complies with FTC request for information Expects transaction to be completed by April 1980

1/28/80 — Under agreement with FTC, Bendix postpones purchase of W&S shares until 2/5/80

2/5/80 — Bendix reaches agreement with staff of FTC

3/10/80 — Stockholders approve merger with Warner & Swasey effective 4/1/80

A. Parity Calculation

Terms: 1 Warner & Swasey ($54) = $83 up to 45 percent of outstanding stock. The remaining Warner & Swasey shares each = 2 Bendix B $9^3/_4$ percent cumulative convertible preferred stock ($38), convertible to .768 shares Bendix common ($54).

Gross Spread: On tender = (.69)($83 − 54) = $20.01

On Bendix Common = (.47)($54 − 51) = $1.41

On Warner & Swasey and Bendix

Preferred = (.69)($83) − $.31($54) = $9.48

Gross Spread = $30.90

B. Practical Application

(1) Position taken: 100 Warner & Swasey long at $54

(2) Date position taken: November 15, 1979

(3) Shares tendered on: December 18, 1979

(4) Cash received for 69 shares: February 8, 1980

(5) Position taken: 47 Bendix short at $54

(6) Date taken: January 15, 1980

(7) Position covered: 47 Bendix long at $51

(8) Date covered: February 19, 1980

(9) Position taken: Bendix Preferred (W/I) 62 shares at $38

(10) Date taken: April 3, 1980

(11) Merger consummated: March 18, 1980

(12) Exchange effective: April 1, 1980

(13) Net Spread:

$3,090	Gross Spread
(191.40)	Interest Cost on $5,400 @ 15.22 Percent for 85 Days
(38.34)	Interest Cost on $1674 @ 15.20 Percent for 55 Days
14	Warner & Swasey Dividends (.45 Record 2/7)
—0—	Bendix Dividends
$2,874	Net Spread

(14) Annualized Return on Capital

  (a) Average Statement of Financial Condition

  November 15, 1979–December 31, 1979

Assets

    100 Warner & Swasey (long) $5,400

Liabilities and Capital

    Bank Borrowings $4,590

    15 Percent "Haircut" .... _810_

    $5,400

  (b) Average Statement of Financial Condition

  December 31, 1979–January 15, 1980

Assets

    69 Warner & Swasey to be

    accepted from tender $3,726

    31 Warner & Swasey (long) 1,674

Liabilities and Capital

    Bank Borrowings $4,590

    15 Percent "Haircut" .... _810_

    $5,400

  (c) Average Statement of Financial Condition

  January 15, 1980–February 8, 1980

Assets

    69 Warner & Swasey to be

    accepted from tender $3,726

    31 Warner & Swasey (long) .... _1,674_

    $5,400

Liabilities and Capital

    47 Bendix (short) $2,538

    Less 47 Bendix (borrowed)   ($2,538) $—0—

    Bank Borrowings $4,234

    Haircut[5] 1,166

    $5,400

(d) Average Statement of Financial Condition
February 8, 1980–February 19, 1980
Assets

31 Warner & Swasey (long)	$1,674

Liabilities and Capital

47 Bendix (short)	$2,538		
Less 47 Bendix (borrowed)	($2,538)	$—0—	
Bank Borrowings			913
"Haircut" (30 percent on short)			761
			$1,674

(e) Average Statement of Financial Condition
February 19, 1980–April 1, 1980
Assets

31 Warner & Swasey (long)	$1,674

Liabilities and Capital

Bank Borrowings	$1,423
15 Percent "Haircut"	251
	$1,674

(f) Average Statement of Financial Condition
April 1, 1980–April 3, 1980
Assets

62 Bendix preferred W/I	$2,356

Liabilities and Capital

Bank Borrowings	$2,003
"Haircut"	353
	$2,356

Average Capital Employed:

$$\frac{61}{365}(810) + \frac{24}{365}(1166) + \frac{11}{365}(761) + \frac{42}{365}$$

$$(251) + \$353\frac{(2)}{365} = 266$$

$$\text{Return on Capital} = \frac{2874}{266} \times 100$$

$$= 1080 \text{ Percent per Annum (pre-tax)}$$

Pullman / Wheelabrator Frye / McDermott

7/1/80 — J. Ray McDermott announces plans for a $28/share offer for 2,000,000 shares

7/18/80 — Justice Department requests additional information

8/22/80 — Pullman accepts merger offer from Wheelabrator-Frye, Inc. $43/share for 2 million Pullman common expires Sept. 19

8/29/80 — Proxy McDermott increases offer to $43.50/share

9/4/80 — Wheelabrator Frye & Pullman boards approve merger offer of $52.50/share for 3M shares and 1.1 shares Wheelabrator common for remainder
Preliminary injunction granted against McDermott's latest offer

9/8/80 — McDermott extends offer two weeks

9/11/80 — McDermott revises offer to include 51 percent of Pullman common

9/16/80 — Justice Dept. clears Wheelabrator-Frye Inc.

9/22/80 — Federal District judge ruled Wheelabrator-Frye's ammendment to offer requires extending bid to Oct. 17. Wheelabrator had been drawn tenders of 7.30M shares by 9/19. McDermott raises offer to $54 9/19

9/23/80 — McDermott, responding to court order extends $54 bid to October 17

9/25/80 — McDermott clears Federal appeals court of antitrust violations

9/25/80 — Proxy—Court of Appeals vacates preliminary injunction against termination of WFI offer allowing WFI to purchase 5,500,000 shares

Pullman Inc./Wheelabrator Frye Inc.

A. Parity Calculation

Terms: 1 Pullman ($47) = $52.5 for 49.3 percent of Pullman's outstanding stock[6]

    1 Pullman ($47) = 1.1 Wheelabrator-Frye ($46) remainder

Parity: 46 × 1.1 = $50.0

Gross Spread: On tender .74 (52.5−47)   = $4.07

             On exchange .26 (50.6−52.5) =   (.49)

                                        $3.58

B. Practical Application

    (1) Position taken: 100 Pullman long at $47

    (2) Date position taken: September 10, 1980

    (3) Shares accepted on tender: 74

    (4) Date tendered: September 19, 1980

    (5) Date proceeds received: September 30, 1980

    (6) Position taken: 28.6 Wheelabrator-Frye @ $46 (short)

    (7) Date position taken: September 30, 1980

    (8) Merger consummated: November 6, 1980

    (9) Exchange effective: November 6, 1980

  (10) Total time involvement [(9)−(12)] = 57 days

  (11) Net Spread

    $358   Gross Spread

       (29) Interest Cost (11.4 Percent on $4700 for 20 Days)

       (18) Interest Cost (14.7 Percent on 1222 for 37 Days)

       (10) Dividends Short (.35 of Record Oct. 17)

    $301   Net Spreads

  (12) Annualized Return on Capital

    (a) Average Statement of Financial Condition

        September 10, 1980–September 19, 1980

        Assets

        100 Pullman (long) $4,700

        Liabilities and Capital

        Bank Borrowings $3,995

        15 Percent "Haircut" . . . . _705_

                                    $4,700

(b) Average Statement of Financial Condition
September 19, 1980–September 30, 1980
Assets

74 Pullman tendered	$3,478
26 Pullman (long)	1,222
	$4,700

Liabilities and Capital

Bank Borrowings	$3,995
15 Percent "Haircut"	705
	$4,700

(c) Average Statement of Financial Condition
September 30, 1980–November 6, 1980
Assets

26 Pullman (long)	$1,222

Liabilities and Capital

28.6 Wheelabrator-Frye (short)	$1,316	
Less 28.6 Wheelabrator-Frye (borrowed)	(1,316)	$—0—
Bank Borrowings		827
30 Percent "Haircut"		395
		$1,222

Average Capital Employed:

$$\frac{(20 \text{ days})}{(365 \text{ days})}(\$705) + \frac{(37)}{(365)}(\$395) = \$79$$

$$\text{Return on Capital} = \frac{301}{79}$$

$$+ 381 \text{ Percent per Annum (pre-tax)}$$

Liggett Meyers / Grand Metropolitan Hotels / Standard Brands

3/26/80 — Disclosed that Grand Metropolitan doubled its 4.4
percent stake in Liggett during December
3/26/80 — NC judge issues temporary restraining order barring
Grand Metropolitan from buying any more shares
4/3/80 — Restraining order extended

4/15/80 — Grand Metropolitan hopes to begin $50/share offer 4/21/80. $415 million value—$67.50 for 7 percent preferred $114.94 for $5.25 convertible preferred

4/21/80 — Formal offer by GM Sub Corp. expiration date: 5/15/80 withdrawal date 5/12/80

4/22/80 — Temporary restraining order

4/23/80 — Liggett proposes to sell Austin Nichols & Co. to Pernod Ricard, Paris for $97.50M (Wild Turkey Bourbon)

5/1/80 — Liggett discussing friendly takeover offer with unnamed suitor

5/7/80 — Standard Brands proposes $65/share for 45 percent of Liggett's shares value $565M. Remainder $5.80 convert stock plus $70 for 7 percent preferred

5/9/80 — Signs that Grand Metropolitan will increase bid—told South Carolina judge it was considering higher offer if cleared from legal delays

5/12/80 — Standard Brands offer made official withdrawal date 5/16/80

5/13/80 — GM Sub Corp. offer made official withdrawal date 5/28/80

5/15/80 — Grand Metropolitan Ltd. increases offer to $69/share common $158.62/share for 5.25 percent convertible preferred, and $70/share for 7 percent preferred

5/15/80 — Standard Brands withdraws offer

Liggett/Grand Metropolitan Hotels

A. Parity Calculation
Terms: 1 Liggett ($43) = $69
Gross Spread: = $26

B. Practical Application
(1) Position taken: 100 shares Liggett at $43
(2) Date taken: April 21, 1980
(3) Shares tendered: May 23, 1980

(4) Proceeds received: May 30, 1980
(5) Total time involvement: 39 days
(6) Net Spread

$2,600 Gross Spread
(71) Interest Cost (15.5 Percent on 4300 for 39 Days)
<u>62</u> Dividends (.625 Record 5/15)
$2,591 Net Spread

(7) Annualized Return on Capital
    (a) Average Statement of Financial Condition
        April 21, 1980–May 23, 1980
        Assets
          100 Liggett (long) $4,300

        Liabilities and Capital
          Bank Borrowings $3,655
          15 Percent "Haircut" .... <u>645</u>
                                 $4,300

    (b) Average Statement of Financial Condition
        May 23, 1980–May 30, 1980
        Assets
          100 Liggett long tendered $4,300

        Liabilities and Capital
          Bank Borrowings $3,655
          15 Percent "Haircut" .... <u>645</u>
                                 $4,300

Average Capital Employed:

$$\frac{(39 \text{ days})}{(365 \text{ days})}(\$645) = \$69$$

$$\text{Return on Capital} = \frac{2,591}{69}$$

$$= 3755 \text{ Percent per Annum (pre-tax)}$$

Hobart/Canadian Pacific/Dart & Kraft

12/6/80 — Canadian Pacific Enterprises Ltd. offers $23.50/share for all stock, $380 million value. Hobart obtains temporary restraining order in Ohio Federal Court

1/8/81 — Hobart sues to enjoin Canadian Pacific Enterprises from proceeding. Basis of suit: offer violates federal securities laws and regulation of the Federal Reserve Board

1/9/81 — Hobart looking for suitor to top Canadian Pacific Enterprises offer

2/17/81 — Ohio Division of Securities approves Canadian Pacific Enterprises offer

2/18/81 — DKI Holdings offers $40/share any and all. $460M value withdrawal date 3/12/81

Hobart/Dart & Kraft

A. Parity Calculation

Terms: 1 Hobart ($31\frac{1}{2}$) = $40 any and all

Gross Spread = $40 − 31.5 = $8.50

B. Practical Application

(1) Position taken: 100 Hobart long at $31\frac{1}{2}$

(2) Date position taken: December 15, 1980

(3) Shares tendered: March 4, 1981

(4) Proceeds received: March 16, 1981

(5) Total time involvement 91 days

(6) Net Spread

$850	Gross Spread
(150)	Interest Cost (19.1 Percent for 91 Days on $3,150)
33	Dividends
$733	Net Spread

(7) Annualized Return on Capital

    (a) Statement of Financial Condition

        December 15, 1980–March 4, 1981

Assets
100 Hobart (long) $3,150

Liabilities and Capital
Bank Borrowings $2,677
"Haircut"   473
                                        $3,150

(b) Average Statement of Financial Condition
March 4, 1981–March 10, 1981
Assets
100 Hobart long tendered $3,150

Liabilities and Capital
Bank Borrowings $2,677
15 Percent "Haircut"   473
                                        $3,150

Average Capital Employed:

$$\frac{(91)}{(365)}(\$473)$$

$$\text{Return on Capital} = \frac{733}{118}$$

$$= 621 \text{ Percent}$$

St. Joe Minerals / Seagrams / Fluor Corp.

3/11/81 — $45 a share bid by Seagrams Co. $2.13 billion value
3/12/81 — St. Joe Directors reject Seagrams' bid 3/11/81
3/17/81 — St. Joe files lawsuit to block Seagrams offer
3/23/81 — St. Joe agrees to suspend court actions to block
          Seagram's bid. The offer expires April 10.
3/30/81 — St. Joe accepts $549.9 million by Sulpetro
          ($44.45/share) for Can Del Oil Ltd, which is 92
          percent owned by St. Joe
3/31/81 — Fluor offer at $60/share for 45 percent of
          stock—preliminary agreement

4/4/81 — Formal offer by Fluor, withdrawal date 4/24/81, prorated

4/10/81 — Seagram withdraws offer

5/5/81 — First part of merger completed, prorate acceptance 78 percent

8/3/81 — St. Joe stockholders approve merger basis 1.2 shares Fluor per share St. Joe effective 8/3/81

St. Joe Minerals Corp./Fluor Corp.

A. Parity Calculation

Terms: 1 St. Joe ($52 $^3/_8$) = $60 for 45 percent of outstanding shares

1 St. Joe ($52 $^3/_8$) = 1.2 shares Fluor ($43^1/_4$) for remainder

Spread: .78 (60-52 $^3/_8$) on tender

$$\frac{+ (.1)(43^1/_4) + (.164)34 - (.22)(52^3/_8)}{4.33 \text{ Gross Spread}} \text{ on exchange}$$

B. Practical Application

(1) Position taken: 100 St. Joe long @ 52 $^3/_8$ 10 Fluor short @ 43 $^1/_4$

(2) Date position taken: April 8, 1981

(3) Shares tendered: April 13, 1981

(4) Proceeds received for 78 shares: May 4, 1981

(5) Position taken: 16.4 Fluor short @ 34

(6) Date position taken: June 3, 1981

(7) Merger consummated and effective: August 3, 1981

(8) Total time involvement: 117 days

(9) Net Spread

433	Gross Spread
(135)	Interest Cost (16.5 Percent on $5238 for 26 Days + 20 Percent on $1466, 91 Days)
5	Dividends Long ($.225) Record 6/5
(5)	Dividends Short (.26) Record 6/30
298	Net Spread

(10) Annualized Return on Capital

    (a) Average Statement of Financial Condition

    April 8, 1981–May 4, 1981

    Assets

100 St. Joe Mineral (long)		$5,238
Liabilities and Capital		
10 Fluor (short)	432.5	
Less 10 Fluor (borrowed)	(432.5)	—0—
Bank Borrowings		$4,452
"Haircut" 15 Percent on long		786
		$5,238

    (b) Average Statement of Financial Condition

    May 4, 1981–June 3, 1981

    Assets

28 St. Joe Mineral (long)		$1,467
Liabilities and Capital		
10 Fluor (short)	$433	
Less 10 Fluor (borrowed)	(433)	—0—
Bank Borrowings		$1,227
"Haircut"[7]		240
		$1,467

    (c) Average Statement of Financial Condition

    June 3, 1981–August 3, 1981

    Assets

28 St. Joe Mineral (long)		$1,467
Liabilities and Capital		
26.4 Fluor (short)	$898	
Less 26.4 Fluor (borrowed)	(898)	—0—
Bank Borrowings		$1,088
"Haircut"[8]		379
		$1,467

Average Capital Employed:

$$\frac{(26 \text{ days})}{365 \text{ days}}(\$786) + \frac{30}{365}(\$240) + \frac{61}{365}(\$379) = \$139$$

$$\text{Return on Capital} = \frac{\$298}{\$139}$$

$$= 214 \text{ Percent}$$

When one compares the returns on capital that were obtained in cash tender offers during this current period to the returns available in merger arbitrage (see Table 3.1) it becomes readily apparent that the tender offers provide significantly higher returns to professional arbitrageurs (compare Table 4.1). This also explains why there was such a proliferation of arbitrage-related activity and participants in risk arbitrage during the period of the late 1970s and 1980s.

Two other offers that attracted great attention in 1981–82 were the three-way bidding war over Conoco and subsequently the contest over Marathon Oil, both of which turned out to be extremely profitable for arbitrageurs. In summer 1982, however, Wall Street experienced one of the greatest debacles in American corporate merger—and arbitrage—history, namely, the sudden withdrawal of Gulf Oil from its tender offer for Cities Service Company. The

Table 4.1 Comparison of Returns on Merger Arbitrage Tender Offers 1974–1981

	Pre-tax Per Annum Return on Capital
Babcock Wilcox/McDermott	182%
Carborundum/Kennecott	284
Rosario/AMAX	469
Warner Swasey/Bendix	1080
Pullman/Wheelabrator Frye	381
Liggett Meyers/Grand Metropolitan Hotels	3755
Hobart/Dart & Kraft	621
St. Joe Minerals/Fluor Corp	214

estimated losses in Wall Street's community have ranged anywhere from $250 million to $500 million. The fact that a major corporation could essentially renege on an offer of this magnitude under false pretenses may give pause to a number of arbitrage participants in the future.

Chapter 5

Other Risk Arbitrage Situations

Exchange Offers

Offers to exchange the securities of Company Y for the majority of Company X's—either via a type "B" reorganization or simply a bid for a controlling interest—were a highly popular form of takeover vis-a-vis the merger route in the 1960s as the willing supply of sellers failed to keep pace either with the ever-increasing list of buyers or with their individual appetites for external expansion. To the arbitrageur, this form of take-over was particularly attractive because it is normally of much shorter duration than a merger. Normally, only the SEC's approval is required and it must grant clearance of the prospectus describing the exchange offer. No definitive agreement is required, nor is there need for a formal IRS tax ruling prior to making the offer effective. When shareholder approval (to authorize the new shares for the offer) is required on the part of the Groom, the proxy for the meeting is filed with the SEC together with the offering prospectus, and both are usually cleared simultaneously. The exchange offer is considered effective once the SEC has cleared the prospectus or once the required percentage of shares, if specified, is obtained, so that the only remaining technicality is shareholder approval of the new shares. The offer can be completed long before the shareholders actually vote; however, the vote usually either coincides with the offering period or follows it by one to two weeks at most.

Not only is the time involved considerably less than in a merger, small too are the charges to a firm's capital. Capital charges are nil after SEC clearance or shareholders' approval of the new shares, whichever is later. Once these conditions have been met, the Stock Exchange will consider the simultaneous purchase of X and sale of Y as a "bona fide arbitrage," thereby requiring no charge to a firm's capital. A private investor can, under similar circumstances, hold the long X and short Y positions with 10 percent of X.

As a result of these leveraging possibilities for both member firms and their customers, tendering corporations increasingly schedule their shareholder meetings, whenever possible, prior to termination of their tender offer. This has proved to be an essential tactic in either a contested offer or one in which there is competition from another bidder. In any case, this situation is a boon to arbitrageurs, who take gigantic positions due to the absence of charges to their capital. From the point of view of the tendering corporations, the arbitrageurs are extremely useful for, just as in a rights offering, the arbitrageurs in effect underwrite the deal by purchasing the shares that are essentially in weak hands, and tendering them. In a rights offering, the arbitrageurs would buy the rights from those who do not want to subscribe, and subsequently subscribe themselves.

The enormous volume undertaken by arbitrageurs in exchange offers gives rise to a variation of the post-merger selling pressure described in Chapter 2. The latter occurs at the closing of a merger deal. That experience in an exchange offer can run during the entire course of the exchange offer, particularly when the package offered consists of new securities that trade on a "when-issued" basis. Arbitrageurs, who have absolutely no respect for a security's predicted investment value, will sell Y "when-issued" at any bid price in sight—without the need for an "uptick"—just to make a decent $\frac{1}{2}$ or $\frac{3}{4}$ points spread. This will often reduce the Y "when-issued" to ridiculously low levels.

An example of this phenomenon was the exchange offer, in January 1969, for Jones & Laughlin Steel by Jones & Laughlin Industries (a subsidiary of Ling-Temco-Vought). The package consisted, amongst other things, of a new Jones & Laughlin Industries $6\frac{3}{4}$ percent Debenture due 1994. When the registration statement became effective, trading in the debentures began on a "when-issued" basis at 67 percent. Four days later, the bonds were 55 percent bid—a yield to maturity that is so high as to be beyond the scope of most bond tables. A week after the expiration of the offer, the bonds were 62 percent in a deteriorating bond market.

There have been a host of interesting exchange offers, mostly opposed by the target Brides during the 1960s and 1970s. One that attracted great attention on Wall Street was the battle for control of United Fruit. After various suitors, including Textron and Dillingham, had bowed out of the contest, AMK Corporation and Zapata-Norness crossed swords for the hand of the asset-laden Bride. There were several different offers by each Groom, each trying to out-bid the other. AMK's final bid consisted of a package of common, convertible debentures and warrants worth roughly $83. Zapata-Norness offered the unusual convertible preferred which is described in Appendix A (p. 165). The latter security was little understood by the investing public at the time of the offer, but it did later manage to gain respect. This lack of recognition at the outset probably cost Zapata-Norness the battle, along with a few shrewd moves on the part of AMK's investment banker in obtaining strategic blocks of United Fruit.

For the alert arbitrageur who could take the time to figure the value of the new Zapata-Norness Preferred, there was a rich reward. While Zapata-Norness formally surrendered to AMK—and agreed to sell to AMK the United Fruit it had already received by virtue of its own offer, Zapata publicly declared that it would nontheless issue its new Convertible Preferred, pending shareholder approval, for whatever amount of United Fruit it had or would still receive. Thus, while most of the Community was content to make a spread of $2 on the AMK offer, a few arbitrageurs bought United Fruit at around $81 and tendered their stock to Zapata-Norness in order to obtain the new "mystery" stock. When it became apparent that Zapata-Norness would actually issue this security, Swiss investors began aggressively bidding for it at around $90 in the OTC "when-issued" market. Thus, while some were fighting for $2, others were cashing in $9 per United Fruit.

Recapitalizations

The need of American industry to reshape its capital structure was, as mentioned in Chapter 1, one of the cornerstones upon which risk arbitrage was founded and from which it subsequently evolved. Recapitalizations are a fairly common occurrence and are closely scrutinized by arbitrageurs for profit possibilities. Wherever a spread can be anticipated between the value of the securities offered in exchange for a particular class of stock and the market value of that stock, an arbitrageur can derive a profit.

The cash tenders and recapitalizations of Ling-Temco-Vought alone were sufficient to keep arbitrageurs busy and in green pastures during 1966–1970. LTV was being recapitalized annually, either to shrink its equity or to retire the preferred stocks which had been the financing vehicle for the equity reductions.

In October 1966, LTV proposed a recapitalization plan which presented the Community with some interesting alternatives. LTV proposed to exchange cash and its Series B Convertible Preferred for up to 1,000,000 shares of its common stock, with the option to take more than that number if so desired. There were 2.4 million shares outstanding at the time.

The precise terms were: 1 LTV common = $20 cash + 0.5 Series B Preferred, each of which was convertible into 1.25 LTV common. The B Preferred was due to receive a dividend of $1.50 on November 1, 1966, to which tendered shares would be entitled; the B Preferred was listed on the New York Stock Exchange and was trading at $60 per share, while LTV common was trading at $48 after the terms were promulgated (and at $40 before). The Community was willing to completely ignore the proration possibility, should more than one million shares be tendered, due to the widely held belief on the part of private and institutional investors alike that the common price of LTV would rise after the expiration of the offer as a result of the improvement in pro-forma earnings per share. Thus LTV was expected to encounter difficulties in evoking tenders of even the desired one million shares. For the arbitrageur, there was a practically negligible downside risk in case of pro-ration. The problem was to select the most profitable of several profitable alternatives.

This offer was an unusual one for the arbitrageur in that there were five ways of participating in the transaction.

1. Buy and subsequently tender 600

LTV common @ $48 =	$28,800
Receive $20 Cash per share =	(12,000)
Cost of 300 LTV B preferred =	$16,800
Sell short 300 LTV B preferred @ $60 =	$18,000
Cost price of 300 LTV B preferred =	(16,800)
Gross profit = $1,200 per 600 shares, or $2 per share	$1,200

2. Buy 240 LTV @ $48 =   ($11,520)

Borrow 400 LTV and tender a total of 640 LTV for which are exchanged (a) $20 cash per share =	12,800
and (b) 320 LTV B preferred, each of which would receive $1.50 dividend on 15 December =	480
Total Profit =	$1,760

per 240 shares, or $7.33 per share

The 320 preferred after receiving the above dividend, could then be converted into 400 shares of common, which in turn would be delivered against the borrowed position.

3. Borrow 1,000 LTV

Buy 1,000 LTV @ $48 =	$48,000
Tender a total of 2,000 LTV and receive	
(a) $20 cash per share =	(40,000)
Deficit =	$ 8,000
and (b) 1,000 LTV B preferred which are	
sold short[1] @ $60 =	$60,000
Deficit from (a) =	(8,000)
Proceeds on remaining short position	$52,000
Cover borrowed 1,000 common @ $48 =	(48,000)
Net Profit on 1,000 LTV =	$ 4,000
Profit per share = $4.00	

4. Borrow 1,000 LTV

Buy 1,000 @ $48 =	$48,000
Tender 2,000 LTV and receive	
(a) $20 cash per share =	(40,000)
Deficit =	$ 8,000
and (b) 1,000 B preferred plus the $1.50	
dividend per share =	(1,500)
Remaining Deficit =	$ 6,500
Convert the 1,000 B preferred into 1,250	
common (after receipt of preferred	
dividend) of which return 1,000	
LTV against borrowed position and sell	
remaining 250 common @ $48 =	$12,000
less deficit from (b) =	(6,500)
Net profit per 1,000 shares =	$ 5,500
or $5.50 per share	

5. Instead of buying the common directly in (1) through (4), buy the $5^3/_4$ percent convertible bonds as follows:

$1M bonds @ 138 percent	=	$13,800.00
Conversion costs	=	25.00
Accrued interest	=	81.50
Total cost	=	$13,906.50

Since each $1M bond = 293.38 common, the common is created at $13,906.50/293.38 = $47.50, which is a $0.60 discount from the market price of $48 for LTV.

In retrospect, option (2) was truly the most advantageous in that it presented not only the highest profit per share, but the least market risk as well. The important element was to be able to borrow stock to tender. This was, in effect, a short-tender, which was still permitted in those carefree days.

Spinoffs

As mentioned earlier, risk arbitrage developed in the United States partly as a result of the divestitures that were forced upon the public utility holding companies. There was little market risk in these operations for the arbitrageur as there would develop "when-issued" markets in all the constituent subsidiaries and even for the holding company itself on an "ex-distribution" basis. The arbitrage maneuvers in today's spinoffs involve substantially more risk.

Spinoffs that can be arbitraged effectively are those involving distribution of portfolio assets to shareholders on a pro-rata basis. When there is no existing market for the asset that is to be distributed, one encounters a double risk (that of the spun-off asset and the parent company "ex-distribution") which is not readily taken. This situation rarely occurs. Usually the portfolio asset has an existing market. In this case, the overriding consideration becomes the calculation of a reasonable price for the parent "ex-distribution."

Let us assume that Y is going to spinoff one-tenth of X for each Y held. Y is trading at $30 and X at $50. An arbitrageur's calculation would be the following: If one Y were bought at $30, and one-tenth of X could be sold short at $50, Y "ex-distribution" could be created at $30 − 1/10 × $50 = $25. The decision to take this position would be based on the possible price-earnings ratio for Y on the new pro-forma basis. Thus, if Y would earn $3 per share without X, and the arbitrageur felt that the $3 should be capitalized—conservatively—by a factor of 9, then Y "ex-distribution" should sell at $27, representing a potential $2 profit per Y.

There occurred in September 1967 truly one of the most complicated spinoffs to challenge the Arbitrage Community. Olin

Mathieson Chemical Corporation proposed to spinoff to its share-holders its wholly-owned subsidiary E.R. Squibb & Sons, where-upon the latter would be merged with Beech-Nut Life Savers, Inc. There was naturally no existing market for Squibb. The spinoff itself consisted of $\frac{2}{3}$ of a newly capitalized Squibb for each Olin Mathieson held. Thereafter, a new corporation, Squibb-Beech-Nut, would be formed to effect the consolidation of Squibb and Beech-Nut Life Savers on the following basis:

1 share of new Squibb-Beech-Nut for each share of Squibb

and

1 share of new Squibb-Beech-Nut for each share of Beech-Nut Life Savers

Wall Street shuddered. Arbitrageurs sharpened their pencils.

Since each Olin was to receive $\frac{2}{3}$ share of Squibb as a spinoff and each of the latter would be exchanged for one share of new Squibb-Beech-Nut, then the spun-off $\frac{2}{3}$ Squibb was equal to $\frac{2}{3}$ new Squibb-Beech-Nut. Furthermore, since each share of Beech-Nut would receive one share of the new corpora-tion, then $\frac{2}{3}$ of Beech-Nut would also receive $\frac{2}{3}$ of Squibb-Beech-Nut. Thus, $\frac{2}{3}$ of Squibb was equal to $\frac{2}{3}$ Squibb-Beech-Nut! In view of this arithmetic relationship, the arbitrageur was able to remove one of the two aforementioned variables by in-directly finding a market for the spun-off asset. The remaining task was to calculate where Olin "ex-Squibb" would be cre-ated, and compare this figure with an expected value of the Olin ex-Squibb.

With Beech-Nut at $58 and Olin Mathieson at $73, and by selling short $\frac{2}{3}$ Beech-Nut at $58 for each Olin purchased at $73, an arbitrageur could create Olin "ex-Squibb" at

$$\$73 - \frac{2}{3} \times \$58 = \$34.33$$

There remained the delicate task of determining a pro-forma capitalization rate for Olin. The latter had shown excellent growth in earning per share over the prior five years (pro-forma and fully diluted):

1962 — $1.47
1963 — $1.68
1964 — $1.98
1965 — $2.44
1966 — $3.34

It was estimated that the Company would earn $3.80 for 1967, and that with its particular mix of metals, papers, chemicals, and firearms, those earnings would command a multiple of between 12 and 15. Thus, having created the Olin "ex-Squibb" at $34.33, an arbitrageur had in fact created it at roughly nine times ($34.44/$3.80) estimated earnings for 1967. There could thus be anticipated a profit of from $11.40 per Olin at the low end of the Price-Earnings scale to $22.80 per Olin at the upper end, when the Olin Mathieson would have to be resold by the arbitrageur in order to complete the transaction.

What actually happened in this case is that on, and for some time after, the ex-distribution date, Olin sold at around $36 a share, which, for all the work, yielded a meager $1.77 per share for those who had created the stock at $34.33. The narrowness of the return, in view of potential risks, clearly called for a limited margin of error. It likewise called for intense analysis of all the many factors that interact in the marketplace to give a security its market price: not only earnings, future prospects, and capitalization rates, but the market's probable mood and its changing attitudes towards particular industries. The latter aspect was probably not duly considered in the Olin case; because the chemical industry was not enjoying at that time the type of popularity that merited the capitalization rates anticipated by some of the better chemical analysts on Wall Street.

Stub Situations

There are three types of arbitrage situations based on the potential for future distributions of either cash or stock—after the legal closing of a merger—in addition to what is received immediately upon consummation. These potential future distributions are called "stubs," and may be generated (a) in contingent interest payments to the Bride's shareholders after consummation, (b) through escrow agreements in mergers, and (c) in liquidations.

When the Groom wishes to give the Bride a tangible incentive to be "productive" in earnings, or when a Bride is too demanding as to her value during the course of the negotiations, there is often the basis for compromise by the adoption of an exchange ratio which consists of future distributions in addition to the major initial distribution of stock, based upon what is called an "earnings formula." Upon consummation, the Bride's transfer books are closed, the latter's securities exchanged for those of the Groom, with the right to these future distributions being passed on to the Bride's shareholders as "certificates of contingent interest." These rights are the resulting "stubs." They are often readily marketable securities that can be traded over-the-counter, usually on a "due bill" basis.

There are many formulas upon which "stubs" may be predicated. Those most often encountered occur when successive distributions are to be made annually relative to earnings performance for the respective year and when one balloon-type payment is to be made at the end of a prescribed period, based upon aggregate earnings over that period.

The arbitrageur's interest is to create the stubs before the merger is consummated, as he can normally create them more cheaply, or sometimes even for nothing, by arbitraging the Bride against the Groom's initial distribution. The merger of Hayes International into City Investing in February 1967 provided just such an opportunity. Each share of Hayes was to receive 2/7 of City Investing common plus one non-transferable Contingent Interest Certificate, each of which called for the additional distribution of up to $6.74 market value of City common stock. The level of earnings required for the maximum distribution was the aggregate of $7,500,000 for the five years ending September 30, 1971. Lower aggregate earnings would entitle certificate holders to receive proportionately less of the $6.74 value in City common. For example, if the total earnings were $5,000,000, each certificate would receive $2/3$ of the $6.74, or $4.50. For the calculation of the market value of City common, the average price (over a twenty-day period) was guaranteed down to a price of $15. Below this the average price would be figured at the minimum of $15 per City common.

At the outset arbitrageurs were able to create the stub at a discount. With City at $42 and Hayes at $11, selling 2/7 of a City would yield $12, or a spread of $1 per Hayes. This situation did not last for long, however, as it became apparent that the Hayes stub was a valuable piece of property. There was, in fact, a very high probability that the earnings goal of $7,500,000 would be easily achieved by 1971.

The probability of achieving this figure is naturally a preoccupation of the arbitrageur. The records show that over the preceding five years, Hayes' net income had advanced from $502,242 to $1,014,242, representing a compounded annual growth rate of roughly 15 percent. Sales over the same period had advanced approximately 30 percent. In order to achieve the required level, Hayes would have to earn at an average rate of $1,500,000 for each of the five years, or more representatively, would have to experience compounded earnings growth of 12 percent per year, which would result in earnings of roughly $1,700,000 for fiscal 1971. As Hayes was primarily a government contractor in aircraft parts and aerospace, it was assumed that, with the Vietnam war accelerating and with the heavy budget outlays for the Mercury and Apollo space program, the five-year prospect for Hayes was fairly bright. Yet, to be conservative, assume that Hayes experiences a drop in its annual earnings growth rate by one-third, so that the earnings would increase by 10 percent over the next five-year period. This would result in aggregate earnings for the period of $6,900,000, which would entitle holders of the certificates to 88 percent of the maximum participation, or $5.93. A figure similar to this could have been arrived at by assigning various probabilities to different aggregate earnings levels for the five-year period, the sum of which would yield an expected value. It is to this expected value that one must once again apply a subjective rate of capitalization, in order to determine the present value of the predicted level of earnings. Let us say that the arbitrageur requires, in this type of situation (the results of which will be taxable as a long-term capital gain) a return before taxes of 20 percent per annum. The present value is thus $2.38. If the arbitrageur in fact valued the stub at $2.38, he was, as mentioned above, able to create the stub, for a certain time, at zero or better cost. As time developed, and as the merger approached its consummation, by buying Hayes at $12 and selling 2/7 of City common at $28.50, one was creating, or paying $1 for the stub.

Liquidations are predicated primarily on the same idea. Normally, when a company liquidates, it will establish a schedule of the amounts of the liquidation payments—in either cash or stock—along with the expected distribution dates. The job of the arbitrageur becomes one of properly discounting these distributions in order to arrive at a present value for the "stub." In addition, there is the more delicate determination of the expected value of the various distributions that are often based upon the sale of fixed assets whose real market values are uncertain. The task becomes one of determining the probable market value of these assets and deducing the various liquidation payments; the latter are then discounted at a subjective rate of capitalization. One must again be mindful that liquidation payments will usually be set so as to come within the provision of the IRS Code[2] entitling capital gains treatment. Thus the arbitrageur is in a position to make long-term capital gains.

One of the truly sizable liquidations was that of Peabody Coal Company, which was acquired by Kennecott Copper in 1968. The financing arranged by Kennecott consisted of a Production Payment that was to yield an initial distribution of $45 per Peabody share upon consummation of the acquisition, plus a liquidating distribution of $2.50 within eight months after that consummation. The latter distribution would be a long-term capital gain. As consummation of the merger approached and after Federal Trade Commission objections were disregarded, Peabody traded in the open market from upwards of $44, or a negative cost for the stub to $47 or $2 for the stub (47 − the initial distribution of $45). Thus, arbitrageurs were counting on a long-term capital gain of

$0.50. After consummation, and after the stock of Peabody was delisted, the stubs were traded over-the-counter, where a bid of $2.35 was not uncommon.

Escrow agreements are regarded by arbitrageurs as more of a headache than as a potential source of profit. While they indeed fall within the definition of "stubs," and they can usually be created at a zero cost basis, their existence often appears in a merger agreement well after an arbitrageur has established a position. For all practical purposes, these stubs are not even normally considered as future profits, as the escrow hold-backs are there for a good reason: to meet the contingent liabilities of the Bride. One can safely assume that at least half of stock or cash held in escrow will never be distributed. As a practical matter, the attitude of arbitrageurs is simply to completely discount the escrow, and if it should indeed yield something over time, so much the better. Stubs emanating from escrows are so highly discounted that there is hardly ever an over-the-counter market in them.

Of more immediate concern, as mentioned above, is that the presence of escrow accounts be known, for they are often disguised and overlooked by the investment community. Let us assume, for example, that each X will receive one Y upon consummation of the merger, but that there is an escrow of 10 percent of the Y stock. To the arbitrageur, the exchange ratio automatically becomes one X equals nine-tenths Y, and the remaining tenth is forgotten. The investor who has counted on a share-for-share exchange, and who accordingly takes a long and short position in X and Y, finds himself short one-tenth Y per X upon consummation. If Y is higher than it was when the position was taken, all the efforts may well have been for naught. Even if Y is lower, the original spread works out to be less than was originally envisioned.

Limited Risk Arbitrage

There is yet another series of arbitrage transactions, that fall somewhere between "risk" and "riskless" arbitrages. These "limited risk" arbitrages basically involve convertible securities rather than reorganizations.

"Delayed Conversion" arbitrage can occur when a security is convertible only after a certain lapse of time and the spread between the current price of this convertible and its future parity—i.e., the parity based on the current price which will be realizable only upon the conversion becoming effective at some future time—yields a satisfactory return.

Corporate financial wizardry has also produced convertible instruments whose conversion features either increase or decrease, possibly even both, giving rise to "changing Conversion" arbitrage. A preferred can be convertible, let us say into 1.5 shares of common stock currently, but may be entitled to 1.6 shares at the inception of the following calendar year. Assuming a convertible preferred is selling at $90, and the common at $60, the immediate conversion parity is $90 and thus there is no spread. However, an arbitrageur could establish a profitable situation by selling short 1.6 common instead of .15, which would result in a parity of $96 or a spread of $6.

"Premium" arbitrage involves the premium associated with convertible preferreds, convertible bonds, warrants, and options. If, for example, there were too much of a premium on a convertible instrument over its conversion parity, an arbitrageur would sell short the convertible and take a long position in the underlying equity, closing out the positions when the premium had shrunk. If, on the other hand, there were too little a premium, one could buy the convertible and sell short the common, closing out the positions when a larger premium materialized. Arbitrageurs spend sleepless nights concocting all sorts of fancy premium hedges. The main idea is simply to find two interchangeable items of dissimilar value but with similar prices (or at parity), and to sell that which is of lesser value and buy that which, of the two, has greater value; and sooner or later, if you have been right in your valuation, others will come to a similar conclusion, enabling you to close out the positions with a profit.

Financing of corporations by issuance of "units" is becoming an increasingly popular mechanism, due to the high level of interest rates and the stiff competition for long term capital. Straight debentures or equity securities are thus provided sweeteners in the form of warrants. These warrants are either immediately detachable, or detachable only after a prescribed period of time. In the latter case, "Units" arbitrage can be accomplished effectively by purchasing the Units and selling off the debenture/equity while simultaneously selling the warrant, which will normally sell in the OTC market on a "when-detached" basis.

The available return on capital in these "limited risk" situations will be predicated not only on the spread and related time element, but, just as importantly, on the "haircut" provisions of the New York Stock Exchange's Rule 325.

Chapter 6

Corporate "Freezeins": The Subterfuge Syndrome

Introduction

Martin Lipton and Erica Steinberger have defined a "freezeout" or "going private" as a corporate transaction in which ". . . a shareholder or group of shareholders receive cash, debt, or preferred stock in exchange for their shares."[1] "Freezeouts" are thus, by definition, coercive maneuvers. This writer utilizes the term "freezein" to refer to a phenomenon that is directly opposite to the aforementioned; it is a corporate quasi-transaction to preclude shareholders from acting on a bona fide offer that they receive from a would-be acquirer and are thereby, if not literally "frozen in" to their equity positions in perpetuity, then at least are forced to forego a handsome premium for their shares. In any case, managements are surely "frozen in" to their various emoluments.

Whereas in "freezeouts" shareholders seem to have some remedy at law in attaining fair value for their shares, it would appear that in the case of "freezeins" no such remedy is currently available. The writer feels that this highly inequitable situation merits close attention by regulatory authorities. There have, in the course of the past few years, been some well-publicized cases of the phenomenon involving managements refusing to pass legitimate offers on to their shareholders, thereby devastating the values of shares owned by common stock investors.

The actual "freezein" is accomplished through what is obviously a subterfuge that Webster describes as: "any plan or action used to evade something difficult or unpleasant; device; artifice. Syn: see deception." To apply this to the real world, what would be difficult or unpleasant to a board of directors in these takeover situations is the takeover being accepted by stockholders and the directors losing their privileged positions, their emoluments, and their sinecures; and last but not least their ego-embellishing self-serving right to run their own enterprise regardless of stockholder wishes. The deception involves the utilization of false issues and statements such as: "potential antitrust problems" and "in the shareholders interest," in order to effectuate the plan.

These various practices will be cited in the following examples to see how a number of corporate "freezeins" were accomplished.

Some Notable Examples

a. *Gerber vs. Anderson Clayton:* In 1977 Anderson Clayton made a bid of $40 per share for all the outstanding shares of Gerber Products. Gerber management immediately opposed the transaction on the grounds that there was an antitrust problem and on the rather farfetched proposition that because Anderson Clayton had been involved in some "sensitive payments" overseas, it was not a fit buyer for Gerber Products (such claims are totally irrelevant in strictly cash offers). The antitrust claim was based on the allegation that Gerber had for some time been contemplating entering the salad dressing business in which Anderson was already substantially involved.

At the outset, the question of the "adequacy" of the price offered to Gerber shareholders was never entertained. Only after significant pressure was brought to bear on Gerber management to respond to this question, did Gerber solicit an opinion from its investment bankers, Goldman Sachs. Such opinion has never been publicly released, but at the Gerber annual meeting that occurred during the course of the takeover, Gerber chairman John Suerth indicated that Goldman Sachs thought that, "the Street generally felt that the offer of $40 was a fair offer." He also cited other investment advice to the effect that in several years' time Gerber stock would be worth a lot more than $40 per share.

The nuances in such self-serving statements are not easily analyzed by the investing public who are not generally attuned to discounted cash flow analysis. However, any financial analyst would have been able to calculate the present value of a hypothetical $50 price for Gerber five years hence, which relative to today's interest rate structure would clearly have produced a present value of less than $40. In other words, $40 then was still far more beneficial than some hypothetical future value.

b. *Marshall Field vs. Carter Hawley Hale:* In February 1978, Carter Hawley Hale offered $42 per share in cash and securities for all the outstanding shares of Marshall Field, representing a premium of approximately 100 percent over the then recent trading range of Marshall Field. The response of Marshall Field was startling, as within 24 hours after the offer had been officially promulgated, Marshall Field filed a suit in Federal District Court in Chicago alleging various violations of the antitrust laws. At the same time there were vague references made to the "adequacy" of the offer with the general comment that the offer was "not in the best interests of shareholders," which is the usual phrase applied to the various issues—fictitious or otherwise—that are brought into the public eye.

If there was not already an antitrust issue present in this case—and that is a highly debatable point—then Marshall Field was going to see to it that it created one, and if it couldn't create one which would be substantial, then it was going to so foul its own balance sheet as to discourage the buyer from proceeding. Thus, Marshall Field proposed to buy various stores, all of which were in the proximity of Carter Hawley stores. Marshall Field also informed its prospective suitor that it had plans to buy other properties which would utilize a good deal of the borrowing potential of Marshall Field and (which analysts will corroborate) were not necessarily suitable investments for Marshall Field. Seeing the desirability of its target bride being dissipated by its management, Carter Hawley Hale withdrew from the scene.

What ensued were the usual spate of stockholder class action suits that were subsequently consolidated in Federal District Court in Chicago, Judge Will presiding. What is particularly interesting in this case is that lawyer-client privilege was revoked permitting an unusual view into the defensive strategy employed by counsel for the defense (Skadden, Arps, Slate, Meagher & Flom). It turns out that Marshall Field had been trying to elude the grasp of would-be acquirers for some ten years and in each case had purchased or proposed to purchase a store in the proximity of the stores owned by the acquirers. It presumably would create an antitrust situation. Accordingly, the records show that no less than four previous potential acquirers had lost their appetites as a result of this policy, including Federated Department Stores, Gamble-Skogmo, Dayton Hudson, and Macy's. This also explains why the antitrust suit filed by Marshall Field against Carter Hawley followed so rapidly the announcement of a proposed takeover. There was probably a standard suit on file with only the blanks to be filled in utilizing the name of the latest suitor.

Again, what is particulary revolting to this observer is that corporate managers will go to any length, even to the point of dissipating the assets of their company, in order to maintain their independence.

It is interesting to note that Marshall Field was recently purchased for a price of $30 per share by Batus Corp., a subsidiary of British American Tobacco. This was accomplished by pressure brought to bear by a group of stockholders led by Carl Icahn who were able to gain roughly a 30 percent position in Marshall Field by acting as a group and forcing management's hand in accepting $30 per share. The academic question, of course, becomes: What was it at $42 per share that was not in the stockholders interests that suddenly became in the stockholders interest at $30 per share?

c. *McGraw-Hill vs. American Express:* The McGraw Hill case is a fairly recent one (1979) wherein a management decided to rebuff a legitimate offer by creating the usual smoke screen. In this particular case, however, McGraw–Hill added a new twist: a "scorched earth" policy that was meant to exhaust and finally ward off the potential suitor and any others that may come along. The issues herein raised were the usual ones: antitrust and conflicts of interest, loss of independence of two integral operations (namely, Standard & Poors and McGraw-Hill Publications), and of course, the "Trojan Horse" charge against Roger Morley. In order to overcome these objections, American Express offered to negotiate and resolve all of the issues by withdrawing its unilateral tender offer and introducing a new and higher "friendly" offer at $40 per share that would only proceed on an amicable basis. After some 36 hours of "profound" deliberation, McGraw-Hill's board again rejected the American Express proposal.

One again senses the heavy-handedness of management in trying to stifle an existing offer and squashing any others that may ensue during a contested tender offer. For instance, during the McGraw-Hill annual meeting subsequent to the American Express rebuff, Harold McGraw stated that when he received a telephone call that indicated that the latter company was interested in making an offer, his initial response on the telephone was "no thank you, we would like to remain independent." Thus, regardless of any price considerations the stated objection was one of independence.

The writer would again underline that such a long-term objective should be properly adopted by a formal resolution of the board of directors and subsequently offered for a vote to all shareholders. It would be doubtful that such action would be ratified by McGraw-Hill's board.

Furthermore, although it was widely known in the investment community that other companies expressed an interest in negotiating with McGraw-Hill, Harold McGraw was able to shunt these offers aside by stating that they were "expressions of support." (He might well have found his flexibility somewhat more limited before a court of law, had the class action suits been adjudicated.) A further contortive twist was added to McGraw's defensive strategy, one that it is "not necessarily the right time to sell" regardless of the price offered. Again, the right time is a function of the familiar use of discounted cash flow analysis. A price of $45 in three years would still be significantly less than a current price of $40 at any reasonable discount factor. Nevertheless, executive officers have the ability to glibly talk their way through and around the issues and stockholders are more or less powerless to defend themselves and protect their own interests. Those who should be protecting their interests in similar situations—the board of directors—are too busy thinking about themselves. There is a clear conflict of interest, but it exists not between the two battling companies, but between the board and its shareholders.

An interesting sidelight in this transaction is the result of the stockholders meeting in the aftermath of the rejection of American Express wherein approximately 12 percent of the total shares voted against incumbent management in an uncontested ballot.

The author must acknowledge that in this particular case the defender was right by virtue of its superior management record. Of all the cases cited, it must be fairly stated that the price of McGraw-Hill went above the tender offer price within roughly a year after the tender by American Express was turned down and whereas the author does not agree with the tactics used to do so, he is nonetheless impressed by the results.

d. *Carrier Corp. vs. United Technologies:* This particular case is probably the most sinister of the four and has received no public comment to date. United Technologies offered a price of $28 per share for 49 percent of Carrier and then a combination of securities worth approximately $28 for the balance of the shares. At the very outset, United Technologies said the price was negotiable, thereby indicating a willingness to increase the offer based upon a satisfactory negotiation and resolution of differences. It is fairly common knowledge on Wall Street, in fact, that United Technologies was willing to pay up to $32 for Carrier. Rather than work for their shareholders and get a better price, management preferred to do battle. They cooked up an antitrust case alleging some 15 different violations of Section 7 of the Clayton Antitrust Act and hoped that a hometown judge in Syracuse would see things their way. In fact, the judge found for the defendant, United Technologies, in each and every charge, even though the Justice Department joined in the fray on the side of the plaintiff.

The final result is that Carrier shareholders received $28 for their shares and management spent millons of dollars litigating against United Technologies with whom they instead should have been negotiating. One would think that perhaps if there was any substance to the antitrust charges that perhaps one of the 15 allegations would have been sustained by the court. But not one was!

e. *Amax vs. Standard Oil of California:* Another flagrant example of the "Subterfuge Syndrome," and one of the greatest deceptions in merger takeover history is the Amax case.

Standard Oil of California (Socal) has since 1975 had a 20 percent interest in Amax, which it acquired with the necessary approval of the Federal Trade Commission. It was always Socal's intention to acquire the remaining shares and it was with this understanding that this initial investment was made. In 1978, Socal bid the equivalent of $26 per share. The offer was rejected as inadequate by the Amax board. In March 1981, Amax suddenly announced that it had rejected a new offer from Socal worth approximately

$78.50 per Amax share. At the time of the offer the Amax shares were trading at around $38 per share.

Reasons cited in the rejection were potential antitrust obstacles and various other factors, all pointing to the conclusion that the offer was not in the stockholders' best interests. Socal left the offer open until just before the Amax annual meeting, and then when Socal was unable to effect either a renegotiation or a reconsideration on the part of Amax, Socal abandoned the transaction. Socal is known for its deep aversion to making hostile offers so that its withdrawal was quite understandable—and predictable.

The subterfuge in this case was effected through three clever ploys:

1. The rejection of the offer came simultaneously with the announcement of the offer. The stockholders had no time to urge upon the board that it accept such a lucrative offer. What was not known at the time was that the top hierarchy of Amax management had the offer in hand approximately three weeks prior to the announcement of the rejection without ever revealing it to the stockholders.

2. By citing "potential antitrust obstacles," Amax chairman, Pierre Gousseland, was raising the usual smokescreen, but in this case, he took a decided risk in that the Federal Trade Commission had already approved the Socal investment in Amax under the Antitrust Law back in 1975. Also, there had been parallel transactions over the course of the past few years that had been consummated: viz. Anaconda/Arco; Molycorp/ Union Oil of California; Kennecott/Sohio; Cyprus Mines/ Standard Oil of Indiana, to name the more prominent ones. Mr. Gousseland also purported to have the backing of the board in stating that antitrust reasons formed the basis for the board's rejection of the Socal offer. In response to a shareholder's question at the annual meeting on May 6, 1982—one year later—Walter Hochshild, an Amax director and holder of some two million Amax shares, stated explicitly that Mr. Gousseland had not been given the authority by the board of directors of

Amax to cite antitrust objections as an obstacle to the Socal deal. Here, then, clearly the deception had been revealed!

3. The third subterfuge in this case was the usual "not in the stockholders' best interest," as the price being inadequate. Amax commissioned both Goldman Sachs and Lehman Brothers/Kuhn Loeb to establish theoretical values for the Amax shares to which Amax could then subsequently point and state unashamedly that the offer of $78.50 per share was "inadequate." It has been reported that the two investment banking houses came up with theoretical values somewhere between $100 and $120 per share.

The deception in this particular ploy is that the acquired company shares also have a theoretical value that is far in excess of the current market value and if one had utilized Standard of California's theoretical values in calculating the parity of the offer, then it is safe to assume that the values would have been close to that estimated by Goldman Sachs and Lehman Brothers/Kuhn Loeb. Amax is currently (mid-1982) trading near $20!

Conclusion

Between the Williams Act, the various state antitakeover statutes (which are now, collectively on their way out by virtue of a recent Supreme Court decision[2]), the government antitrust agencies, and last but most importantly, entrenched managements, nowhere is there to be found a spokesman for the investing public. There is, however, a ready example that could remedy the situation and clearly protect the interests of the investing public. Great Britain has a Takeover Panel whose purpose is to sort out the various offers made for a company and to make sure all the laws are adhered to. The SEC could create such a power whose purpose would be to determine whether or not there clearly are issues that warrant either some sort of resolution or, if irreconcilable, whether or not the bidder should be allowed to proceed with his offer. The Takeover

Panel would be empowered to appoint independent legal counsel as to the existence of antitrust and other issues that are normally raised during the course of a contested offer. It is this writer's feeling that such a panel would save a great amount of time, energy expense, and confusion, and in the final analysis assure proper safeguards for the investing public in contested takeover battles.

Chapter 7

Active Arbitrage

The genesis of "active arbitrage" must be seen in the context of the early 1970s and the abuses of entrenched managements, which were highlighted in Chapter 6.

"Active arbitrage" investments can be considered ones in which an investor takes steps to organize shareholders and acts as a catalyst to bring about change. These strategies are relevant in situations where the portfolio manager believes that there is significant value or performance shortfall arising from current corporate policies that is not being adequately addressed by the marketplace. In these situations there would be an opportunity for an investor to employ tactics that go beyond the traditional arbitrage approach in order to catalyze changes that will lead to substantial value gains.

The collapse of takeover activity in the early 1970s and the market for corporate control left a dearth of active catalysts in the investment community. As a consequence, there were numerous examples of situations in which corporate policy choices decreased value but aroused no active response from the market. This created a "value gap" that could be addressed and corrected by "active arbitrage" strategies.

The expertise necessary to engage successfully in "active arbitrage" situations was considered strongly related to the traditional skills necessary for successful risk arbitrage. Traditionally, the arbitrage firm has used its capacity for risk bearing and its expertise in corporate valuation to take positions in mergers or other transactions and insure an efficient outcome. The same skills were thought to be necessary to identify situations where significant "value gaps" had appeared due to inefficient corporate policies, and the same tolerance for risk bearing would be necessary to carry out active strategies to catalyze change. The "active arbitrage" role thus represents a natural extension of an arbitrageur's skills and organizational capability beginning with the post-takeover environment of the 1970s.

The Bache/Pru-Bache Years (1967–1991)

Great Western United Corporation

Corporate abuses such as those described in Chapter 6 suggested to this author that, sooner or later, a new phase in the corporate governance movement might evolve. My own experience with active arbitrage came in 1974. Great Western United (GWU) was a conglomerate located in Denver, Colorado, run by a youngster by the name of Billy White. The company had a number of subsidiaries, the major one of which was the Great Western Sugar Company. GWU had outstanding a series of senior preferred stock, which was cumulative and which was many quarters in arrears. We started purchasing the shares in this cumulative preferred when we noticed that the price of sugar was rising dramatically. It rose to such an extent that, in simple arithmetic, it was obvious that Great Western could now clearly afford to pay off all its cumulative dividend arrears. We therefore contacted the company and asked them to pay the arrears given its new-found financial fortunes. The company, in several telephone conversations, refused to accede to our wishes.

I was then contacted by Mr. Allen Slifka, Managing Partner of L.F. Rothschild & Company and head of its Arbitrage Department, who suggested that we do something together as he, too, had a large position in the preferred shares. So we jointly filed an action in Federal District Court in Denver, Colorado and sent a courtesy copy of the complaint to the Company. Amazingly, within a period of two weeks, and without further ado, we both received a check for the full amount of the preferred dividend arrears, at which point I said to myself: "Aha! There is something to standing up to these entrenched corporate directors who do not pay attention to the legitimate demands of their shareholders." A spark had ignited a bonfire!

Therein are to be found the seeds of the "active arbitrage" revolution, which in this particular case was more of a corporate governance-type of arbitrage, challenging the resistance of entrenched managers to respond to their shareholders. In its subsequent forms, "active arbitrage" came to target a similar resistance by boards of directors; but now, this new strategy would seek to overcome boardmember opposition to accepting a premium share price bids offered by a third party. The spread, or "value gap," was the difference between the market price, which would suffer when a management refused to negotiate with a willing bidder, and the proposed price for the target company's shares.

Gerber Products Company

In the summer of 1977, Anderson Clayton & Company Incorporated offered a rich premium price of $40 per share for each Gerber Products share. The company's board refused to consider this handsome price for Gerber shares or to negotiate a better one. I went out to the annual meeting of Gerber Products on July 27th of that year and challenged the chairman either to consider the adequacy of $40 or to explain why he wouldn't accept such a rich premium for Gerber shareholders. The chairman was unresponsive and evasive.[1,2] The article points out that the chairman, John Suerth, was not only unresponsive to questions posed by Wyser-Pratte, but even had the microphone taken from him in the middle of his questioning.

Eventually, having seen the share price adversely impacted by management's refusal to consider this offer, we determined to file suit with the Federal District Court in Freemont, Michigan. The lawyer handling the case was none other than the granddaddy of class action lawyers and former Nuremberg Prosecutor, Abraham Pomerantz. Unfortunately, a hometown judge from this particular court determined to impede our efforts by bifurcating the trial on the issues into two separate cases, which would have meant an interminable delay and expense. We were forced to withdraw our complaint as a result of this maneuver, but the point had nonetheless been made: the board of directors must rule on the adequacy of a premium offer received for shares or must at least establish a range of values which it considers adequate for shareholders to receive as consideration in a takeover.

Our action against Gerber Products received wide publicity and set the stage for other activists to enter the arena and begin challenging entrenched corporate managements. Activism and arbitrage were now truly morphing. At about this time, one began to see Carl Icahn in his moves against the Tappan Corporation.

The McGraw-Hill Corporation

In early January 1979, the American Express Corporation made an unsolicited offer of $40 per share directly to the board of McGraw-Hill and attempted to convince them to accept its offer. McGraw-Hill stock had been trading in the mid-20s. When McGraw-Hill refused to even negotiate a higher offer, we went on the offensive and protested vehemently about the lack of responsiveness on the part of McGraw-Hill's board of directors to a premium offer to McGraw-Hill shareholders. In order to try to convince the board to react more positively, we first organized a "shareholder protective committee." Once established, we sought via this committee to conduct a poll of McGraw-Hill shareholders in order to show management and the board that the majority of the shareholders wanted to accept the $40-per-share offer.[3] When the protective committee was threatened with litigation, its members folded their tents one by one, and we were finally obliged to withdraw as well. But that didn't end the action. I went to the annual shareholder meeting[4] and purposely and determinedly scolded the chairman of the board, Mr. Harold McGraw, Jr., and the other members of the board for not even having considered the American Express offer and for having hidden behind the vague claim of American Express's offer being illegal. When challenged by numerous shareholders as to why the board considered the offer illegal, no response was forthcoming.

But a school of thought was building in the shareholder and legal communities: that directors had a responsibility to respond to premium offers made for the benefit of shareholders and that such offers could not simply be swept under the rug.[5]

The ERC Corporation of Kansas City, Missouri

In the fall of 1979, the Connecticut General Corporation began courting The ERC Corporation and eventually proposed an offer of $80 per share. The stock had been trading in the upper-40s. Then chairman Stamford Miller resisted the offer, hiding behind the Insurance Commissioner of Missouri, who claimed the offer was anti-competitive; but, we concluded that such a refusal of a premium offer could not go unchallenged. So we implemented a new strategy to manifest the shareholders' discontent and opposition to management's actions. Since there was no place on the proxy ballot at the shareholders' meeting to vote "No," we organized a movement amongst the shareholders to vote to abstain. The abstention vote was very large, almost 45 percent of the shares outstanding, and made a significant impact on the board of directors in reconsidering their opposition to accepting an offer.

We also tried to present six other shareholder resolutions at the shareholders' meeting, including:

1. A vote of no confidence in management;
2. A resolution directing the board to negotiate with any suitable buyer at a price of $80 or better; and

3. Other significant moves to force the board to disclose offers that may have been made in the past.

The chairman refused to allow these resolutions to be proposed officially, allowing me only to read these resolutions aloud.[6]

Ultimately, our resistance and cohesiveness with other shareholders forced the board to reconsider its position. In early June of 1980, ERC's board accepted an offer from the Getty Oil Corporation at $97 per share.[7]

Amax Incorporated

In March of 1981, Amax Incorporated received an unsolicited offer of $78.50 a share from Standard Oil of California. The shares had been in the $50 range, but climbed as high as $68 as a result of this offer. The board of Amax mysteriously declined the offer as "not in the best interests of shareholders." One year later, the shares had plummeted to $26.25. We, as well as many other shareholders, protested vociferously at the annual shareholders' meeting of Amax on May 6, 1982 but to no avail.[8,9] The horse had long before left the barn.

Houston Natural Gas

In February of 1984, the Coastal States Corporation made a merger proposal to the board of Houston Natural Gas. The chairman, M.D. Matthews, refused to accept the offer and in fact evaded the offer by "greenmailing" (buying back the shares at a premium price) Coastal States and by paying $15 million of its takeover expenses. Naturally, the shares of Houston crumbled in the wake of this maneuver.

At about the same time as Coastal States was pulling off this travesty, Peter Jacquith of Lazard Frères contacted me to let me know that a Lazard client, the Transco Corporation, was willing to pay an even higher price than Coastal States, but had not been able to get an offer into the Houston Natural Gas board of directors. A transmittal letter containing the Transco offer had been refused entry at the boardroom door! In other words, the company was going to stonewall any offer that came in to benefit shareholders. With this fact and the highly dubious practice of "greenmailing" that Houston Natural Gas had engineered with the full cooperation of Coastal States, we, as Prudential-Bache, filed a lawsuit in Federal District Court in Houston, Texas. This lawsuit was the undoing of chairman Matthews, as we eventually were able to show that Houston Natural Gas' investment banker, The First Boston Corporation, was illegally gathering potential bidders in a secret basement office and having them sign "standstill" agreements. The idea was that any potential bidder would only get access to confidential data (the data room) if they agreed to "stand still" and not make an offer until authorized to do so. In this manner Houston Natural Gas was able to choke off any prospective offers for the company. The only problem with this was that the agreements were illegal since they weren't authorized by the board of directors.[10,11] This tactic of having potential bidders executing "standstill" agreements, and freezing them out, was subsequently brought out in an important article in *The Economist*.[12]

Houston Natural Gas was subsequently acquired by the Enron Corporation, which, of course, went on to perpetrate one of the greatest scandals in U.S. financial history.

The Wyser-Pratte Years: Years of Increasing Activism (1991–Present)

A New Beginning

Wyser-Pratte and Company was reconstituted in February 1991 after parting company with Pru-Bache.[13] I had determined that upon raising a new fund—The Euro-Partners Arbitrage Fund—.25 percent of all capital raised would be allocated to investing in "active arbitrage" strategies. And now, being a privately owned company, we would be able to tabulate very accurately the returns of our various activist initiatives. Appendix C serves to illustrate a number of initiatives undertaken by Wyser-Pratte and Company that were strictly "active arbitrage" interventions. These were "reactive" rather than "pro-active." The latter involves a more operationally oriented approach to change a company's business model. The former would occur when a company's management resisted a takeover and we attempted, and in most cases succeeded, in resurrecting the transaction or eventually improving the price of the shares by attracting the affections of a "white knight," or forcing a restructuring to improve the market price.

Each example in Appendix C is comprised of four parts, in addition to the initial introductory graph: Part I showing the investment statistics and our investment returns; Part II, a brief description of the company; Part III, a precise chronology of the events surrounding the initiatives; and Part IV, the events subsequent to the initiatives' completion.

The U.S. press quickly tuned into the continuing activism from the reincarnated Wyser-Pratte and Company, Inc., and was soon followed by the European media, which seemed to sense that something new was afoot.[14,15]

Evolution of the Wyser-Pratte Shareholder Rights By-Law

We had been sufficiently frustrated over the years by entrenched managements' refusal to accept premium offers for shares of their companies. Thus, in 1996, we devised a stratagem we labeled the "Shareholder Rights By-Law." We adopted this concept from a combination of European jurisprudence and custom whereupon in most European countries, and particularly the U.K. and France, if a company's management received a premium offer for shares and if it wanted to resist such an offer, it had to ask its shareholders' permission to authorize such resistance. The result of this, of course, was that few managements sought to resist because they knew very well what the response from the shareholders would be: clearly negative!

a) Wallace Computer Services Corporation (see Exhibit 7.1) We got our initial chance to apply this new tactic with Wallace Computer Services (WCS), which received an offer from

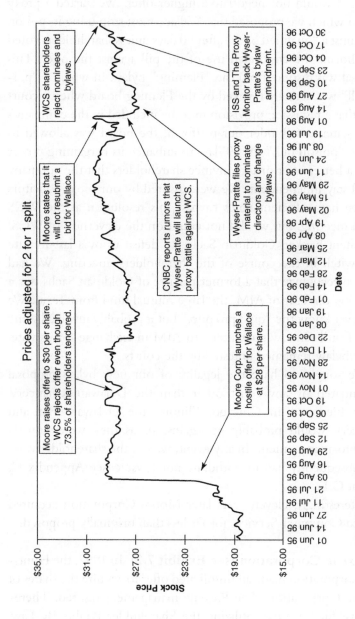

Prices adjusted for 2 for 1 split

WCS shareholders reject nominees and bylaws.

Moore states that it will not resubmit a bid for Wallace.

Moore raises offer to $30 per share. WCS rejects offer even though 73.5% of shareholders tendered.

CNBC reports rumors that Wyser-Pratte will launch a proxy battle against WCS.

ISS and The Proxy Monitor back Wyser-Pratte's bylaw amendment.

Wyser-Pratte files proxy material to nominate directors and change bylaws.

Moore Corp. launches a hostile offer for Wallace at $28 per share.

Stock Price

$35.00
$31.00
$27.00
$23.00
$19.00
$15.00

Date

01 Jun 95
14 Jun 95
27 Jun 95
11 Jul 95
21 Jul 95
03 Aug 95
16 Aug 95
29 Aug 95
12 Sep 95
25 Sep 95
09 Oct 95
19 Oct 95
01 Nov 95
14 Nov 95
28 Nov 95
11 Dec 95
22 Dec 95
08 Jan 96
19 Jan 96
01 Feb 96
14 Feb 96
28 Feb 96
12 Mar 96
25 Mar 96
08 Apr 96
19 Apr 96
02 May 96
15 May 96
29 May 96
11 Jun 96
24 Jun 96
08 Jul 96
19 Jul 96
01 Aug 96
14 Aug 96
27 Aug 96
10 Sep 96
23 Sep 96
04 Oct 96
17 Oct 96
30 Oct 96

Exhibit 7.1 Wallace Computer Services, Inc.

151

The Moore Corporation of Canada. The WCS board refused the offer and would not negotiate a higher offer. We started a proxy fight in which we proposed that Wallace must stop using its poison pill against a "qualified offer" after 90 days unless shareholders voted to authorize the continued use of the pill against the offer. This proposal was distinct from the "Fleming" bylaw, in which a "poison pill" was actually revoked by the Fleming board when a court ruled that a rescission provision must be included in the company's proxy statement. Under our platform, the board was allowed to use the "poison pill," for 90 days to enhance its bargaining power to get a better offer or to convince shareholders that the company should stay independent. We were assured by our proxy solicitors that we had sufficient votes to pass this resolution at the WCS annual meeting, but we did not count on the cleverness of WCS' investment banker, Goldman Sachs, to defeat us by a last-minute vote switch in the course of the shareholders' meeting. We had failed to recognize that a former partner of Goldman Sachs was a managing director of AIM, the large mutual fund from Texas. We will never know the "quid pro quo," but it probably involved some kind of order inflow guaranteed to AIM in exchange for its vote. So the bylaw remained untested by the courts.

We sought to have the legality of our new bylaw proposal substantiated by any court other than the Delaware Chancery, so we filed suit in Chicago, Illinois—the Delaware Bar and Chancery would probably go against us as they were notoriously pro-management. In any event, we lost the shareholder vote, and subsequently had to withdraw our lawsuit (see Appendix C, Exhibit C.1).

Interestingly, eleven years later Moore Corporation acquired Wallace Computer Services for far less than originally proposed.

b) Rexene Corporation (see Exhibit 7.2) In 1997, the Huntsman Corporation made an unsolicited offer to acquire the shares of Rexene Corporation. The Rexene management resisted. Therefore, we filed a proxy utilizing the Shareholder Rights By-Law, but this time sought to propose a slate of directors committed to

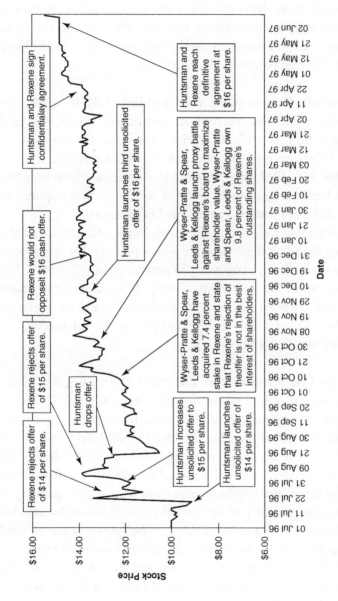

Exhibit 7.2 Rexene Corporation

trying to negotiate a sale of the company to Huntsman. We quickly obtained four qualified dissident director candidates to further our cause. Most of the shareholders became increasingly supportive of our proposal, to such an extent that the company was forced to negotiate a sale to Huntsman on the very eve of the shareholders' meeting[16] (see Appendix C, Exhibit C.2).

c) Pennzoil Corporation (see Exhibit 7.3) In 1998, the Pennzoil Corporation received an unsolicited, hostile cash and share offer from the Union Pacific Resources Corporation. In a proxy filing, we supplemented the Shareholder Rights By-Law with what we called "the Shareholders' Interests Protection By-Law," wherein a unanimous vote of the board was required to approve defensive actions by the board of directors.

Naturally, we were sued by Pennzoil, but in settling the case, the Company did adopt the "chewable poison pill" (a pill withdrawn to facilitate a fully financed offer at a 35 percent premium approved by $66^2/_3$ percent of the outstanding shares). This was a case in which we won our corporate governance platform, but lost on the transaction because of a subsequent collapse in the oil market.[17,18] (See Appendix C, Exhibit C.3.)

d) Telxon Corporation (See Exhibit 7.4) In 1998, the Telxon Corporation received a negotiable offer from Symbol Technologies. Again the target company resisted. In response, we created something we called the "Shareholder Friendly By-Law," which stipulated that if an acquisition proposal is made, holders of 10 percent of the stock can call a special meeting and a majority of the shares represented at the meeting can require the company to stop using the "poison pill" to block the offer. This is what avoided the problem of defining "a qualified offer." Again we were sued by the target, but in a settlement the Telxon Company appointed a Wyser-Pratte nominee to the board and agreed not to use the "poison pill" to block a fully financed offer at $40 per share or more. Little by little, we were making inroads against entrenched corporate boards with our bylaw proposals strategy (see Appendix C, Exhibit C.4).

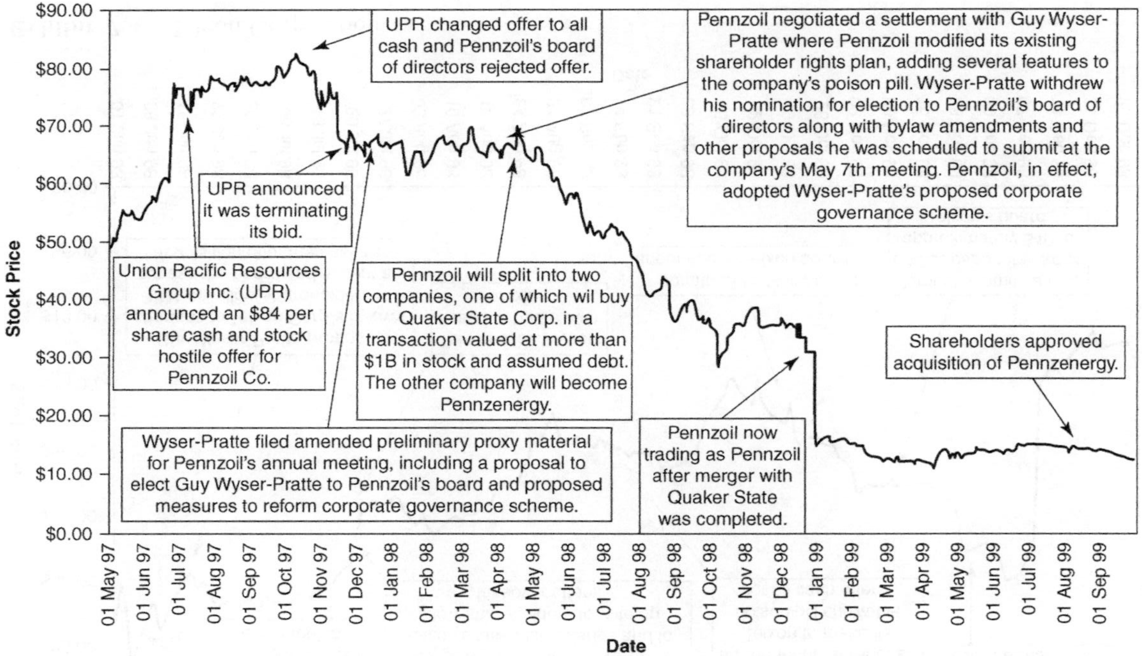
Stock Price
$90.00
$80.00
$70.00
$60.00
$50.00
$40.00
$30.00
$20.00
$10.00
$0.00
UPR changed offer to all cash and Pennzoil's board of directors rejected offer.
Pennzoil negotiated a settlement with Guy Wyser-Pratte where Pennzoil modified its existing shareholder rights plan, adding several features to the company's poison pill. Wyser-Pratte withdrew his nomination for election to Pennzoil's board of directors along with bylaw amendments and other proposals he was scheduled to submit at the company's May 7th meeting. Pennzoil, in effect, adopted Wyser-Pratte's proposed corporate governance scheme.
UPR announced it was terminating its bid.
Union Pacific Resources Group Inc. (UPR) announced an $84 per share cash and stock hostile offer for Pennzoil Co.
Pennzoil will split into two companies, one of which wil buy Quaker State Corp. in a transaction valued at more than $1B in stock and assumed debt. The other company will become Pennzenergy.
Shareholders approved acquisition of Pennzenergy.
Wyser-Pratte filed amended preliminary proxy material for Pennzoil's annual meeting, including a proposal to elect Guy Wyser-Pratte to Pennzoil's board and proposed measures to reform corporate governance scheme.
Pennzoil now trading as Pennzoil after merger with Quaker State was completed.
01 May 97
01 Jun 97
01 Jul 97
01 Aug 97
01 Sep 97
01 Oct 97
01 Nov 97
01 Dec 97
01 Jan 98
01 Feb 98
01 Mar 98
01 Apr 98
01 May 98
01 Jun 98
01 Jul 98
01 Aug 98
01 Sep 98
01 Oct 98
01 Nov 98
01 Dec 98
01 Jan 99
01 Feb 99
01 Mar 99
01 Apr 99
01 May 99
01 Jun 99
01 Jul 99
01 Aug 99
01 Sep 99
Date

Exhibit 7.3 Pennzoil Corporation

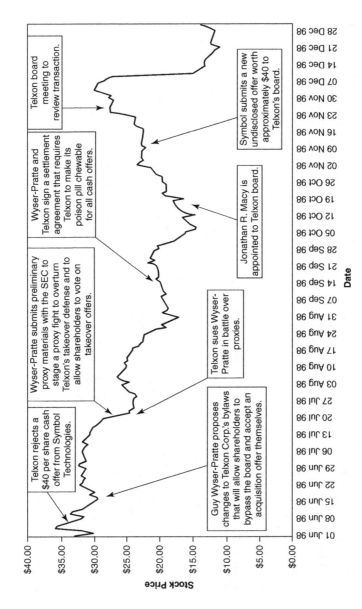

The chart shows Telxon Corporation stock price from 01 Jun 98 to 28 Dec 98, with the following annotations:

Telxon rejects a $40 per share cash offer from Symbol Technologies.

Wyser-Pratte submits preliminary proxy materials with the SEC to stage a proxy fight to overturn Telxon's takeover defense and to allow shareholders to vote on takeover offers.

Wyser-Pratte and Telxon sign a settlement agreement that requires Telxon to make its poison pill chewable for all cash offers.

Telxon board meeting to review transaction.

Guy Wyser-Pratte proposes changes to Telxon Corp.'s bylaws that will allow shareholders to bypass the board and accept an acquisition offer themselves.

Telxon sues Wyser-Pratte in battle over proxies.

Jonathan R. Macy is appointed to Telxon's board.

Symbol submits a new undisclosed offer worth approximately $40 to Telxon's board.

Stock Price axis: $0.00, $5.00, $10.00, $15.00, $20.00, $25.00, $30.00, $35.00, $40.00

Date

Exhibit 7.4 Telxon Corporation

156

e) Anti-Poison Pill Crusade: Union Carbide Based on the success of our bylaw proposals, we determined to lead a poison pill revolt. There were dozens of companies with "poison pills'" set to expire in the subsequent year, all likely targets to receive a binding "poison pill" resolution. Sponsored by our partner, the State of Wisconsin Investment Board (SWIB), along with other funds, a proposal would purport to amend a company's bylaws to require shareholder approval before a "poison pill" could be renewed.

Our goal was to get a number of corporations to adopt our more shareholder-friendly "chewable poison pill." It started with our trying to prevent companies with expiring pills simply to renew their existing pills without shareholder approval.

As our lead target we selected the Union Carbide Corporation. The ensuing fight was protracted and hard fought indeed, as the "father of the poison pill," Martin Lipton, Esq., of the redoubtable firm of Wachtel, Lipton, etc., was going to support Union Carbide to the end. In an alarming turn of events for this latter group, we and SWIB won the shareholder vote that eliminated Union Carbide's "poison pill." The outcome? Shortly thereafter Union Carbide received a takeover offer from the Dow Chemical Corporation, an offer which Union Carbide, newly denuded of its protective armor, was unable to fend off. The acquisition went through without a hitch with the godfather of the "poison pill" a very unhappy individual. Martin Lipton's huge client base was now in jeopardy. This victory was an interesting and rewarding turn of events, but not for reasons you might expect. We did not own Union Carbide shares. We acted purely on principle.[19]

There was much attention devoted to our Shareholder Rights By-Law by the legal community, some of which is enclosed.[20,21] Interestingly, as of 2008, Delaware has not challenged our bylaw creations.

Transition

Eventually our "active arbitrage" interventions attracted the attention of our colleagues in Europe, leading Wyser-Pratte and

Company into "pro-active activism" in continental Europe. This is a permutation of the activist métier in which one assesses the reasons for a stock's undervaluation, be it management problems, strategy problems, the blend of assets to achieve a particular strategy, corporate governance problems, shareholder conflicts between majority and minority shareholders, or local contrivances such as "double voting rights"—or in some cases, no voting rights, such as under the "Structured Regime" in the Netherlands. Having established the reason for the undervaluation, one calculates the spread by a peer group analysis and other related financial statistics in order to determine the prospective value of an unencumbered, restructured target company. This becomes the "value gap" and establishes the potential return, vis-a-vis the "active arbitrage" approach wherein one gauges the difference between the takeover premium and the actual market price.

By the year 2000, the active arbitrage call-to-arms was being echoed internationally. *Capital*, the French financial magazine, ran an article[22] about all of our French initiatives, and its headline and graphics said it all: "This Former Marine is Terrorizing Our Bosses," ran the title; shown were bulls-eyes projected over the photo of each of six French CEOs. This led us eventually to initiatives in Germany, Belgium, Austria, Spain, and the Netherlands. In each case we attempted to first persuade managements and, if not, then the shareholders to follow us in putting pressure on managements to effect the necessary change in order to achieve the potential values that we had calculated.

Since 1995, we have undertaken forty such initiatives in Europe, most examples of the operational, "proactive" type of activism that has been the mainstay of the sport. "Active arbitrage" is still very much in force as this book goes to press. For instance, Carl Icahn in May 2008 launched a proxy fight to convince a reluctant Yahoo board of directors to accept an unsolicited offer from Microsoft.

Chapter 8

Summary and
Conclusions

A rbitrageurs participate in a great variety of situations that
arise from the various forms of corporate financial reorganizations and refinancing. The author has been chiefly
concerned with those situations that involve some degree of risk.
The risk factor manifests itself in the spread and thus provides the
arbitrageur with the requisite maneuverability and potential profit
which permits him to assume that risk.

To understand and predict the behavior of securities involved
in the various types of situations requires deeper analysis than is
generally manifested by the investing public. Statements by the
financial press and by company officials as to the value of a particular
offer should be regarded skeptically.

The same holds for statements by research departments of brokerage firms attempting to explain either the market action of a

proposed Bride, or her technical chart pattern. She is selling at a price not for any reason of over- or under-supply, but due solely to the collective activity of professional arbitrageurs who are together setting the price based on:

• Their calculation of the parity
• Their assessment of the risks
• Their estimation of the probable timetable
• Their availability and cost of capital
• Alternative rates of return available to them

The activity of arbitrageurs moving in and out of these situations produces certain other phenomena in the marketplace; e.g., post-merger selling pressure, exchange offer pressures, tax reversals, and "swap" arrangements. All of these leave special traces in the marketplace.

Arbitrageurs are able to reap handsome profits because of their ability to commit large amounts of capital to a highly diversified portfolio for risk arbitrage situations. They particularly benefit from low capital requirements to finance these positions, and from their membership in the Arbitrage Community. Lacking any of the above requisites, the private and institutional investor is advised to invest not in deals, but in securities!

But there are yet for the investing public and institutions some alternatives to total avoidance of involvement in risk arbitrage. Every proposed merger, tender offer, or recapitalization involves the issuance of existing or new classes of securities. In practically every one of these, there will sooner or later be a spread, the existence of which can be translated into a discount. Therefore, the public is presented with the opportunity to purchase securities that they would wish to buy—the Grooms—at a discount to their actual or expected (in the case of new classes of securities) market prices, by buying the proposed Brides. This is described throughout this writing and in Appendix A as the "creation" of securities. Thus with a share for share exchange of Y, selling at $10, for X, selling at $5, if one would like to buy Y on its own merits, one could instead simply buy X, thereby making a saving of $5. This procedure seems even more enticing when new high grade convertible securities are involved. If, for instance, a new convertible preferred is to be offered and is expected to sell at a yield of 10 percent, an investor, by working through the discount, might possibly create the preferred at a yield of 15 percent. In such instances, investor participation on the long side of risk arbitrage seems warranted. The underlying assumption, of course, is that the merger or reorganization will be effected. While the private investor is not usually in a position to estimate the probabilities, the institutional investor, thanks to his economic striking power, is often made privy to the essential facts necessary to make the requisite judgment. There are strong indications that institutions are increasingly utilizing such discount creations produced by corporate reorganizations. For performance conscious institutions, this process carries a built-in performance factor in the realization of the discount.

A variation of these "discount creations" involves selling long the Groom and repurchasing it—at a discount—through the Bride. Utilizing the above example of X and Y, if one is long Y, one can sell it long at $10 and immediately reestablish the position by purchasing X at $5 for a paper profit of $5, so long as the merger goes through. This has an important tax implication: one can avoid activating the "wash sale" rule in reestablishing a position, the sole requirement being that a long sale of Y and the purchase of X occur at a time when X and Y are considered to be not substantially identical securities, i.e., before the shareholders' meeting.

There is also the simple possibility of profiting from arbitrage activity through the purchase of technically depressed Grooms. Where concentrated arbitrage selling pressure can be discerned, both the private and institutional investor can make some very reasonable and sound investments by bidding for securities that arbitrageurs are liquidating. They would appear to be the least risky involvement of all; and sometimes quite rewarding. Arbitrageurs have absolutely no patience when it comes to inventorying prospective Grooms. A little patience on the part of the true investor in these securities often will yield a return greater than that which could have been realized on the risk arbitrage transaction itself.

It should be emphasized at the same time that the activity of arbitrageurs lends an additional element of liquidity to the marketplace, although their motive is exclusively the rate of return. Arbitrageurs will make block bids for Brides and make block offerings of Grooms simply to establish their arbitrage hedge position. So, in locating a potential source of supply, or a source of demand, an institutional portfolio manager should always check to see whether the security in question is involved in some form of arbitrage. His task is greatly facilitated if he can find a congenial and smiling arbitrageur on the opposite side of his market.

It is apparent then that the Arbitrageur provides greater marketability to securities, thereby earning his economic justification. Marketability is a major prerequisite to large-scale or institutional investment and thus provides a strong incentive to savings. Moreover, when securities are marketable, investors are willing to accept lower returns on their investments and speculators are willing to assume risks they would otherwise avoid, knowing that they will be able to limit their losses through immediate resales. Accordingly, marketability induces the purchase of securities by those with savings to invest, which, in turn, reduces the cost of capital to the economy.

Morgan Evans goes one step further: "Since all arbitrageurs have almost identical costs and no arbitrageur's firm is big enough to dominate the scene, we have pure competition in the classic sense ..."[1] Thus the arbitrage community plays its indispensable economic role by stabilizing prices of securities in the various types of situations in which they participate.

Appendix A

The following are sample reorganization proposals for which the parities have been calculated. The calculations were predicated on interest rate structures and transaction costs that existed at the time the particular proposals were promulgated; accordingly, the resulting calculations would prove to be vastly different under current fee structures and money rates.

The "spread" or potential profit is determined along with the parity for each case. This is figured on a gross basis before taxes. From this figure one would normally make adjustments for such transaction factors as brokerage, state and transfer taxes, long and short dividends, and for private investors, commissions.

Prices of all securities involved in each case were taken on the same day.

A New Issue of Convertible Preferred with Two Simultaneous Conversion Rates

Terms: 1 Landis Machine ($115) = $90 market value of Teledyne $3.50 convertible preferred stock (226\frac{1}{2}$) + $\frac{1}{2}$ share of a new $6 preferred stock, each share of which would be convertible at any time into 0.67 Teledyne common (113\frac{5}{8}$), but for 30 days after the closing date would be convertible into $100 market value of Teledyne common, such market value to be determined by the closing price of Teledyne common on the closing date.

Parity: Each part of the package must be dealt with separately. Taking first the $3.50 preferred, which is convertible into two shares of Teledyne common, we note that this preferred trades at a discount to its conversion parity on the common.

$$226\tfrac{1}{2} \text{ versus } 2 \times \$113\tfrac{5}{8} = \$227\tfrac{1}{4}$$

The $90 market value for this preferred was to be determined by its average closing price for the ten business days ending April 10, 1968. With the above price of Teledyne taken on April 3, 1968, calculating a probable ratio for the common should not prove too difficult a task in spite of its volatility (remember that whatever ratio is determined for the preferred, multiplying by a factor of two will yield the amount of common to be received per preferred, which is what we should want to do in view of the discount on the preferred, and thereby receiving slightly more than the value in preferred). There is a very high probability that the price of the common will not fluctuate during the course of the next five trading days outside the limits of $105 to $125. Taking a fairly even probability distribution of these values, we come to an expected value of $115 for the common during the averaging period. This would mean a price of roughly $230 for the preferred. Thus,

$$90/\$230 = 0.391 \text{ preferred, or } 0.782 \text{ common}$$

Applying this ratio to the current price of Teledyne, the first part of the package is worth

$$0.782 \times \$113\tfrac{5}{8} = \$89.05$$

The treatment of the new $6 convertible preferred is somewhat less obvious but in practice quite simpler. The conversion ratio of 0.67 per preferred would yield

$$\$113\tfrac{5}{8} \times 0.67 = \$76.13$$

Mindful that for a thirty-day period we are assured to receive $100 per preferred—rather than $76.13—we would naturally want to obtain the higher figure. Since the $100 is to be calculated on the closing price on the closing date, all one has to do is to ascertain the chosen date, and mark a sell order for Teledyne common with the specialist "at the close of the market," thereby assuring that one will fall exactly on the ratio.

Gross Spread: $89.05 + ½ ($100) − $115 = $25.05

A New Issue of Convertible Preferred with a Delayed Conversion Privilege

Terms: 1 United Fruit ($82) = 1 new $2 Zapata-Norness preferred convertible into 1.4 common ($61) after 90 days and into $120 market value of common stock beginning on 1 February 1971, with the stipulation that the preferred shall be convertible into not more than 2 common shares at a later date.

Parity: The preferred should have a present value that deserves only slight discount from the conversion parity in 90 days; $61 × 1.4 = $85.40. For the long-term view, figuring that at worst (from a market value point of view) one will receive 2 common shares on conversion: by buying United Fruit at $82 one is buying Zapata two years hence at 41. One will receive the $120 market value per preferred so long as Zapata-Norness common will be $60 or above two years hence. Thus one must assign a discount factor to the $120 based on, first that Zapata will be $60 or above in two years, and second, the return that one expects to earn on one's investment in the common stock of a similar company, or the opportunity cost on some other investment possibility. The latter is a rather subjective calculation. One must also be mindful that the common stock of Zapata-Norness pays no dividend, while the new preferred will pay $2. In view of the (then) high regard of the Investment Community for the company, and its impressive growth record, the probability that the stock two years hence would be at least $60 could be considered high. Let us say that Zapata at $61, probability estimates would yield an expected value of $54 for February 1, 1971. Thus $2 \times \$54 = \$108$, which is the figure that will be discounted at some selected rate to arrive at present value. Having chosen a desired per annum return of 10 percent, one must deduct the yearly dividend yield on the now preferred or roughly 2.35 percent: 2/$85 ($85 taken as the conversion value). Using the compound interest tables, and a discount factor of 10 percent − 2.35 percent, one arrives at a present value of $92 for the preferred.

Gross Spread: On conversion in 90 days—$85.40 − $82 = $3.40 with premium on conversion = $92 − $82 = $10

Common Stock of a New Corporation for Shares of Both Merging Companies (a Typical "Consolidation")

Terms: 1 Imperial Eastman ($30) = 0.86 new ITE Imperial Corp
1 ITE Circuitbreaker ($80) = 2 new ITE-Imperial Corp

Parity: The calculation of parities when merging parties form a new corporation, and are given varying proportions of same, is undoubtedly one of the most elusive. One might be first tempted to figure the parity by determining a capitalization rate for the pro-forma earnings of the new company. This approach is a bit too theoretical for the arbitrageur, who must be able to somehow hedge against the whims of the market. What is considered a "proper" capitalization rate when the arbitrageur takes a position may no longer be the case three months later when the deal is consummated and the arbitrageur tries to sell—with a profit—shares of the new company. In the actual case, then, one must find a way to hedge: something must be sold short! The answer lies in the fact that since both companies are receiving new shares of the ITE-Imperial and, according to the axiom, "things equal to the same things are equal to each other," a ratio can be calculated which will express the relationship between Imperial Eastman and ITE Circuitbreaker. Since 1 Imperial Eastman = 0.86 of the new concern, then 1 Imperial Eastman = 0.86/2 = 0.43 ITE Circuitbreaker. So, one can sell short 0.43 ITE for each Imperial purchased and thereby, "lock in" his profit. When the merger is consummated, each Imperial will receive the 0.86 ITE Imperial, which will be delivered to close out the short position of 0.43 ITE Circuitbreaker (since 0.43 ITE Circuitbreaker = 0.86 ITE Imperial).

Gross Spread: 0.43 × $80 − $30 = $34.40 − $30 = $4.40 per Imperial-Eastman

A New Convertible Preferred Stock in a New Corporation with the Preferred Having a Delayed Conversion Privilege

Terms: 1 Amerada Oil ($102) = 1 new $3.50 preferred of a new corporation convertible after 1 year into 2.2 common shares of the new corporation.

1 Hess Oil ($54) = 1 common of the new corporation

Parity: Had the new preferred been immediately convertible, it would be an easy matter of establishing a ratio whereby, assuming conversion of the new preferred into 2.2 common, 1 Hess Oil = 1/2.2 Amerada = 0.455 Amerada. However, since there is a delayed conversion feature, one must calculate a value for the preferred and thus the parity per Amerada. Since each Hess = 1 new common one could now sell short 2.2 Hess and calculate a value of 2.2 × $54 = $118 for the new preferred. Yet this is the value only one year hence, so we must calculate a present value for the preferred. Once again, this will be a calculation of some subjective elements, but let us assume that since we could obtain a risk free gain by shorting 2.2 Hess at $54, that our desired rate of return on this type of instrument should be somewhere around 10 percent. Since the preferred will pay $3.50 in dividends during the one year for which we will have to hold the preferred in order to be able to convert and get $118, we will have a dividend yield of roughly 3 percent, so that our net discount factor should be approximately 7 percent, giving the preferred a present value of $109.75.

Gross Spread: $109.75 − $102 = $7.75 per Amerada

A New Issue of Convertible Debentures

Terms: 1 Union Pacific 4 percent Preferred ($10) = $10 principal amount of new Union Pacific $4^3/_4$ percent debenture due 1999, convertible into 1.75 common ($54.50).

Parity: By purchasing 1 preferred at $10, one is creating the $10 principal amount at $10, or the equivalent bond at par. On conversion, the debenture is worth 1.75 × $54.50 = $95.375. Employing once again the analysis such as was utilized in Chapter 3, the author arrives at a probable current yield of $4^5/_8$ percent, or a price of 103 per debenture. This would amount to a premium on conversion of 8.4 percent. The calculation was also based on the fact that the common is yielding 3.6 percent, that a debenture was marginable at 60 percent, which means that a lot of speculative money would buy them, and that the Railroad, then being reorganized into a holding company, had an impressive record and excellent growth potential in view of its diversification prospects, its valuable land holdings, etc.

Gross Spread: $10.30 per $10 principal amount − $10 =
$0.30 per 4 percent preferred

Common Plus a New Issue of Straight Preferred

Terms: 1 Bullard ($32) = 0.44 common White Consolidated ($42) plus 0.43 new $3 preferred $50 par value.

Parity: By purchasing 1 Bullard at $32 and selling 0.44 White Consolidated common at $42, one creates 0.43 of the new $4 preferred at:

$$\$32 - (0.44 \times \$42) = \$13.42$$

Therefore, 1 full share of the new preferred is created at $\frac{\$13.42}{0.43} = \$31.21$. At this price the preferred would have a current yield of 9.612 percent. Based on a comparison with two issues of straight preferred of White Consolidated already traded on the Big Board, one could safely calculate a probable current yield of 7.9 percent for the new preferred, or a price of $38.

Gross Spread: $38 − $31.21 = $6.79 per preferred

or

$$(\$42 \times 0.44 = 0.43 \times \$38) - \$32 =$$
$$\$35.78 - \$32 = \$3.78 \text{ per Bullard}$$

Common with a Put Provision

Terms: 1 Allied Radio ($17.50) = 0.9 LTV Ling Altec ($21) with a provision that one can resell—to LTV Altec—80 percent of the securities received for the guaranteed price of $22.20.

Parity: With the common stock below the price of the put, one must figure on putting 80 percent of 0.9 = 0.72 shares to the company. Thus, 0.72 × $22.20 = $15.90. There remains 0.9 − 0.72 = 0.18 which can be sold at $21. Thus, 0.18 × $21 − $3.78 plus $15.98 = $19.76.

Gross Spread: $19.76 − $17.50 = $2.26

Common Stock Plus Warrants

Terms: 1 Clevite ($87) = 1.55 U.S. Smelting common ($55) plus 1 10-year warrant to purchase $1/2$ share of common at $60.

Parity: By buying 1 Clevite at $87 and selling 1.55 U.S. Smelting at $55, one creates the warrant (to buy $1/2$ share) at $87 − 1.55 × $55 = $1.75. Thus one creates a warrant to buy one full share at $3.50.

The valuation of warrants is a developing art, but given certain guidelines one can approach a reasonable appraisal. The value of a warrant depends upon (1) its maturity, (2) its exercise price, (3) the price of the common stock, (4) the volatility and speculative nature of the common stock, and (5) the growth prospects for the company. In a study prepared by the Investment Bankers' Association, it was pointed out that a warrant has a premium and an intrinsic value. "Premium is defined as the market value of the option less intrinsic value." A premium normally arises because the buyer of an option purchases a participation in the future value of the underlying security itself. The lower money requirement creates a leverage in the potential return as a percentage of the funds at risk, and limits the potential dollar loss, and the buyer therefore is willing to pay for the option something more than mere intrinsic value. To illustrate, if a stock sells at $25 while an option to purchase that stock at $22 sells at $12, the intrinsic value is $3, namely $25 (the price of the stock) less $22 (the exercise price). The premium is $9, namely $12 (the price of the option) less $3 (the intrinsic value). Alternatively, assume that the stock sells at $20 while the option to purchase the stock at $22 sells at $7. Then because the stock is below exercise price there is no intrinsic value. The premium is $7, which is the price of the option. Parity means the equivalence of exercise price and the market value of the optioned security.[1]

The report of the IBA purported that there is only a slight addition to a warrant's premium for a maturity going beyond two years. Thus, a 10-year warrant should have roughly the same value as a two-year warrant. The report further showed that the following average values were prevalent.[2]

Ratio of Market Value of Optioned Stock to Exercise Price	Ratio of Market Value of Option to Exercise Price
80%	28%
90	34
100	41
110	48
120	55

Based on the above, then, one could ascribe a value of 34 percent of exercise price to the U.S. Smelting warrant, as the ratio of the common stock price to the exercise is roughly 90 percent. Thus, 34 percent of $55 = $18.

Gross Spread: $18 − $3.50 = $14.50 per warrant, or
$85.25 plus $1/2 \times \$18 = \$94.25 − \$87 =$
$7.25 per Clevite

A New Issue of Convertible Preferred with a Built-in (Non-detachable) Warrant

Terms: 1 Miehle-Goss-Dexter ($34) = 1 new North American Rockwell $1.35 preferred convertible into 0.9 common ($41) with a right to buy 0.225 common shares for 10 years with payment of $10.125.

Parity: One must first view the convertible preferred on its own merits, without regard for the additional purchase right, which is really a warrant. The preferred itself will have no yield advantage over the common as the latter pays $2 yearly, so that the preferred would on conversion pay $1.80 (0.9 × $2) versus $1.35 on the preferred itself. Thus the preferred should not command a premium and be worth approximately its conversion parity, which at the actual price is $0.9 \times \$41 = \$36.90$. The additional attached right is, when translated to one full warrant, the right to buy one share of common at $45.55. With the market price of the common at 90 percent of the exercise price, using the table, the warrant should have a market of approximately 34 percent of its exercise price, or 34 percent of $45.55 = $15.49. Thus, 0.225 of a warrant would have a value of roughly $3.50. The parity at the given prices is therefore $36.90 + $3.50 = $40.40.

Gross Spread: $40.40 − $34 − $6.40

Common Plus a New Issue of Debentures Plus a New Issue of Warrants

Terms: 1 Glen Alden ($16) = $^{1}/_{4}$ Rapid American common ($33) + $^{1}/_{2}$ 25-year warrant to buy 1 share of common at $35 + $4 principal amount of a new 7 percent 25-year subordinated debenture.

Parity: In this type of situation one must determine whether one will create warrants or create debentures. This is done by establishing a conservative price for the debentures if one wishes to create warrants, and likewise for warrants if one wishes to create debentures. A Glen Alden debenture is a speculative one that normally sells at a very high yield to maturity, and thus a large discount. Comparing this issue with other Glen Alden debt issues, one could visualize a price of roughly 65 percent for the new debenture. Thus, the warrant, or in this case $^{1}/_{2}$ a warrant, is created at $16 − $^{1}/_{4}$ × $33 − .65 × $4 − $16 − $8.25 − $2.60 = $5.15. Thus a full warrant is created at $10.30. The question now is, will this new warrant have a value greater than $10.30? In view of the speculative character of Rapid American, and with the common stock selling at 95 percent of the exercise price, the warrant should have a market value of about 40 percent of the exercise price, or 40 percent of $35 = $14.

Gross Spread: $14 − $10.30 + $3.70 per warrant, or
($8.25 − $2.60 + $7) − 16 = $17.85
− $16 = $1.85 per Glen Alden

A New Issue of Debentures Plus Warrants, with the Face Value of the Debentures Utilizable in lieu of Cash to Exercise the Warrants (Both Trading on a "When-Issued" Basis)

Terms: 1 Sharon Steel ($41) = $70 principal amount of a new NVF 5 percent subordinated debenture due 1994 (trades "W.I." at 41 percent bid) plus $1\frac{1}{2}$ 10-year warrants to buy a total of $1\frac{1}{2}$ shares at $22 (traded "W.I." at $10 bid).

Parity: On the surface, this appears as a relatively simple calculation: ($70 × .41) + ($1\frac{1}{2}$ × $10) = $28.70 plus $15 = $43.70. But if one views the situation from the point of view that the face value of the bonds may be utilized in lieu of cash to exercise the warrants, the result is quite different. The price of the bond (.41) × the exercise price of the warrant ($22) gives you the true exercise price of the warrant, $9.02. The intrinsic value, or parity, of the warrant is thus the price of the common ($21\frac{1}{8}$) − the real exercise price or $21.125 − $9.02 = $12.325. Since the warrant is selling at only $10, it is at a discount from its intrinsic value. So in this case it would behoove one to exercise the warrant and receive one share of common stock per warrant. In this case, since the package consists of $1\frac{1}{2}$ warrants, $1\frac{1}{2}$ × 21.125 = $31.6875. But in exercising the warrants, one has used up $1\frac{1}{2}$ × $22 (the exercise price) = $33 of principal amount of debenture. Therefore, one is left with $70 − $33 = $37 principal amount of debentures. Since the latter is bid at 41, (.41 × $37) = $15.17. Added to the value of the common received by exercising the warrants, the total value is $15.17 + $31.69 = $46.86, which is $3 plus higher than the more obvious calculation:

Gross Spread: $46.86 − $41 = $5.86

Common Stock, the Exact Amount of Which is Based on an Average Price Formula

Terms: 1 Ginn Corp ($33) = $40.50 market value of Xerox ($280) the exact amount of which is to be determined by the average closing price of Xerox on the New York Stock Exchange for 15 business days prior to the closing of the merger. The price of $40.50 was to be guaranteed per Ginn as long as the price of Xerox was between $239 and $312.

Parity: One might be tempted at first glance to establish the parity at the guaranteed price of $40.50. The important fact to keep in mind, however, is that the price is only good within certain limits. The parameters of $239 and $312 for Xerox mean that the distributions per Ginn may range anywhere from 0.13 Xerox to 0.17 Xerox (40.50/312 = 0.13, 40.50/239 = 0.17). Thus, at below $239 for Xerox, 1 Ginn will still get only the maximum permissible distribution (0.17) under the formula, and at above $312, 1 Ginn will get not more than the minimum distribution of 0.13. So what is the deal worth? One must figure that, regardless of the actual price of Xerox, or even the final average price that will establish the final ratio, one can only count for sure on minimum distribution of 0.13 at the present time. If an arbitrageur were to count on the maximum of 0.17 and Xerox went to $350, he would find himself in serious trouble, having sold short the maximum portion of Xerox and being entitled to only the minimum portion. If, on the other hand, he had sold nothing short and Xerox slipped to $200, he would also be in trouble because by virtue of his long position in Ginn he would be correspondingly long Xerox at a much higher price. So, the arbitrageur must do the safe thing and short 0.13 Xerox per Ginn. At the stated prices, this would mean $280 × 0.13 = $36.40. If at a later time the average price of Xerox should later be established at $255 (which is what actually happened in this merger) then the arbitrageur is entitled to an additional 0.0225 Xerox per Ginn, which means an additional $5.74 per

Ginn, or a real parity of $42.14—which is more than the guaranteed price.

Gross Spread: $36.40 − $33 = $3.40 at the stated prices

New Issue of Convertible Preferred where the Conversion Price is to Be Established at a Given Percentage over an Average Price (to Be Determined over a Specified Period), with Specified Limits on the Conversion Price to Be So Determined

Terms: 1 Island Creek Coal (64\frac{1}{2}$) = 0.65 new $4 preferred of Occidental Petroleum (113\frac{1}{2}$) convertible at 12$\frac{1}{2}$ percent over an average market price, with a minimum conversion price of $75, and a maximum conversion price of $105.

Parity: First, the conversion price must be translated into ratios of Occidental Petroleum common per Island Creek Coal. Thus, the minimum per Island Creek Coal would be

$$0.65\,(100/105) = 0.6189 \text{ Occidental Petroleum}$$

and the maximum

$$0.65\,(100/75) = 0.8665 \text{ Occidental Petroleum}$$

Multiplying each ratio by the common price of Occidental, we arrive at an upward limit of $98.35 and a lower limit of $70.25. Once again, conservatism must be the guiding criterion for the arbitrageur, so that, at the present time, the only amount that he can absolutely count on is the higher conversion price, and thus the lower dollar value. Because, were he to sell short 0.8665 Occidental per Island Creek Coal and subsequently have the higher conversion price established during the averaging period, he would be short 0.248 Occidental, which at the prevailing price would amount to a potential loss of $28.15. If, on the other hand, he had shorted the lesser amount, and thereafter a lower conversion price were to be established, he would be entitled to more Occidental shares, and therefore greater profit.

Thus, the parity is $70.25. Since the new preferred would yield 3.7 percent on its conversion parity based on the actual price, it is doubtful that there would be a premium on the preferred. Should the common stock go lower, however, a premium might well crystallize.

Gross Spread: $70.25 − $64.50 = $5.75 per Island Creek Coal

New Issue of Convertible Preferred Where the Conversion Price Is to Be Established at a Given Percentage over an Average Market Price (to Be Determined over a Specified Period) with No Limits on Such Conversion Price

Terms: 1 Electrolux ($28) = 0.32 new $4.50 preferred of Consolidated Foods ($64) to be convertible at $12\frac{1}{2}$ percent over an average market price during a three week period prior to the shareholders meeting.

Parity: The average price of Consolidated Foods common stock was to be determined during the three weeks prior either to the mailing of the proxy to shareholders, or to the shareholders meeting itself, whichever was most favorable to Electrolux. Evidently, the latter would hope for the lower conversion price.

For the arbitrage, the problem was to determine a probable price range for Consolidated Foods during the averaging period. Since the prices in this case existed one or two months (depending on which three week period one had in mind) from the time that the conversion price would be determined, an arbitrageur had to establish a confidence internal around the current price of $64. Based on the strength and direction of the general market condition at the time one could predict with 95 percent assuredness that the stock would be between $60 and $68 two months hence. Since the conversion price was to be calculated at $12^{1}/_{2}$ percent above the average price, these limits would have meant conversion prices between $67.50 and $76.50, or 1.48 common to 1.31 common per new preferred share. Based on the current price, this would have been equal to a range on the conversion parity $83.84 to $95.72 or a yield on parity from 5.3 percent to 4.7 percent. In view of the then existing interest rate structure, and based on a yield advantage over the common of 1.35 percent to 1.85 percent, the new preferred could be expected to sell at prices from $93 to $100.

Once again, one must choose the lower end of the range. So that the parity per Electrolux is

$$0.32 \times \$93 = \$29.76$$

Gross Spread: $29.76 − $28 = $1.76

Securities of Company A Offered to Company B Who is in Turn Acquiring Securities of Company C

Terms: 1 St. Regis Paper ($40) = 0.1 RCA common ($43) + 0.425 $4 convertible preferred ($101).

1 Eastern States ($62) = 1.6 St. Regis Paper ($40)

Parity: Taking the latter merger itself, the parity would be 1.6 × $40 = $64. However, if one can correctly assume that both mergers will be consummated, then 1 Eastern States = 1.6 × 0.1 RCA common + 1.6 × 0.425 $4 preferred or 0.16 RCA common + 0.68 $4 preferred. The parity per Eastern States is thus 0.16 × $43 × 0.68 × $4 preferred. The parity per Eastern States is thus 0.16 × $43 × 0.68 × $101 = $75.56, compared to the earlier parity of $64. In other words, one can create the RCA preferred by buying either Eastern States or St. Regis Paper. If the latter, one creates the preferred at ($40 − 0.1 × $43)/0.425 = $84. If the former at ($39 − 0.1 × $43)/0.425 = $81.61.

Gross Spread: $75.45 − $62 = $13.45 per Eastern States, or $101 − $81.61 = $19.39 per RCA preferred by creating it through Eastern States

An Exchange Offer for 49 percent of the Stock of Company A for Debentures of Company B, to Be Followed by a Merger for Convertible Preferred in B for the Remainder of A, with the Initial Exchange Offer (a) to Be Prorated if More than 49 percent Request Debentures, or (b) to Be Selected by Lots if More Than 49 percent Request Debentures

Terms: 1 Youngstown Sheet & Tube (48\frac{1}{2}$) = $70 principal amount of a new 7$\frac{1}{2}$ percent Lykes Corp., 25-year subordinated debenture for a maximum of 49 percent of the outstanding common stock of Youngstown. For the remaining 51 percent, a new $2.50 preferred of Lykes convertible at 110 percent of the market price during an average period prior to the closing, with a maximum of 1.98 and a minimum of 1.36 Lykes common ($30) on conversion.

Parity: The first task is to determine separately the market value of each part of the package. The debenture, with its 7$\frac{1}{2}$ percent coupon, can be shown to have a value of roughly 85 percent, which would mean a value of .85 × $70 = $59.50 per Youngstown. The preferred, if the actual price of the common prevails during the averaging period, would have a conversion price of $33, or a conversion parity of $54. The preferred should also command a premium, so that the market value should be around $57. The debenture is obviously the more interesting choice from a market value point of view. However, assuming pro-rata treatment of the exchange offer, one can only safely count on 49 percent of his stock receiving the debenture. Thus, the worst that one can do is 49 percent of \$59.50 + 51 percent of \$56 = \$29.15 + \$28.56 = \$57.71. However, since receipt of the debenture is a taxable exchange, there is a strong likelihood that many shareholders will not request the debenture, so that those who do request it will receive proportionately more of it, and thus may achieve a total valuation of closer to the full \$59.50.

It should be noted that if the exchange offer were not to be pro-rated, but rather that the 49 percent would be selected by lots, there would be an even chance that all of a single shareholder's stock would receive either debentures or the preferred, but not both. In this case, one would conservatively have to assume that his stock would only receive the preferred stock and none of the debentures. In this case, the parity would be strictly that of the preferred. If by chance one were to receive some amount of debentures, so much the better.

Gross Spread: Pro-rata selection—\$57.71 − \$48.50 = \$9.21
By lot—\$56 − \$48.50 = \$7.50

Appendix B

The Department of Justice, in June, 1982, published a new set of guidelines describing the general principles and specific standards used by the Department in analyzing mergers (see Figure B.1). The Federal Trade Commission immediately embraced the guidelines as indicative of its policies as well. These guidelines represent the first changes since 1968 and go a long way to improve the predictability of the Department's merger enforcement policy. There will, of course, still be many mergers that do not fit exactly into the specific guidelines that will require a judgement call by the arbitrageur. The flow chart gives a good schematic idea of the Department's guidelines regarding anticompetitiveness in the three various types of mergers.

While policy on conglomerate and vertical mergers appears largely unchanged, as an aid to the interpretation of market concentration in horizontal mergers the Department has proposed use of the Herfindahl-Hirschman Index (HHI). The HHI is calculated by summing the squares of the individual market shares of all the firms in the relevant product and geographic markets.

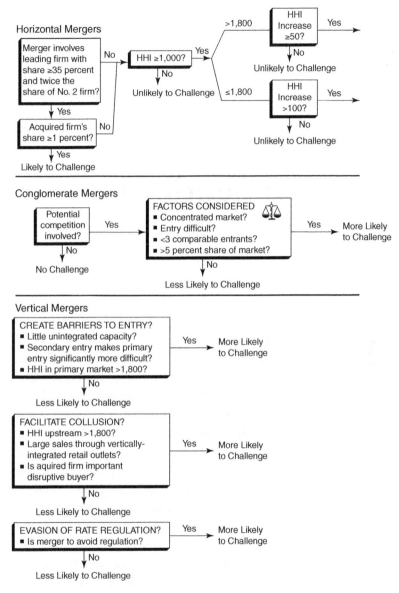

Figure B.1 Department of Justice Merger Guidelines

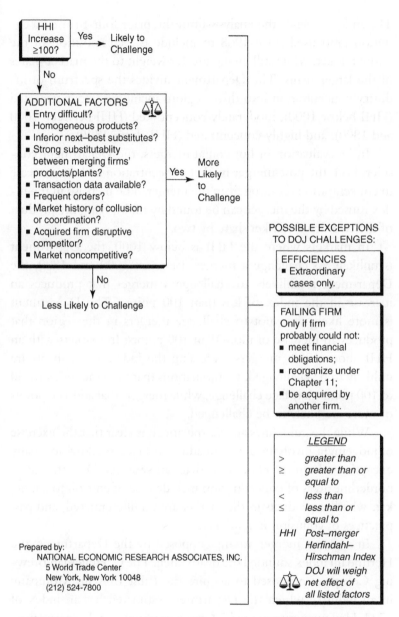

Figure B.1 (*Continued*) NERA Flow Chart of Enforcement Policies

The index expands the analysis from the prior four-firm concentration ratio used since 1968 to include the composition of the entire market, while still giving greater weight to the market shares of the larger firms. The Department divides the spectrum of industry concentration into three regions including unconcentrated (HHI below 1000), moderately concentrated (HHI between 1000 and 1800), and highly concentrated (HHI above 1800).

In its evaluation of horizontal mergers, the Department considers both the post-merger market concentration and the increase in concentration resulting from the merger. The increase in the index caused by the merger can be found by multiplying the product of the two firms' market share by two.

In markets where the HHI is below 1000, the Department is unlikely to challenge a merger. Between 1000 and 1800, the Department is unlikely to challenge a merger that produces an increase in the index of less than 100 points. The Department is more likely than not to challenge mergers in the region that produces an increase of more than 100 points. In markets with an HHI above 1800, mergers increasing the index less than 50 are unlikely to be challenged. Combinations that raise the index by 50 to 100 points may face challenge, while mergers that add 100 points or more are likely to be challenged.

While the guidelines appear specific, it is clear that the exercise of judgement involving a host of additional factors allows for many exceptions. Industry conditions that can sway the Department in borderline areas of concentration include ease of entry into a market, whether products in the market are undifferentiated, and past practices of collusion in a market.

In a recent merger attempt opposed by the Department, the Herfindahl index sounded the death knell. The G. Heileman Brewing Company proposed to acquire the Pabst Brewing Company in an industry which the Department estimated has an index of 1722. Heileman represented 7.6 percent of industry beer barrelage shipped in 1981 while Pabst represented 7.4 percent of the total. The combination would have increased the index by 112 points to 1834, falling outside of the guidelines.

APPENDIX C

Active Arbitrage Initiatives

Wyser-Pratte activist initiatives comprise two separate and distinctive styles. One style—"active arbitrage"—is described in Chapter 7. It is a corporate governance-type of activism in which the activist must overcome an entrenched management that is reluctant to accept a proposed or contemplated takeover offer to shareholders, even at a substantial premium.

The second style of activist initiative is called "pro-active" or "operational" activism. Here the activist seeks to change the strategy, blend of assets, management, capital structure, or local contrivances such as "double voting rights" for the purpose of maximizing shareholder value.

Since 1991, the author has engaged in 65 activist initiatives, both active arbitrage and pro-active activism. Appendix C delineates 23 of the former category that projects the fusion of arbitrage and activism. Each example is comprised of a graphic illustration or chart of the share price evolution of the target company with concomitant annotations marking key events during the course of each initiative. This is followed by Section II, which highlights the key financial characteristics of the company. Section III presents the chronology of events over the course of the initiative and includes the financial results of the activist initiative undertaken by Wyser-Pratte on a "ticket-in, ticket-out" basis. It also includes returns from the commencement of the activist initiative through to its completion. Section IV describes subsequent events relative to the initiative.

Van Dorn Corporation
USA   Defensive

I. Investment Statistics

Market Capitalization	April 1992	$121.20M
Capital Invested*		$4.90M
Wyser-Pratte Initial Purchase	January 7, 1992	$18.56
Wyser-Pratte Initiates CG Action	April 22, 1992	$15.13
Wyser-Pratte Ends CG Action	December 18, 1992	$20.38
Wyser-Pratte Sale Date**	January 28, 1993	$20.38
Annualized Rate of Return— Period of Corporate Governance Action		52.76%
Ticket In/Ticket Out Return		20.41%

* For all Wyser-Pratte managed accounts invested in this stock.
** Final 100 shares were sold on April 26, 1993.

II. Company

At the time of investment, Van Dorn was engaged primarily in the manufacture of containers for the paint, coatings, food, and other industries, and in the manufacture of plastic injection molding machinery for the plastics industry. Van Dorn was made up of primarily three segments: Central States Can, Davies Can, and Van Dorn Plastic Machinery. Central States Can Division manufactured metal, plastic, and composite containers for a variety of processed and unprocessed foods, pet foods, and household, garden, institutional, and industrial chemicals. Davies Can was a regional manufacturer of metal and plastic containers. The Machinery Division was a leader in the manufacture of injection molding machinery for both custom and captive plastic processors.

III. Chronology of Events/Investment Rationale/Wyser-Pratte's Role

December 20, 1991	Crown Cork & Seal delivered to Van Dorn a proposal under which Crown would acquire Van Dorn in a merger of stock and cash at a price stated to be in excess of $16 per share.
January 6, 1992	Van Dorn rejected the proposal.
January 7	Crown announced a proposal to acquire Van Dorn at a price of $18 per share.
January 14, 1992	Van Dorn rejected the offer.
February 6	Crown increased the proposed price to $20 per share. Van Dorn rejected the offer and stated that it was not in Van Dorn's interest to pursue Crown Cork's proposal.
February 25	Wyser-Pratte sent a letter to the president and CEO of Van Dorn, which requested that a special meeting of Van Dorn's shareholders be called for the purpose of shareholder consideration of measures with respect to the corporate governance of Van Dorn.
March 31	Along with other shareholders, Wyser-Pratte filed a Statement on Schedule 13D

with the SEC, which disclosed its intent to take actions to call a special meeting of the shareholders for the purpose of addressing proposals.

April 23   Wyser-Pratte filed with the SEC definitive proxy material urging Van Dorn's shareholders to withhold their vote for the election to director status of the three candidates nominated by Van Dorn's board, and instead, to attend the 1992 Annual Meeting and vote in person.

May 28   A letter was sent by Wyser-Pratte to each of Van Dorn's directors, proposing that the board appoint a special committee which would have the authority to evaluate and make recommendations to the board regarding acquisition proposals and would undertake an analysis of whether all or part of Van Dorn's assets should be sold.

June 25   Wyser-Pratte filed definitive proxy material with the SEC relating to the solicitation of demands to call a special meeting of Van Dorn's shareholders to consider and vote on four proposals.

August 6   Wyser-Pratte presented to Van Dorn demands for a special meeting of Van Dorn's shareholders. The purpose was to present a series of proposals to amend certain provisions of Van Dorn's Articles of Incorporation and Regulations and to recommend that Van Dorn's board of directors appoint a special committee of non-employee directors to review and make recommendations with respect to any acquisition proposals. At the annual meeting,

Wyser–Pratte made a floor nomination of William Frazier to be a director of the company. Mr. Frazier became a director.

December 18

Van Dorn finally agreed to be acquired for $21 per share by Crown Cork & Seal Co. Based on the negotiations conducted with Crown and the solicitation process, the Special Advisory Committee and the board of directors believed that the possibility of obtaining a higher price in the near term was not sufficient to warrant turning down the $21 offer. Therefore, they decided to recommend that Van Dorn's board of directors accept Crown's offer, and the board of directors decided to accept Crown's offer and recommended that Van Dorn's shareholders vote in favor of the merger.

IV. Subsequent Events

December 1992 through April 26, 1993

Wyser–Pratte held its position to take advantage of the remaining merger arbitrage opportunities in the stock.

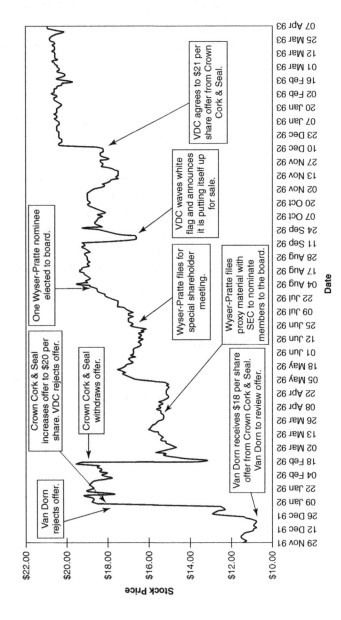

Figure C.1 Van Dorn Corporation (USA)

190

LAC Minerals Ltd.

Canada   Defensive

I. Investment Statistics

Capital Invested*		$6.10M
Wyser-Pratte Initial Purchase	July 11, 1994	$9.45
Wyser-Pratte Initiates CG Action	July 20, 1994	$9.50
Wyser-Pratte Ends CG Action	September 19, 1994	$13.50
Wyser-Pratte Sale Date	September 16, 1994	$12.00
Annualized Rate of Return— Period of Corporate Governance Action		251.95%
Ticket In/Ticket Out Return		97.18%

* For all Wyser-Pratte managed accounts invested in this stock.

II. Company Description

Lac Minerals Ltd. is a leading North America based gold mining company that owns and operates mines located in Canada, the United States, and Chile and is active in the exploration of gold and other metals in North and South America and Australia. The company specializes in the exploration and development of hard-rock mineral deposits. The company is primarily a gold producer but also produces significant amounts of copper, zinc, silver, and aggregates.

III. Chronology of Events/Investment Rationale/Wyser-Pratte's Role

July 7, 1994	Royal Oak announces its C$2 billion offer for LAC Minerals.
July 18	LAC Minerals board of directors rejected Royal Oak's offer.

July 20	Wyser-Pratte sends a letter to the board of LAC urging the board to "either accept Royal Oak Mines Inc.'s offer or work for a better one." Wyser-Pratte further warned the board that "any attempt by the board of directors to return to the status-quo or pursue a scorched earth policy will be met with the utmost resistance on our part and the part of other shareholders."
July 25	American Barrick Resources said it would join the bidding for LAC Minerals with an offer of C$2.08 billion or C$0.45 a share more than the bid from Royal Oak.
August 8	Royal Oak increased its bid to C$2.4 billion, C$5, in cash, and 2 Royal Oak shares for each LAC share.
August 11	LAC Minerals announced its board of directors determined that the revised offer of Royal Oak to purchase all of LAC's outstanding shares was inadequate and rejected the offer.
August 24	American Barrick Resources announced that it had signed an agreement with LAC to make an increased offer to C$5 in cash and 0.325 shares of Barrick.

IV. Subsequent Events

September 6, 1994	American Barrick successfully acquired over 80 percent of LAC Minerals common shares.
September 20	More than 90 percent of the shares of LAC Minerals Ltd. were tendered for the takeover offer by American Barrick Resources.

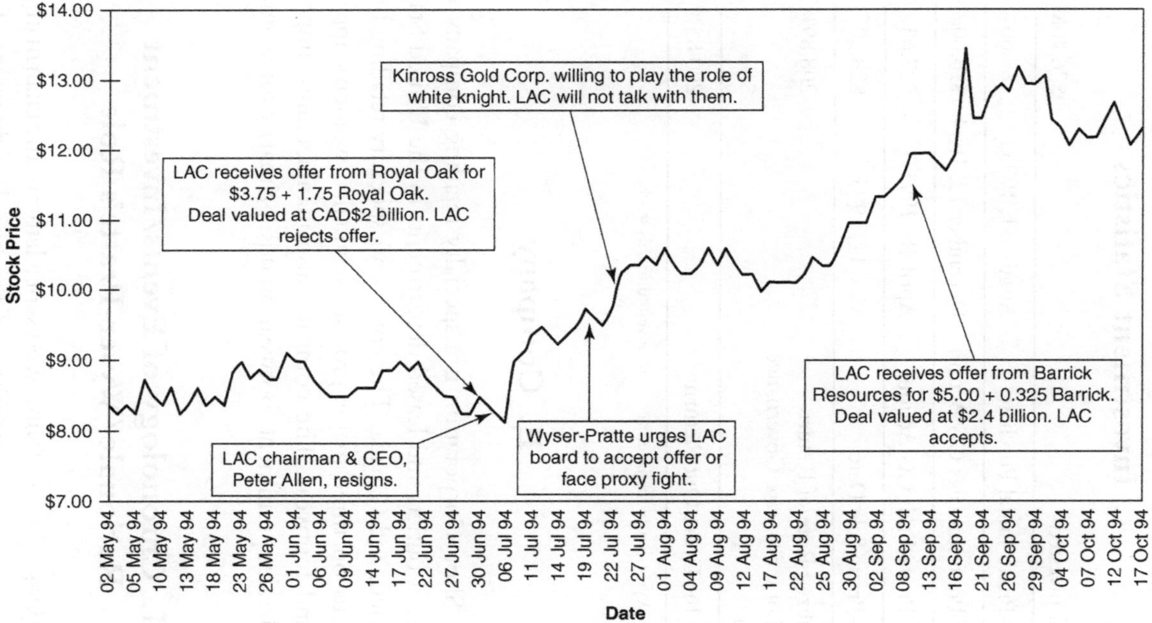
$14.00
$13.00
$12.00
$11.00
$10.00
$9.00
$8.00
$7.00
Stock Price
Kinross Gold Corp. willing to play the role of white knight. LAC will not talk with them.
LAC receives offer from Royal Oak for $3.75 + 1.75 Royal Oak. Deal valued at CAD$2 billion. LAC rejects offer.
LAC receives offer from Barrick Resources for $5.00 + 0.325 Barrick. Deal valued at $2.4 billion. LAC accepts.
LAC chairman & CEO, Peter Allen, resigns.
Wyser-Pratte urges LAC board to accept offer or face proxy fight.
02 May 94
05 May 94
10 May 94
13 May 94
18 May 94
23 May 94
26 May 94
01 Jun 94
06 Jun 94
09 Jun 94
14 Jun 94
17 Jun 94
22 Jun 94
27 Jun 94
30 Jun 94
06 Jul 94
11 Jul 94
14 Jul 94
19 Jul 94
22 Jul 94
27 Jul 94
01 Aug 94
04 Aug 94
09 Aug 94
12 Aug 94
17 Aug 94
22 Aug 94
25 Aug 94
30 Aug 94
02 Sep 94
08 Sep 94
13 Sep 94
16 Sep 94
21 Sep 94
26 Sep 94
29 Sep 94
04 Oct 94
07 Oct 94
12 Oct 94
17 Oct 94
Date

Figure C.2 LAC Minerals Ltd. (Canada)

U.S. Shoe Corporation
USA   Defensive

I. Investment Statistics

Capital Invested*		$26.40M
Wyser-Pratte Initial Purchase	August 11, 1993	$9.00
Wyser-Pratte Initiates CG Action	December 12, 1994	$16.00
Wyser-Pratte Ends CG Action	April 18, 1995	$27.63
Wyser-Pratte Sale Date	May 12, 1995	$28.00
Annualized Rate of Return— Period of Corporate Governance Action		208.89%
Ticket In/Ticket Out Return		200.83%

* For all Wyser-Pratte managed accounts invested in this stock.

II. Company

The U.S. Shoe Corporation is a specialty retailing company operating retail outlets and leased departments in the United States, Puerto Rico, and Canada. The company's specialty retailing businesses focus on three major product segments: women's apparel, optical, and footwear. The company also manufactures, imports, and wholesales prominent footwear brands, primarily for women.

III. Chronology of Events/Investment Rationale/Wyser-Pratte's Role

July 27, 1994   Nine West sent a letter to the chairman and members of the board of directors of the U.S. Shoe Corporation proposing a combination of the footwear businesses of the

two companies. U.S. Shoe rejected the proposal two days later.

December 12   Wyser-Pratte urged the company to split
itself into three parts: sell or spinoff its
footwear, apparel, and eye-care units.

December 19   Wyser-Pratte filed a proxy to nominate
William Frazier to be an independent director of U.S. Shoe's board.

March 3, 1995   Luxottica Group made a $24 per share
offer, which U.S. Shoe rejected.

IV. Subsequent Events

April 17, 1995   Luxottica won its battle to take over U.S.
Shoe with an increased offer worth $1.3
billion. Both companies reached an agreement of $28 in cash for each U.S. Shoe
share.

May 12   A shareholder meeting took place at which
time U.S. Shoe shareholders approved the
acquisition. The deal closed shortly after
the meeting.

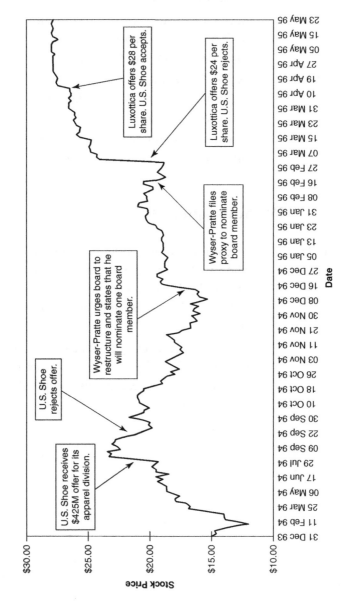

Figure C.3 U.S. Shoe Corporation (USA)

196

American Maize Corporation
USA/France   Defensive

I. Investment Statistics

Capital Invested*		$17.50M
Wyser-Pratte Initial Purchase	January 27, 1995	$33.50
Wyser-Pratte Initiates CG Action	June 28, 1995	$30.63
Wyser-Pratte Ends CG Action	July 10, 1995	$40.00
Wyser-Pratte Sale Date	July 12, 1995	$39.50
Annualized Rate of Return—Period of Corporate Governance Action		930.24%
Ticket In/Ticket Out Return		22.30%

* For all Wyser-Pratte managed accounts invested in this stock.

II. Company

At the time of investment, American Maize, based in Stamford, CT, was engaged primarily in the manufacture and sale of products derived from corn wet milling, such as corn sweeteners and starches, and a variety of specialty foods and industrial starches. It also manufactured and marketed cigars and smokeless tobacco products.

III. Chronology of Events/Investment Rationale/Wyser-Pratte's Role

January 6, 1995   American Maize received an offer of $32 per share from Eridania Beghin-Say, which was rejected by William Ziegler III, the owner of a majority of the voting shares.

January 20	American Maize announced that it had received a revised proposal to acquire the company for $37 per share, which Ziegler also thought was inadequate.
February 22	A definitive agreement was announced with Eridania Beghin-Say, announcing a tender offer at a purchase price of $40 per share.
March 13	The board voted 8-1 to accept the $40 per share offer and Ziegler was the only vote on the board to reject the offer.
Early June	Wyser-Pratte prepared a lawsuit against Ziegler and the board for its breach of fiduciary duty to shareholders.
June 28	At the annual board meeting Wyser-Pratte challenged Ziegler and the board about its blatant disregard for minority shareholders and disclosed the existence of an improper transaction between Ziegler and his general counsel.

IV. Subsequent Events

July 27, 1995	Eridania Beghin-Say reached an agreement to buy American Maize for $40 per share, or about $430 million, after Ziegler was removed and the board of directors approved the deal. Under the agreement, Eridania Beghin-Say sold 88 percent of American Maize's tobacco operations to Ziegler for $165 million.

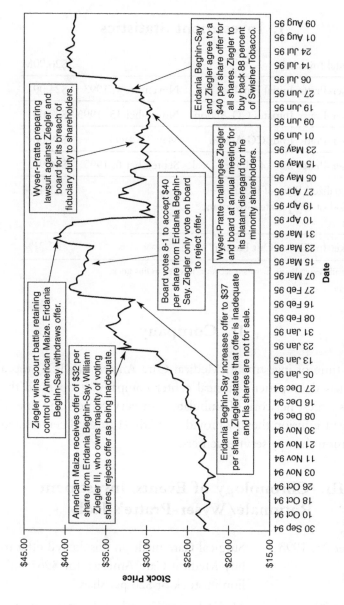

Figure C.4 American Maize Corporation (USA/France)

The chart contains the following annotations:

- Ziegler wins court battle retaining control of American Maize. Eridania Beghin-Say withdraws offer.
- American Maize receives offer of $32 per share from Eridania Beghin-Say. William Ziegler III, who owns majority of voting shares, rejects offer as being inadequate.
- Wyser-Pratte preparing lawsuit against Ziegler and board for its breach of fiduciary duty to shareholders.
- Board votes 8-1 to accept $40 per share from Eridania Beghin-Say. Ziegler only vote on board to reject offer.
- Wyser-Pratte challenges Ziegler and board at annual meeting for its blatant disregard for the minority shareholders.
- Eridania Beghin-Say increases offer to $37 per share. Ziegler states that offer is inadequate and his shares are not for sale.
- Eridania Beghin-Say and Ziegler agree to a $40 per share offer for all shares. Ziegler to buy back 88 percent of Swisher Tobacco.

Y-axis (Stock Price): $15.00, $20.00, $25.00, $30.00, $35.00, $40.00, $45.00

X-axis (Date): 30 Sep 94, 10 Oct 94, 18 Oct 94, 26 Oct 94, 03 Nov 94, 11 Nov 94, 21 Nov 94, 30 Nov 94, 08 Dec 94, 16 Dec 94, 27 Dec 94, 05 Jan 95, 13 Jan 95, 23 Jan 95, 31 Jan 95, 08 Feb 95, 16 Feb 95, 27 Feb 95, 07 Mar 95, 15 Mar 95, 23 Mar 95, 31 Mar 95, 10 Apr 95, 19 Apr 95, 27 Apr 95, 05 May 95, 15 May 95, 23 May 95, 01 Jun 95, 09 Jun 95, 19 Jun 95, 27 Jun 95, 06 Jul 95, 14 Jul 95, 24 Jul 95, 01 Aug 95, 09 Aug 95

Medical Care America
USA   Defensive

I. Investment Statistics

Capital Invested*		$26.90M
Wyser-Pratte Initial Purchase	November 1, 1993	$24.00
Wyser-Pratte Initiates CG Action	November 15, 1993	$22.00
Wyser-Pratte Ends CG Action	May 23, 1994	$29.00
Wyser-Pratte Sale of Merger Deal	September 6, 1995	$46.97
Annualized Rate of Return—Period of Corporate Governance Action		61.45%
Ticket In/Ticket Out Return		62.21%

* For all Wyser-Pratte managed accounts invested in this stock.

II. Company

At the time of investment, Medical Care America (MRX) was a Dallas-based outpatient surgical center company. It operated the nation's largest network of ambulatory surgery centers and one of the largest infusion therapy providers, with 91 surgical centers and 47 infusion therapy service centers.

III. Chronology of Events/Investment Rationale/Wyser-Pratte's Role

October 25, 1993   Surgical Care made an unsolicited offer to buy Medical Care America for $967 million in stock or $26 per share.

October 29   Medical Care's board of directors rejected Surgical Care's proposal.

November 19   After Medical Care talked with other po-
                     tential buyers, it suggested that Surgical
                     Care raise its offer and Surgical Care re-
                     jected its request.

November 21   Wyser-Pratte sent a letter to the board
                     of Medical Care demanding negotiations
                     with Surgical Care and threatened a proxy
                     fight, which was reported in Medical Care's
                     home state of Texas. Shortly thereafter,
                     Medical Care began to act in ways that
                     were more shareholder friendly.

December 1   Medical Care asked to meet with Surgical
                     Care to discuss the advantages of a merger.

December 8   Medical Care reaffirmed that the previ-
                     ously announced proposal to merge was
                     not in the best interest of the company or
                     its shareholders.

IV. Subsequent Events

May 23, 1994   Columbia Healthcare agreed to buy Med-
                     ical Care for $29 per share, about $850
                     million in stock.

September 14   The deal was completed. The FTC ap-
                     proved after they agreed to divest an
                     outpatient surgery center, Alaska Surgery
                     Center.

September 1994   Wyser-Pratte Management remained
through September   in the stock until consummation to take
1995   advantage of further merger arbitrage
                     activity.

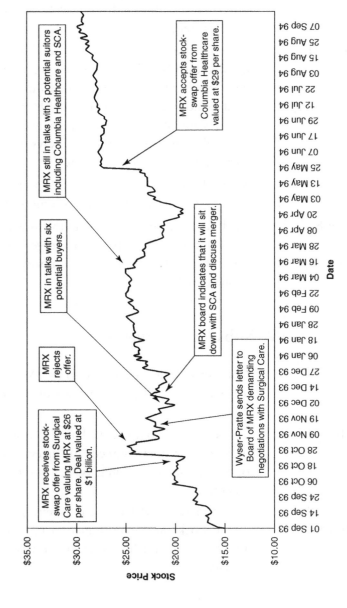

Figure C.5 Medical Care America, Inc. (USA)

202

Hillhaven Corporation
USA Defensive

I. Investment Statistics

Capital Invested*		$20.50M
Wyser-Pratte Initial Purchase	January 27, 1995	$26.27
Wyser-Pratte Initiates CG Action	March 2, 1995	$24.13
Wyser-Pratte Ends CG Action	April 22, 1995	$28.88
Wyser-Pratte Sale Date	September 14, 1995	$31.38
Annualized Rate of Return— Period of Corporate Governance Action		140.87%
Ticket in/Ticket Out Return		46.09%

* For all Wyser-Pratte managed accounts invested in this stock.

II. Company

At the time of investment, Hillhaven Corporation operated nursing centers, pharmacies, and retirement housing communities. The company provided a wide range of diversified health care services, including long-term care and sub-acute medical and rehabilitation services, such as wound care, oncology treatment, brain injury care, stroke therapy, and orthopedic therapy.

III. Chronology of Events/Investment Rationale/Wyser-Pratte's Role

February 6, 1995	Horizon made a hostile bid to acquire Hillhaven for $803.6 million or $28 per share.
March 1	Wyser-Pratte urged Hillhaven's board to negotiate a friendly deal or face a proxy fight.

March 7   The offer was increased to $31 per share. Hillhaven rejected both offers.

March 17   Wyser-Pratte threatened a proxy fight at Hillhaven's annual meeting if Hillhaven refused a merger with Horizon. Also, Wyser-Pratte filed a preliminary proxy statement with the SEC to nominate William Frazier to the Hillhaven board.

April 24, 1995   Vencor Inc. and Hillhaven jointly announced that they had entered into a definitive merger agreement. Under the terms of the agreement, Hillhaven stockholders received $32.25 per share, or $1.5 billion in value.

June through   Wyser-Pratte held discussions with
September   investors and the media about its proxy battle, within the limits of the law.

IV. Subsequent Events

September 27, 1995   Stockholders approved the merger of Hillhaven and Vencor, which created one of the nation's largest healthcare providers. The deal officially closed on September 28.

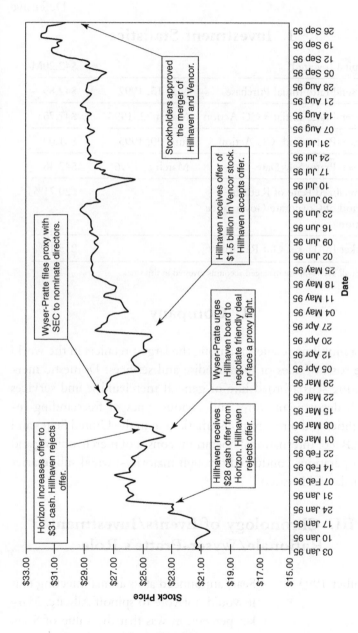

Figure C.6 Hillhaven Corporation (USA)

The following text boxes appear on the figure:

- Horizon increases offer to $31 cash. Hillhaven rejects offer.
- Wyser-Pratte files proxy with SEC to nominate directors.
- Stockholders approved the merger of Hillhaven and Vencor.
- Hillhaven receives offer of $1.5 billion in Vencor stock. Hillhaven accepts offer.
- Wyser-Pratte urges Hillhaven board to negotiate friendly deal or face a proxy fight.
- Hillhaven receives $28 cash offer from Horizon. Hillhaven rejects offer.

Y-axis (Stock Price): $15.00, $17.00, $19.00, $21.00, $23.00, $25.00, $27.00, $29.00, $31.00, $33.00

X-axis (Date): 03 Jan 95, 10 Jan 95, 17 Jan 95, 24 Jan 95, 31 Jan 95, 07 Feb 95, 14 Feb 95, 22 Feb 95, 01 Mar 95, 08 Mar 95, 15 Mar 95, 22 Mar 95, 29 Mar 95, 05 Apr 95, 12 Apr 95, 20 Apr 95, 27 Apr 95, 04 May 95, 11 May 95, 18 May 95, 25 May 95, 02 Jun 95, 09 Jun 95, 16 Jun 95, 23 Jun 95, 30 Jun 95, 10 Jul 95, 17 Jul 95, 24 Jul 95, 31 Jul 95, 07 Aug 95, 14 Aug 95, 21 Aug 95, 28 Aug 95, 05 Sep 95, 12 Sep 95, 19 Sep 95, 26 Sep 95

Sears Roebuck & Co./Allstate
USA   Defensive

I. Investment Statistics

Capital Invested*		$42.20M
Wyser-Pratte Initial Purchase	May 15, 1992	$42.89
Wyser-Pratte Initiates CG Action	March 22, 1994	$47.75
Wyser-Pratte Ends CG Action	June 30, 1995	$61.00
Wyser-Pratte Sale Date	March 5, 1996	$43.48
Annualized Rate of Return— Period of Corporate Governance Action		20.71%
Ticket In/Ticket Out Return		215.16%

* For all Wyser-Pratte managed accounts invested in this stock.

II. Company

Sears, a multiline retailer, is among the largest retailers in the world on the basis of sales of merchandise and services. Domestic merchandising sells a broad line of general merchandise and services through department stores and various types of freestanding retail facilities and direct response marketing in the United States and Puerto Rico. International operations consist of merchandising and credit operations conducted through majority-owned subsidiaries in Canada and Mexico.

III. Chronology of Events/Investment Rationale/Wyser-Pratte's Role

November 1993   Sears announced at its annual meeting that it would not vote to spinoff Allstate. Market perception was that the value of Sears would rise if Allstate was spun off.

March 11, 1994	Wyser-Pratte wrote a letter to the board of Sears urging them to spinoff Allstate. Wyser-Pratte stated "investors and analysts simply do not like the volatility and unpredictability of Sears EPS caused by Allstate, and they would prefer eliminating that source of uncertainty."
March 21	Wyser-Pratte filed a proxy with the SEC for a spinoff proposal to be included in the Sears proxy.
April 4, 1994	The Sears board blocked shareholders from voting on the spinoff proposal at the annual meeting by not putting the issue on the proxy.
May 13	Sears' shareholders overwhelmingly defeated a proposal calling for the retailer to spinoff its Allstate insurance unit.
	Wyser-Pratte attended Sears' annual meeting, and publicly voted the proxy of the LA Police and Fire Department Fund, a major California public pension fund, in favor of the spinoff proposal.
November 10	Sears stated it would spinoff its remaining 80.2 percent stake in Allstate through a stock dividend to Sears' shareholders, leaving Sears to be solely a retail company.
February 22, 1995	Sears said it would hold a special meeting for shareholders to vote on the proposed spinoff.
March 31	Sears announced that its shareholders approved the company's proposal to spinoff its ownership in Allstate. Of the shares voted, over 99 percent were in favor of the spinoff.

IV. Subsequent Events

July 1, 1995

Sears finished the spinoff of its majority stake in Allstate Corp., representing the biggest spinoff ever at $10.7 billion, Sears' shareholders received 0.93 of an Allstate share for every share of Sears' common stock.

July 1995 through
March 1996

Wyser-Pratte remained in the stock after the spinoff as it believed there was additional value in the stock.

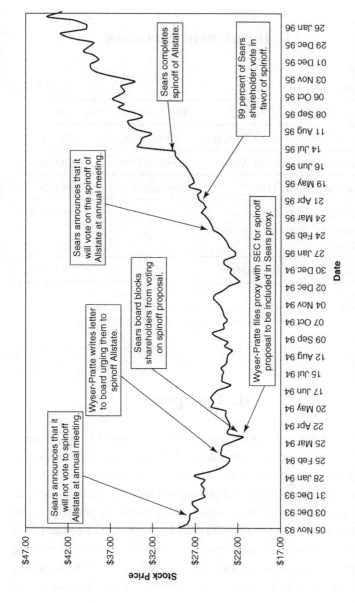

Figure C.7 Sears Roebuck & Co./Allstate Insurance Company; prices include Allstate spinoff (USA)

209

Teledyne, Inc.
USA   Defensive

I. Investment Statistics

Capital Invested*		$36.00M
Wyser-Pratte Initial Purchase**	December 22, 1994	$20.50
Wyser-Pratte Initiates CG Action	February 15, 1996	$27.38
Wyser-Pratte Ends CG Action	April 2, 1996	$33.50
Wyser-Pratte Sale Date	September 13, 1996	$23.48
Annualized Rate of Return— Period of Corporate Governance Action		166.63%
Ticket In/Ticket Out Return		83.09%

   * For all Wyser-Pratte managed accounts invested in this stock.
   ** Initial purchase of Teledyne stock occurred on December 22, 1994, the initial
   merger arbitrage position involving Teledyne was established on June 10, 1993.

II. Company

Teledyne, Inc. was incorporated in the state of Delaware in 1960. At the time of investment, Teledyne was a federation of technology-based manufacturing business serving worldwide customers with commercial and goverment-related aviation and electronic products; specialty metals for consumer, industrial, and aerospace applications; and industrial and consumer products. This diversified manufacturing corporation served customers worldwide through 18 operating companies focused in four business segments: Aviation and Electronics, Specialty Metals, Industrial, and Consumer.

III. Chronology of Events/Investment Rationale/Wyser-Pratte's Role

November 28, 1994   The board of directors of Teledyne rejected WHX's (formerly Allegheny Ludlum) first offer, in which Teledyne shareholders would have received $22 per share in cash and stock, because they believed that Teledyne's long-term strategic business plans suggested substantial increases in future values.

December 22   WHX Inc. announced it was seeking federal approval to buy up to 15 percent of the outstanding shares of Teledyne stock.

March 29, 1995   Teledyne announced it had put the company up for sale and had retained an outside advisor to assist it in soliciting bids.

October 9   Wyser-Pratte wrote a letter to Teledyne's board urging the company to actively pursue a sale of the company or one or more of its divisions. Also, Wyser-Pratte demanded public disclosures of any legitimate offers to buy the company or various units and of any updated offers from WHX.

October 26   Teledyne officially discontinued its search for a potential buyer, claiming that months of behind-the-scenes talks with several parties failed to produce adequate offers.

February 9, 1996   The board of directors of WHX offered $30 to acquire Teledyne.

February 15   Wyser-Pratte threatened a proxy fight unless there was an immediate sale of Teledyne.

February 26   WHX raised its offer to $32. Teledyne later
                     rejected the offer.

V. Subsequent Events

April 1, 1996   Teledyne and Allegheny Ludlum Corpora-
                     tion agreed to merge in a $3.2 billion deal.
                     The offer stated that Teledyne's sharehold-
                     ers would receive 1.925 shares in the new
                     entity for each of their Teledyne shares.

August 15   Shareholders approved Ludlum's acquisi-
                     tion of Teledyne, which closed shortly
                     after.

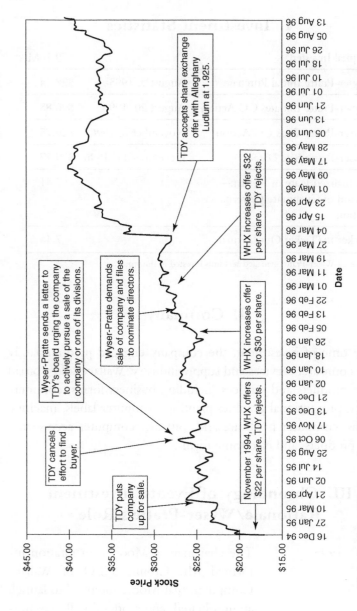

Figure C.8 Teledyne, Inc. (USA)

The following labels appear on the chart:

- TDY puts company up for sale.
- TDY cancels effort to find buyer.
- November 1994, WHX offers $22 per share. TDY rejects.
- WHX increases offer to $30 per share.
- WHX increases offer $32 per share. TDY rejects.
- Wyser-Pratte sends a letter to TDY's board urging the company to actively pursue a sale of the company or one of its divisions.
- Wyser-Pratte demands sale of company and files to nominate directors.
- TDY accepts share exchange offer with Allegheny Ludlum at 1.925.

Y-axis (Stock Price): $15.00, $20.00, $25.00, $30.00, $35.00, $40.00, $45.00

X-axis (Date): 16 Dec 94, 27 Jan 95, 10 Mar 95, 21 Apr 95, 02 Jun 95, 14 Jul 95, 25 Aug 95, 06 Oct 95, 17 Nov 95, 13 Dec 95, 21 Dec 95, 02 Jan 96, 10 Jan 96, 18 Jan 96, 26 Jan 96, 05 Feb 96, 13 Feb 96, 22 Feb 96, 01 Mar 96, 11 Mar 96, 19 Mar 96, 27 Mar 96, 04 Mar 96, 15 Apr 96, 23 Apr 96, 01 May 96, 09 May 96, 17 May 96, 28 May 96, 05 Jun 96, 13 Jun 96, 21 Jun 96, 01 Jul 96, 10 Jul 96, 18 Jul 96, 26 Jul 96, 05 Aug 96, 13 Aug 96

Wallace Computer Services
USA   Defensive

I. Investment Statistics

Capital Invested*		$39.10M
Wyser-Pratte Initial Purchase	August 1, 1995	$28.94
Wyser-Pratte Initiates CG Action	August 20, 1996	$26.88
Wyser-Pratte Ends CG Action	November 6, 1996	$29.75
Wyser-Pratte Sale Date	November 11, 1996	$29.77
Annualized Rate of Return—Period of Corporate Governance Action		67.41%
Ticket In/Ticket Out Return		7.46%

* For all Wyser-Pratte managed accounts invested in this stock.

II. Company

At the time of investment, the company engaged predominantly in the computer services and supply industry. Wallace sold a broad line of products and services including business forms, commercial and promotional graphics printing, computer labels, machine ribbons, computer hardware and software, computer accessories, office products, and electronic forms.

III. Chronology of Events/Investment Rationale/Wyser-Pratte's Role

July 30, 1995   The chairman of Moore Corporation informed Mr. Cronin, CEO of Wallace Computer, that Moore intended to launch an unsolicited tender offer for all outstanding shares of the company's common stock, at $28 per share, a $1.3 billion cash offer. Three days later, Moore commenced its tender offer.

October 12   Moore amended its tender offer to increase the cash price offered for the company's common stock from $28 to $30 per share. Wallace rejected this offer even though 73.5 percent of the shares were tendered.

August 8, 1996   Moore announced that it was abandoning its efforts to acquire Wallace.

                    Guy Wyser-Pratte announced his intention to seek to elect three candidates at the annual meeting of Wallace Computer.

August 19   Wyser-Pratte launched a proxy challenge to put three new representatives on Wallace's board of directors and planned to present proposals to boost the value of the company's stock. The main proposal was to force the company to hold a shareholder vote within 90 days on any fully financed cash bid for the company that was at least 25 percent more than the company's stock price.

October 31   The Proxy Monitor published a report in 1996 recommending that Wallace shareholders supported the three Wyser-Pratte director nominees and both the tender offer bylaw proposal and the business combination statute proposal. The report followed just two days after a recommendation by ISS that Wallace holders support the tender offer bylaw proposal.

November 6   At the annual meeting, Wyser-Pratte's
                        nominees and bylaws were rejected, after
                        AIM Management changed its vote "for"
                        to an "abstain" on the day of the meet-
                        ing. Technically, any "abstain" vote had the
                        same affect as an "against" vote.

IV. Subsequent Events

By using the poison pill and other defensive tactics, the Wallace
board was able to rebuff Moore, without giving shareholders an
alternative means of getting a premium for their stock.

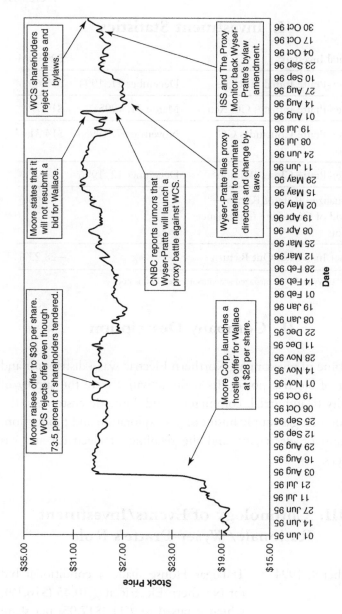

Figure C.9 Wallace Computer Services, Inc.; prices adjusted for 2 for 1 split (USA)

217

Northern Electric, plc
USA   Defensive

I. Investment Statistics

Capital Invested*		$29.90M
Wyser–Pratte Initial Purchase	December 21, 1994	$15.63
Wyser–Pratte Initiates CG Action	March 31, 1995	$11.70
Wyser–Pratte Concludes CG Action	November 7, 1995	$14.31
Wyser–Pratte Closes Position	December 12, 1996	$9.97
Annualized Rate of Return— Period of Corporate Governance Action		101.03%
Ticket In/Ticket Out Return		−28.23%

* For all Wyser-Pratte managed accounts invested in this stock.

II. Company Description

At the time of investment, Northern Electric was a distributor and supplier of electric power. Its main activities were the supply of electricity to industrial, commercial, and domestic customers; the operation of a gas supply business; gas exploration and production; generation of electricity; and the retailing of electrical and gas appliances.

III. Chronology of Events/Investment Rationale/Wyser-Pratte's Role

December 9, 1994	Trafalgar House made a conditional bid for Northern Electric at £10.45 ($16.19), which it raised to £11 ($17.05) per share in February 1995.

December 1994	During the pendency of this offer, a new pricing scheme for electricity was introduced by the applicable regulatory authority, which made Northern Electric unattractive at the price offered by Trafalgar House.
	Trafalgar House decided to allow the bid to lapse, triggering a mandatory one-year waiting period that had to elapse before Trafalgar House could make a new bid (£9.5 or $14.72). Trafalgar House wanted to re-enter the bidding prior to the passage of the one-year waiting period but could only do so with the acquiescence of the board of directors of Northern Electric, which refused to do so.
April 1995	Wyser-Pratte was determined to lead a call for an extraordinary general meeting of Northern Electric's shareholders and quickly obtained the 10 percent of shareholder votes required to do so. Northern Electric reluctantly agreed to call the meeting.
May 1995	Although the extraordinary general meeting did not support allowing Trafalgar House to renew its bid prior to the end of the waiting period, Northern Electric later permitted Trafalgar House to do so.
	Wyser-Pratte continued to put pressure on Northern Electric's board of directors to restructure and recapitalize the company to enhance the shareholder value.

IV. Subsequent Events

June 1995

Under pressure by stockholders, Northern Electric's board of directors restructured and recapitalized the company in a package worth £5 per share. Shareholder value was enhanced significantly even in the face of a lapsed bid. It also gave Trafalgar House the go ahead to launch a new bid.

Late July 1995

Trafalgar House decided not to launch a new bid for Northern Electric.

November 1995 through December 1996

Once the period of corporate governance intervention had ended, the Wyser-Pratte team continued to hold the stock for another year for the arbitrage opportunities.

1996

CalEnergy acquired Northern Electric in a hostile bid.

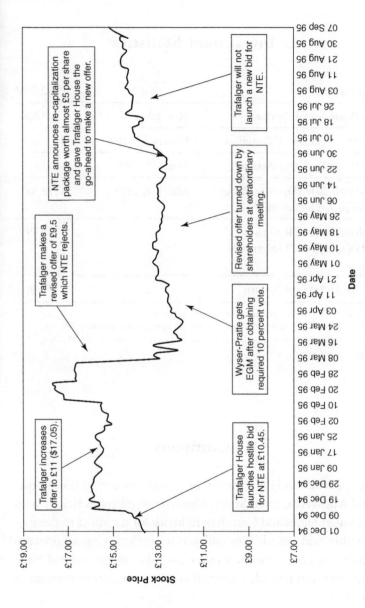

Stock Price

£19.00
£17.00
£15.00
£13.00
£11.00
£9.00
£7.00

Trafalger increases offer to £11 ($17.05).

Trafalger makes a revised offer of £9.5 which NTE rejects.

NTE announces re-capitalization package worth almost £5 per share and gave Trafalger House the go-ahead to make a new offer.

Trafalger House launches hostile bid for NTE at £10.45.

Wyser-Pratte gets EGM after obtaining required 10 percent vote.

Revised offer turned down by shareholders at extraordinary meeting.

Trafalger will not launch a new bid for NTE.

Date

01 Dec 94
09 Dec 94
19 Dec 94
29 Dec 94
09 Jan 95
17 Jan 95
25 Jan 95
02 Feb 95
10 Feb 95
20 Feb 95
28 Feb 95
08 Mar 95
16 Mar 95
24 Mar 95
03 Apr 95
11 Apr 95
21 Apr 95
01 May 95
10 May 95
18 May 95
26 May 95
06 Jun 95
14 Jun 95
22 Jun 95
30 Jun 95
10 Jul 95
18 Jul 95
26 Jul 95
03 Aug 95
11 Aug 95
21 Aug 95
30 Aug 95
07 Sep 95

Figure C.10 Northern Electric, plc (United Kingdom)

221

Conrail
USA   Defensive

I. Investment Statistics

Capital Invested*		$52.70M
Wyser-Pratte Initial Purchase	November 21, 1996	$94.63
Wyser-Pratte Initiates CG Action	January 13, 1997	$100.50
Wyser-Pratte Ends CG Action**	March 7, 1997	$113.63
Wyser-Pratte Sale Date—tender of shares in partial tender offer	March 4, 1997	$112.88
Annualized Rate of Return— Period of Corporate Governance Action		91.59%
Ticket In/Ticket Out Return		74.46%

   * For all Wyser-Pratte managed accounts invested in this stock.
 ** Although the official notice of the definitive merger agreement was made public on
    March 7, 1997, Wyser-Pratte tendered its shares in a partial tender offer on March 4, 1997.

II. Company

Conrail provides freight transportation services within the Northeast and Midwest United States. Conrail interchanges freight with other United States and Canadian railroads for transport to destinations within and outside Conrail's service region. Conrail operates no significant line of business other than the freight railroad business and does not provide common carrier passenger or commuter train service.

III. Chronology of Events/Investment Rationale/Wyser-Pratte's Role

October 15, 1996	CSX announced its plans to buy Conrail for $8.4 billion to create the nation's third-largest railroad.
December 19	Norfolk Southern entered the picture by offering a bid of $115 per share, which represented total value of approximately $10.4 billion.
January 13, 1997	Wyser-Pratte announced that it intended to conduct a proxy fight and seek an amendment to the bylaws of Conrail, which would encourage greater responsiveness by Conrail to the views of its shareholders. Under the proposal, anti-takeover defenses against certain premium cash tender offers had to be terminated after ninety days unless shareholders approved the board's opposition to the offer.
January 17	Shareholders voted down the proposal by CSX.
January 22	Wyser-Pratte announced its proposal that Norfolk Southern sponsor a voting trust that would seek to control at least 50 percent of the vote of Conrail's shareholders concerning the repeal of Conrail's anti-takeover provisions.
January 23	Wyser-Pratte attended the annual meeting, during which time he made a speech to management demanding that it accept Norfolk's offer. Wyser-Pratte also sought to rally the shareholders around this goal.

March 7   Conrail announced that Conrail and CSX
                           amended their merger agreement to in-
                           crease the consideration to $115 per share
                           and to include Norfolk Southern.

IV. Subsequent Events

May 23, 1997   The joint $115 per share cash tender of-
                           fer was completed, and CSX and Norfolk
                           Southern came to hold 96 percent of Con-
                           rail's shares.

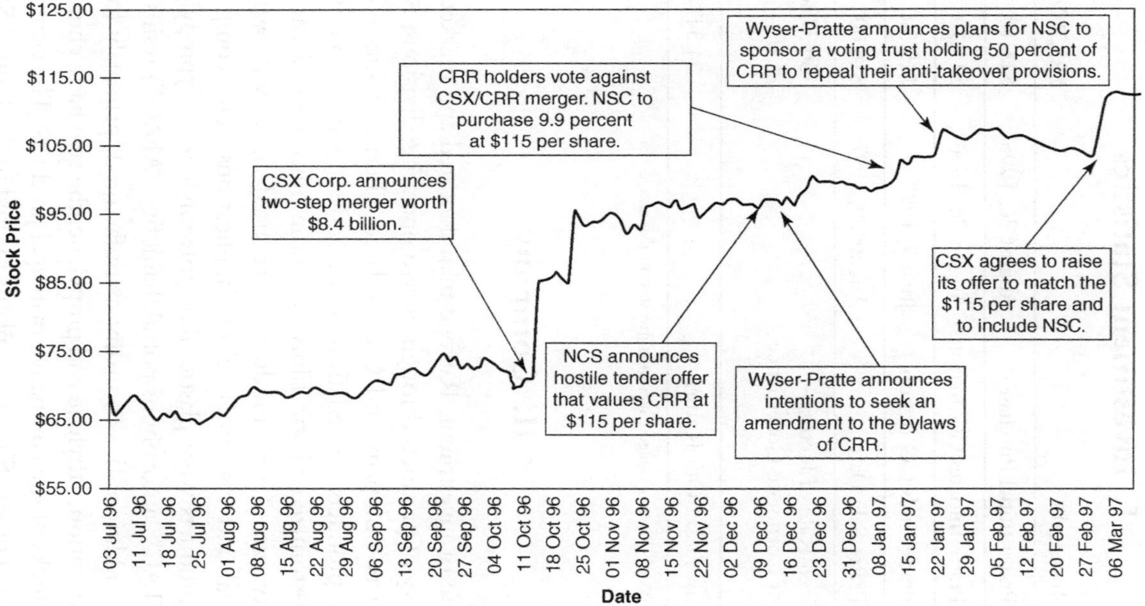
$125.00
$115.00
$105.00
$95.00
$85.00
$75.00
$65.00
$55.00
Stock Price
CSX Corp. announces two-step merger worth $8.4 billion.
CRR holders vote against CSX/CRR merger. NSC to purchase 9.9 percent at $115 per share.
Wyser-Pratte announces plans for NSC to sponsor a voting trust holding 50 percent of CRR to repeal their anti-takeover provisions.
NCS announces hostile tender offer that values CRR at $115 per share.
Wyser-Pratte announces intentions to seek an amendment to the bylaws of CRR.
CSX agrees to raise its offer to match the $115 per share and to include NSC.
03 Jul 96
11 Jul 96
18 Jul 96
25 Jul 96
01 Aug 96
08 Aug 96
15 Aug 96
22 Aug 96
29 Aug 96
06 Sep 96
13 Sep 96
20 Sep 96
27 Sep 96
04 Oct 96
11 Oct 96
18 Oct 96
25 Oct 96
01 Nov 96
08 Nov 96
15 Nov 96
22 Nov 96
02 Dec 96
09 Dec 96
16 Dec 96
23 Dec 96
31 Dec 96
08 Jan 97
15 Jan 97
22 Jan 97
29 Jan 97
05 Feb 97
12 Feb 97
20 Feb 97
27 Feb 97
06 Mar 97
Date

Figure C.11 Conrail (USA)

Rexene Corporation
USA   Proactive

I. Investment Statistics

Capital Invested*		$25.70M
Wyser-Pratte Initial Purchase	August 26, 1996	$11.10
Wyser-Pratte Initiates CG Action	August 26, 1996	$11.10
Wyser-Pratte Ends CG Action	June 9, 1997	$15.50
Wyser-Pratte Sale Date	August 29, 1997	$16.00
Annualized Rate of Return— Period of Corporate Governance Action		50.37%
Ticket In/Ticket Out Return		34.34%

* For all Wyser-Pratte managed accounts invested in this stock.

II. Company

At the time of investment, Rexene manufactured and marketed a wide variety of products through its two operating divisions, Rexene Products Company and Consolidated Thermoplastics Company. The products ranged from value added specialty products, such as customized plastic films, to commodity petrochemicals, such as styrene. These products were used in a wide variety of industrial and consumer-related applications. The company's principal products were plastic film, polyethylene, polypropylene, and REXTAC® amorphous polyalphaolefin ("APAO") resins and styrene. In addition, the company manufactured, primarily for its own consumption, ethylene and propylene, the two basic chemical building blocks of the company's principal products. The company manufactured plastic film at five plants located in the United States and England and polymers and petrochemicals at an integrated facility in Odessa, Texas, which was located near supplies of most of its raw materials.

III. Chronology of Events/Investment Rationale/Wyser-Pratte's Role

June 19, 1996   Rexene received an unsolicited proposal from Huntsman Corporation to acquire all of its outstanding shares at $14 per share.

July 22, 1996   Rexene's board of directors rejected the proposal. The board considered a wide range of factors, including the historical and present market valuation of the company's common stock, the then present condition of the commodity chemical industry and the company's future prospects in reaching its conclusions.

August 1   Rexene received a second unsolicited acquisition proposal on August 1 from Huntsman for $15 per share.

August 5   Rexene's board unanimously rejected the proposal.

August 21   Huntsman dropped its $286.5 million unsuccessful bid.

October 3   Wyser-Pratte filed a Form 13D with the SEC soon after Rexene rejected Huntsman's $15 per share offer. The filing said Wyser-Pratte hoped to make changes in the company's management and board of directors that would lead it to consider purchase offers from third parties.

November 12   Wyser-Pratte and the investment firm Spear, Leeds & Kellogg increased their respective stakes to 9.8 percent in November.

     Wyser-Pratte also launched a proxy battle to remove Rexene's board members and sell the company, and to adopt bylaw provisions designed to give shareholders a greater say in takeover matters.

December 4

Huntsman returned with a new proposal to acquire Rexene in a merger transaction for $16 per share.

January 3, 1997

Rexene reported a willingness to accept an offer of $16 per share, as long as it was fully financed and completed in 60 days.

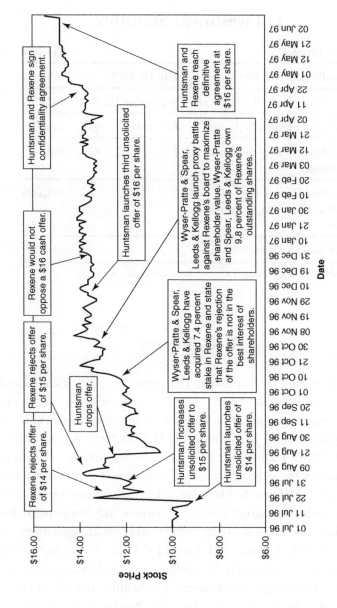

Figure C.12 Rexene Corporation (USA)

ITT Corporation
USA   Defensive

I. Investment Statistics

Capital Invested*		$54.40M
Wyser-Pratte Initial Purchase	July 17, 1997	$65.56
Wyser-Pratte Initiates CG Action	September 16, 1997	$62.63
Wyser-Pratte Ends CG Action	November 7, 1997	$80.31
Wyser-Pratte Sale of final piece after merger	February 27, 1998	$68.04
Annualized Rate of Return— Period of Corporate Governance Action		198.14%
Ticket In/Ticket Out Return		91.72%

* For all Wyser-Pratte managed accounts invested in this stock.

II. Company

ITT Industries is a worldwide enterprise engaged directly and through its subsidiaries in the design and manufacture of a wide range of engineered products, focused on the three principal business segments of ITT Automotive, ITT Defense & Electronics and ITT Fluid Technology. ITT Automotive designs, engineers and manufactures a broad range of automotive components and systems. ITT Defense & Electronics develops, manufactures, and supports high technology electronic systems and components for worldwide defense and commercial markets with operations in North America, Europe, and Asia. ITT Fluid Technology, with 1996 sales of approximately $1.3 billion, is a worldwide enterprise engaged in the design, development, production, and sale of products, systems, and services used to move, handle, transfer, control, and contain fluids.

III. Chronology of Events/Investment Rationale/Wyser-Pratte's Role

July 15, 1997

ITT announced that its board of directors approved a plan where ITT would split into three separate companies.

August 7

Hilton Hotels announced that it had increased its bid to acquire ITT from $55 to $70, valuing the deal at $11.5 billion. ITT's board rejected this offer.

September 17

Wyser-Pratte filed an amicus brief in federal court (Nevada) against the ITT breakup. The amicus brief demonstrated that Wyser-Pratte had presented novel arguments against ITT's Comprehensive Plan. Wyser-Pratte argued that the plan violated Nevada corporate law since it would involve an illegal distribution. Also, the brief alerted the Court to the damage that would be occasioned by the plan in creating a loophole in Nevada corporate law that would eliminate the veto power enjoyed by shareholders over the creation of a staggered-term board of directors.

September 30

Due to a filing by Wyser-Pratte, the Court made a decision that urged the ITT board to end its resistance to the Hilton Corporation acquisition immediately.

October 20

Starwood Lodging Trust agreed to buy ITT for $15 in cash and $67 in stock, resulting in a $13.3 billion deal, which would create the world's largest hotel chain and apparently ended Hilton Hotel's long running effort to buy ITT.

| November 3 | Hilton raised its cash bid to $80 per share. |
| November 7 | Starwood Lodging raised its offer again to $85 per share in cash and stock. |

IV. Subsequent Events

February 18, 1998	Shareholders of Starwood Hotels approved their company's takeover of ITT Corporation.
February 23	The deal became official share in cash and stock.
February 27	Wyser-Pratte completed the sale of its stock, reflecting the completion of the deal.

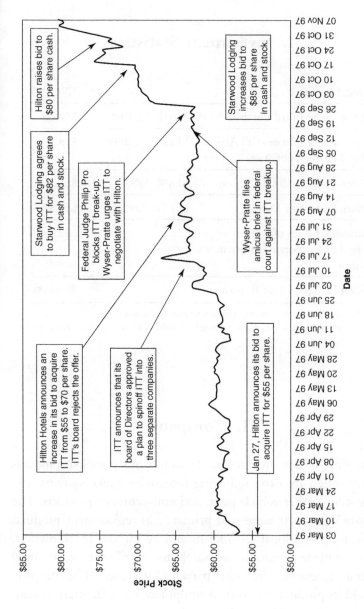

Figure C.13 ITT Corporation (USA)

The following text appears as labels within the figure:

Hilton raises bid to $80 per share cash.

Starwood Lodging agrees to buy ITT for $82 per share in cash and stock.

Federal Judge Philip Pro blocks ITT break-up. Wyser-Pratte urges ITT to negotiate with Hilton.

Starwood Lodging increases bid to $85 per share in cash and stock.

Hilton Hotels announces an increase in its bid to acquire ITT from $55 to $70 per share. ITT's board rejects the offer.

ITT announces that its board of Directors approved a plan to spinoff ITT into three separate companies.

Wyser-Pratte files amicus brief in federal court against ITT breakup.

Jan 27, Hilton announces its bid to acquire ITT for $55 per share.

Stock Price axis: $50.00, $55.00, $60.00, $65.00, $70.00, $75.00, $80.00, $85.00

Date axis: 03 Mar 97, 10 Mar 97, 17 Mar 97, 24 Mar 97, 01 Apr 97, 08 Apr 97, 15 Apr 97, 22 Apr 97, 29 Apr 97, 06 May 97, 13 May 97, 20 May 97, 28 May 97, 04 Jun 97, 11 Jun 97, 18 Jun 97, 25 Jun 97, 02 Jul 97, 10 Jul 97, 17 Jul 97, 24 Jul 97, 31 Jul 97, 07 Aug 97, 14 Aug 97, 21 Aug 97, 28 Aug 97, 05 Sep 97, 12 Sep 97, 19 Sep 97, 26 Sep 97, 03 Oct 97, 10 Oct 97, 17 Oct 97, 24 Oct 97, 31 Oct 97, 07 Nov 97

Echlin Manufacturing
USA   Proactive

I. Investment Statistics

Capital Invested*		$36.90M
Wyser-Pratte Initial Purchase**	March 26, 1998	$52.00
Wyser-Pratte Initiates CG Action (ahead of stock purchase)	March 17, 1998	$48.81
Wyser-Pratte Ends CG Action	May 4, 1998	$51.56
Wyser-Pratte Sale Date	July 10, 1998	$50.52
Annualized Rate of Return— Period of Corporate Governance Action		42.88%
Ticket In/Ticket Out Return		219.51%

  * For all Wyser-Pratte managed accounts invested in this stock.
 ** The actual accumulation of the position began after the intervention date, due to capital restraints.

II. Company

At the time of the investment, the company's principal products were classified into the following categories: brake systems, engine systems, other vehicle parts, and non-vehicular products. The company's products were sold primarily as replacement products for use by professional technicians and by car and truck owners. Sales were made to automotive warehouse distributors, heavy-duty distributors, retailers, and other parts manufacturers. The company also sold its products to original equipment manufacturers in both the automotive and heavy-duty markets.

III. Chronology of Events/Investment Rationale/Wyser-Pratte's Role

February 17, 1998   SPX announced its bid for Echlin, offering cash and shares worth $3 billion or $48 per share.

March 6   The head of SPX launched his appeal for shareholders to call a special meeting by April 24 and sent a letter to Echlin's board calling Echlin's defense misguided and extreme.

March 17, 1998   Guy Wyser-Pratte sent and publicized a powerfully-worded letter to Echlin CEO and all members of the Connecticut Legislature, criticizing the anti-shareholder bill drafted by Echlin supporters. The bill, once expected to pass, was quickly abandoned, allowing SPX to buy Echlin. (Please note this letter was sent prior to actual investment in the stock by Wyser-Pratte.)

March 25   Defeat of the Echlin-backed bill in the Connecticut State House that would have effectively delayed a special shareholder's meeting.

March 25   SPX announced that it had delivered to Echlin demands from owners of approximately 29 million Echlin shares, representing approximately 46 percent of Echlin's outstanding shares, to hold a special meeting.

April 6   Echlin announced that, contrary to SPX Corporation's announcement, SPX had not delivered sufficient valid demands to Echlin to require Echlin to call a special meeting of Echlin's shareholders. Echlin initiated a suit against SPX for making misleading statements.

May 4   Echlin's board of directors voted unanimously to recommend that Echlin's shareholders reject SPX Corporation's exchange offer, while Dana Corporation emerged as a "white knight" bidder for Echlin.

May 6   SPX said it abandoned its hostile takeover bid for Echlin because it appeared Echlin would join forces with Dana Corp.

May 11   Dana Corp. and Echlin said their boards agreed to a definitive merger agreement that would create a global auto parts supplier in a tax-free stock swap transaction valued at $3.6 billion. The merger had to meet approval from shareholders and federal regulators before it was finalized.

IV. Subsequent Events

July 8, 1998   The European Union approved the deal.

July 9   The merger was completed. It created one of the world's largest independent companies supplying components to both automotive original equipment manufacturers and the aftermath. With the merger complete, Dana now manufactures products used on more than 95 percent of the world's motor vehicles. The combined company offers more comprehensive product lines including fuel systems and engine management components, brakes, and vehicular drivetrain components and systems.

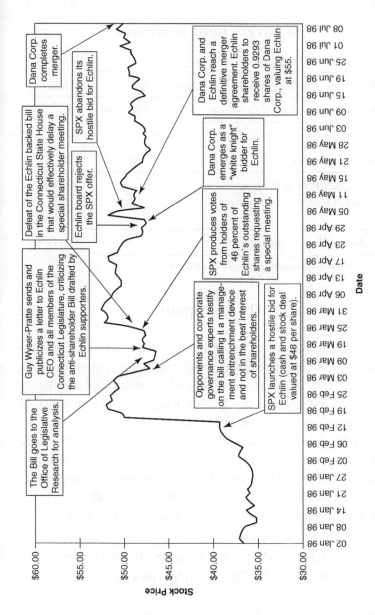

Figure C.14 Echlin Manufacturing (USA)

American Bankers Insurance
USA   Defensive

I. Investment Statistics

Capital Invested*		$56.30M
Wyser-Pratte Initial Purchase	January 27, 1998	$55.875
Wyser-Pratte Initiates CG Action	February 19, 1998	$55.00
Wyser-Pratte Ends CG Action	March 16, 1998	$65.75
Wyser-Pratte Sale Date	March 8, 1999	$51.95
Annualized Rate of Return— Period of Corporate Governance Action		285.49%
Ticket In/Ticket Out Return		−13.19%

* For all Wyser-Pratte managed accounts invested in this stock.

II. Company

At the time of the investment, American Bankers Insurance (ABI) was a specialty insurer providing primarily credit-related insurance products in the United States and Canada as well as in Latin America, the Caribbean, and the United Kingdom. The majority of the company's gross collected premiums were derived from credit-related insurance products sold through financial institutions and other entities which provided consumer financing as a regular part of their businesses. ABI differed from most insurance companies in that a substantial portion of its property and casualty segment is credit property and unemployment versus traditional property.

III. Chronology of Events/Investment Rationale/Wyser-Pratte's Role

December 22, 1997   American Bankers Insurance agreed to be acquired by AIG for $47 per share.

January 27, 1998	Cendant Corporation launched a hostile offer to acquire ABI for $58 per share.
February 19	Wyser-Pratte filed a petition with the Florida Department of Insurance to consolidate the filings of AIG and Cendant in order to protect the best interests of ABI, depriving AIG of its timing advantage. The Florida State Insurance Commissioner ruled in favor of Wyser-Pratte and agreed to consolidate the filings on a parallel basis.
February	The Florida Insurance Commissioner ruled in favor of Wyser-Pratte and agreed to consolidate the filings on a parallel basis.
March 2	AIG and ABI said they reached an amended agreement under which AIG would pay $58 in stock and cash for each ABI share.
March 16	Cendant increased the offer to acquire ABI to $67 per share.
March 23	Cendant and ABI announced they signed a definitive agreement for Cendant to acquire ABI for a combination of cash and stock valued at about $3.1 billion.

IV. Subsequent Events

| April 15, 1998 | The deal became questionable when Cendant revealed that it had accounting problems. News of Cendant's accounting irregularities sent its stock tumbling, and the shares traded at about 35 percent of their level at the time. Cendant offered to |

purchase ABI. Cendant had to provide almost three times the number of shares
it had originally expected. The company
stated that it might seek to alter the terms
of the agreement to include more cash;
however, such a deal was less attractive to
ABI.

October 14, 1998   Cendant announced a mutual decision to
                            terminate the merger agreement.

October 1998
through March 1999   Wyser-Pratte remained in the stock in
                            an effort to take advantage of perceived
                            arbitrage opportunities. It believed that
                            American Bankers was a valuable property
                            that ultimately would be bought.

March 8, 1999   Fortis announced that it would buy
                            American Bankers at $55 per share. Wyser-
                            Pratte Management sold its stock at that
                            time.

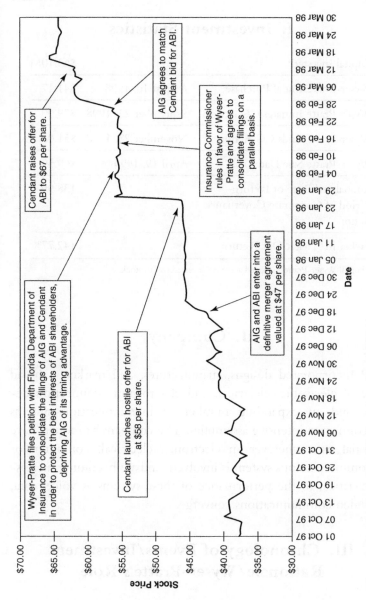

The following text labels appear within the figure:

Wyser-Pratte files petition with Florida Department of Insurance to consolidate the filings of AIG and Cendant in order to protect the best interests of ABI shareholders, depriving AIG of its timing advantage.

Cendant raises offer for ABI to $67 per share.

AIG agrees to match Cendant bid for ABI.

Insurance Commissioner rules in favor of Wyser-Pratte and agrees to consolidate filings on a parallel basis.

Cendant launches hostile offer for ABI at $58 per share.

AIG and ABI enter into a definitive merger agreement valued at $47 per share.

Figure C.15 American Bankers Insurance (USA)

241

AMP, Inc.
USA   Defensive

I. Investment Statistics

Capital Invested*		$63.10M
Wyser–Pratte Initial Purchase	August 10, 1998	$41.17
Wyser–Pratte Initiates CG Action	September 23, 1998	$39.00
Wyser–Pratte Ends CG Action	November 23, 1998	$51.00
Wyser–Pratte Sale Date	April 19, 1999	$69.59
Annualized Rate of Return— Period of Corporate Governance Action		138.99%
Ticket In/Ticket Out Return		142.77%

* For all Wyser-Pratte managed accounts invested in this stock.

II. Company

AMP Incorporated designs, manufactures, and markets a broad range of electronic, electrical, and electro–optic connection devices, and an expanding number of interconnection systems and connector-intensive assemblies. The company's products have potential uses wherever an electronic, electrical, computer, or telecommunications system is involved, and are becoming increasingly critical to the performance of these systems as voice, data, and video communications converge.

III. Chronology of Events/Investment Rationale/Wyser-Pratte's Role

August 4, 1998   Allied Signal announced plans to acquire AMP for $44.50 per share.

August 21	AMP rejected the offer as inadequate and said it would produce more value for shareholders through its profit-improvement plan that it began that summer. Just a few days later, AMP filed a lawsuit in federal court to stop Allied Signal from placing its representatives on the AMP board of directors as part of its $10 billion takeover attempt.
September 23	Wyser-Pratte sent a letter to Representative Bruce Smith severely criticizing his support of the Pennsylvania legislation to block Allied Signal's takeover bid. Wyser-Pratte began to prepare a lawsuit attacking potential legislation on constitutional grounds. The Pennsylvania legislative action failed to block Allied Signal's bid.
September 24	AMP filed a complaint in Pennsylvania State Court that said Allied Signal's effort to delegate authority over the poison pill to non-directors violated state law. This was AMP's attempt to convince the Pennsylvania legislature to block Allied Signal's takeover bid and prevent hostile bidders from conducting consent solicitations for an 18-month period.
October 12	AMP Inc. announced it was commencing its self-tender offer to repurchase up to 30 million shares of AMP common stock, at a price of $55 per share in cash.

IV. Subsequent Events

November 22, 1998   AMP agreed to a rival bid of $11.3 billion in stock from Tyco International Ltd. The Tyco deal gave AMP shareholders $51 in Tyco stock for each of their AMP shares. The boards of Tyco and AMP approved their agreement to merge into a company with more than $22 billion in annual revenues and operations in more than 80 countries.

April 2, 1999   Tyco announced the completion of the merger.

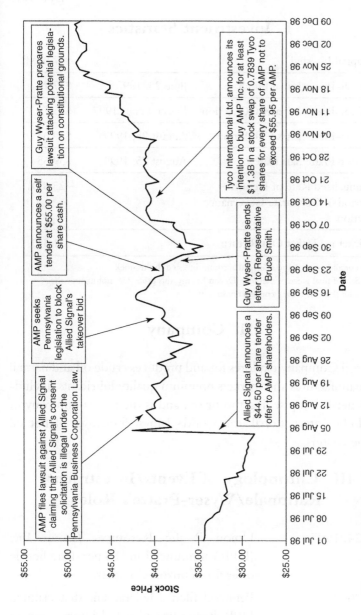

Figure C.16 Amp, Inc. (USA)

245

Pennzoil Company
USA   Defensive

I. Investment Statistics

Capital Invested*		$67.00M
Wyser-Pratte Initial Purchase	June 23, 1997	$77.77
Wyser-Pratte Initiates CG Action	December 1, 1997	$65.75
Wyser-Pratte Ends CG Action**	August 25, 1999	$39.65
Wyser-Pratte Sale Date**	August 25, 1999	$39.65
Annualized Rate of Return— Period of Corporate Governance Action		−25.87%
Ticket in/Ticket Out Return		−31.31%

 * For all Wyser-Pratte managed accounts invested in this stock.
 ** Sale of final piece of merger—Devon Energy, this price does not include the
    cash flow from the Pennzenergy spinoff.

II. Company

Pennzoil Company explores for and produces crude oil and natural
gas, manufactures and markets premium quality lubricants, including America's top selling motor oil, and is the parent company of
Jiffy Lube International, the world's largest franchiser of fast oil
change centers.

III. Chronology of Events/Investment Rationale/Wyser-Pratte's Role

June 24, 1997	Union Pacific Resources Group Inc. (UPR) announced an $84 per share hostile offer for Pennzoil Company.
June 26	Pennzoil filed a federal suit that claimed UPR hadn't provided full information to shareholders on the negative aspects of the offer.

July 1	Pennzoil's board of directors recommended Pennzoil's shareholders reject UPR's proposed tender offer and merger as inadequate and not in the best interest of the shareholders.
July 22	61.5 percent of Pennzoil shares were tendered.
September 11	Union Pacific said a federal judge denied a motion by Pennzoil for preliminary injunction against Union Pacific's unsolicited tender offer.
October 7, 1997	Union Pacific changed its $84 a share cash and stock bid to an all cash offer.
October 14	Pennzoil's board of directors rejected Union Pacific's revised offer.
November 11	Union Pacific announced it would terminate its offer unless Pennzoil entered into good faith negotiations with UPR on or prior to November 17.
November 17	UPR announced it was terminating is bid.
December 9	Wyser-Pratte filed amended preliminary proxy material for Pennzoil's annual meeting, including:

- Adopt a "Shareholder Rights Bylaw"
- Adopt a "Shareholder Interests Protection Bylaw"
- Allow the holders of 10 percent of the company's shares to call a special meeting of shareholders.
- Allow shareholders to submit proposals and director nominations for the annual meeting between 60 and 120 days in advance of the anniversary of the prior annual meeting.

- Require the vote of a majority of the outstanding shares to change any of the foregoing bylaws.
- Repeal any bylaws adopted by the board of directors after November 1,1997.

April 3, 1998   Pennzoil negotiated a settlement with Guy Wyser-Pratte where Pennzoil modified its existing shareholder rights plan, adding several features to the company's position pill. Wyser-Pratte withdrew his nomination for election to Pennzoil's board of directors along with the bylaw amendments and other proposals he was scheduled to submit at the company's May 7th meeting. Pennzoil, in effect, adopted Wyser-Pratte's proposed corporate governance scheme.

April 16   Pennzoil announced it would split into two companies, one of which would buy Quaker State Corp. in a transaction valued at more than $1 billion in stock and assumed debt. The other company was to become Pennzenergy.

IV. Subsequent Events

January 4, 1999   Pennzoil and Quaker State announced the completion of its restructuring, including the spinoff of Pennzoil's Product Group.

May 20   Devon Energy proposes acquisition of Pennzenergy.

August 17   Pennzenergy and Devon Energy shareholders approve the acquisition of Pennzenergy.

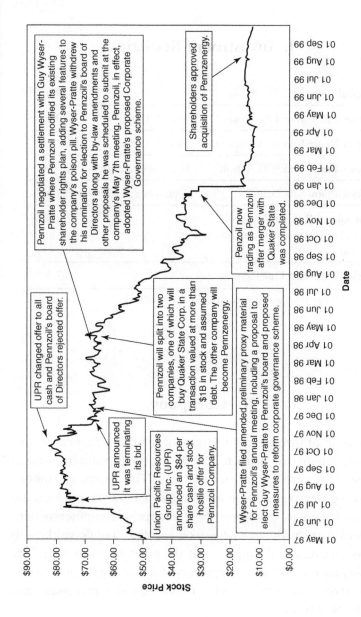

Figure C.17 Pennzoil Company (USA)

The following labels appear on the figure:

- UPR changed offer to all cash and Pennzoil's board of Directors rejected offer.

- Pennzoil negotiated a settlement with Guy Wyser-Pratte where Pennzoil modified its existing shareholder rights plan, adding several features to the company's poison pill. Wyser-Pratte withdrew his nomination for election to Pennzoil's board of Directors along with by-law amendments and other proposals he was scheduled to submit at the company's May 7th meeting. Pennzoil, in effect, adopted Wyser-Pratte's proposed Corporate Governance scheme.

- Shareholders approved acquisition of Pennzenergy.

- UPR announced it was terminating its bid.

- Union Pacific Resources Group Inc. (UPR) announced an $84 per share cash and stock hostile offer for Pennzoil Company.

- Pennzoil will split into two companies, one of which will buy Quaker State Corp. in a transaction valued at more than $1B in stock and assumed debt. The other company will become Pennzenergy.

- Penzoil now trading as Pennzoil after merger with Quaker State was completed.

- Wyser-Pratte filed amended preliminary proxy material for Pennzoil's annual meeting, including a proposal to elect Guy Wyser-Pratte to Pennzoil's board and proposed measures to reform corporate governance scheme.

Y-axis (Stock Price): $0.00, $10.00, $20.00, $30.00, $40.00, $50.00, $60.00, $70.00, $80.00, $90.00

X-axis (Date): 01 May 97, 01 Jun 97, 01 Jul 97, 01 Aug 97, 01 Sep 97, 01 Oct 97, 01 Nov 97, 01 Dec 97, 01 Jan 98, 01 Feb 98, 01 Mar 98, 01 Apr 98, 01 May 98, 01 Jun 98, 01 Jul 98, 01 Aug 98, 01 Sep 98, 01 Oct 98, 01 Nov 98, 01 Dec 98, 01 Jan 99, 01 Feb 99, 01 Mar 99, 01 Apr 99, 01 May 99, 01 Jun 99, 01 Jul 99, 01 Aug 99, 01 Sep 99

Telxon Corporation
USA   Proactive

I. Investment Statistics

Capital Invested*		$28.00M
Wyser-Pratte Initial Purchase	June 2, 1998	$30.13
Wyser-Pratte Initiates CG Action	June 8, 1998	$31.26
Wyser-Pratte Ends CG Action	November 30, 1998	$27.00
Wyser-Pratte Sale Date	September 21, 1999	$8.00
Annualized Rate of Return— Period of Corporate Governance Action		−28.42%
Ticket In/Ticket Out Return		−67.30%

* For all Wyser-Pratte managed accounts invested in this stock.

II. Company

At the time of investment, Telxon Corporation designed, manu-factured, integrated, marketed, and supported transaction-based wireless workforce automation systems. The company's mobile computing devices and wireless local area network products are integrated with its customers' host enterprise computer systems and third-party wide area networks, enabling mobile workers to process data on a real-time basis at the point of transaction. The company also served several segments of the emerging mobile ser-vices market, such as field service, insurance claims processing, and work force automation.

III. Chronology of Events/Investment Rationale/Wyser-Pratte's Role

June 1, 1998

Symbol Technologies announced its bid for Telxon of $40 per share in cash or up to $42 per share in cash and stock. The following day, Telxon ultimately rejected that offer aggravating some shareholders that expected to gain a substantial premium from the deal. Telxon had a poison pill provision, which allowed it to fight off hostile takeovers.

June 18

Wyser-Pratte launched a campaign to attempt to amend Telxon's bylaws after Telxon rejected the $40 per share cash offer. Wyser-Pratte launched a proxy fight in an attempt to bypass Telxon's unwilling board of directors and force a vote by shareholders on the proposal.

July 15

Telxon retaliated by filing a lawsuit in the US District Court for the District of Delaware charging that Wyser-Pratte made false and misleading statements to the SEC.

August 27

The rejected takeover attempt inspired a proxy battle led by Wyser-Pratte that was settled when Telxon agreed to accept any future all-cash offers valued above $40 per share. Wyser-Pratte and Telxon signed a settlement agreement that required Telxon to make its poison pill chewable for all cash offers, which would force the board of a company to introduce a tender offer to its shareholders for a 90-day period, and to accept his director nominee on the board.

IV. Subsequent Events

December 11, 1998

Telxon rejected the $40 per share offer as "insincere," dismissing it as an attempt to sabotage the company. Allegations of accounting fraud by Telxon caused Symbol to rescind its offer.

December 1998 through September 1999

Wyser-Pratte remained in the stock as it was not totally clear that the allegations of accounting fraud leveled against Telxon were well-founded. It sold the stock at the point at which the Wyser-Pratte team believed it had recovered as much value as the circumstances permitted.

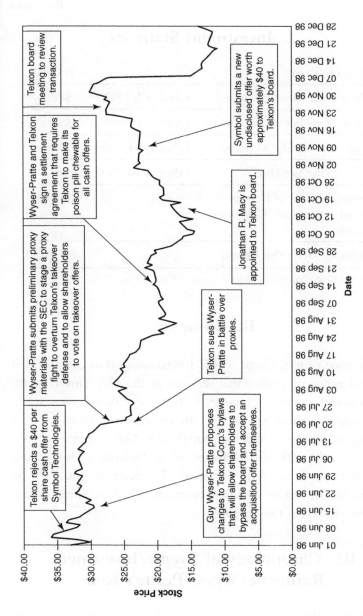

Telxon board meeting to review transaction.

Wyser-Pratte and Telxon sign a settlement agreement that requires Telxon to make its poison pill chewable for all cash offers.

Wyser-Pratte submits preliminary proxy materials with the SEC to stage a proxy fight to overturn Telxon's takeover defense and to allow shareholders to vote on takeover offers.

Telxon rejects a $40 per share cash offer from Symbol Technologies.

Telxon sues Wyser-Pratte in battle over proxies.

Jonathan R. Macy is appointed to Telxon board.

Symbol submits a new undisclosed offer worth approximately $40 to Telxon's board.

Guy Wyser-Pratte proposes changes to Telxon Corp.'s bylaws that will allow shareholders to bypass the board and accept an acquisition offer themselves.

Figure C.18 Telxon Corporation (USA)

253

GRC International
USA   Proactive

I. Investment Statistics

Capital Invested*		$0.40M
Wyser-Pratte Initial Purchase	October 7, 1999	$8.50
Wyser-Pratte Initiates CG Action	October 7, 1999	$8.50
Wyser-Pratte Ends CG Action	February 14, 2000	$15.00
Wyser-Pratte Sale Date	February 14, 2000	$15.00
Annualized Rate of Return— Period of Corporate Governance Action		214.66%
Ticket In/Ticket Out Return		214.71%

* For all Wyser-Pratte managed accounts invested in this stock.

II. Company

At the time of investment, GRC International (GRCI) provided a broad range of professional services to the U.S. Government. Government services represented 96 percent of revenues while information technology services to commercial clients were 4 percent of revenues. The company's U.S. Government business was primarily with the Department of Defense ("DoD") and its instrumentalities. Approximately 17 percent of the business was performed under classified contracts, which required special security clearances for employees.

III. Chronology of Events/Investment Rationale/Wyser-Pratte's Role

August 5, 1999   Wyser-Pratte was granted options in GRC International by Frank Cilliffo from his own holdings to entice him to go on to the GRC board of directors.

Early October

Frank Cilliffo filed documents with the SEC to nominate Wyser-Pratte to the board of GRC International. Cilliffo complained that GRCI's board had ignored advisory votes by shareholders calling on the company to repeal its "poison pill" antitakeover defense and restructure its board to make it easier to vote in new directors.

December 13

Wyser-Pratte associates, Neal B. Freeman and Richard N. Perle, were elected to the board of directors as a condition of the settlement of the litigation.

IV. Subsequent Events

February 14, 2000

GRCI entered into an Agreement and Plan of Merger with AT&T Corporation for a cash price of $15.00 per share. Following the acquisition, GRCI came to operate as a unit of AT&T Government Markets within AT&T Business Services.

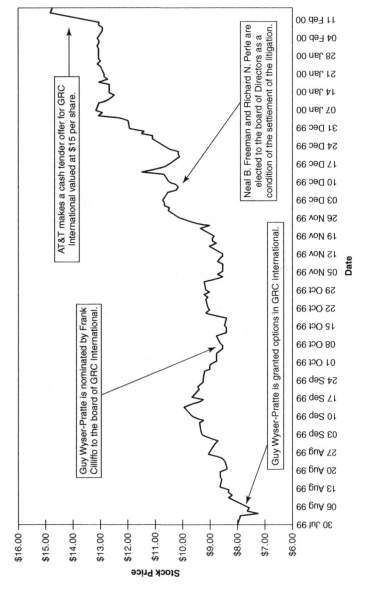

Figure C.19 GRC International (USA)

256

Mannesmann AG
Germany   Defensive

I. Investment Statistics

Capital-Invested*		$34.50M
Wyser-Pratte Initial Purchase	November 24, 1999	€187.40
Wyser-Pratte Initiates CG Action	December 22, 1999	€231.60
Wyser-Pratte Concludes CG Action	February 9, 2000	€278.57
Wyser-Pratte Closes Position	March 13, 2000	€360
Annualized Rate of Return— Period of Corporate Governance Action		€151.09%
Ticket In/Ticket Out Return		€186.09%

* For all Wyser-Pratte managed accounts invested in this stock.

II. Company Description

Mannesmann is a globally operating diversified group of companies active in the engineering, automotive, and telecommunications industries. Mannesmann's acquisition in 1998 of Orange, UK's third largest mobile phone company, made it Europe's top wireless company.

III. Chronology of Events/Investment Rationale/Wyser-Pratte's Role

October 21, 1999   Mannesmann's price dropped 10 percent to €140 on the announcement of its bid for Orange. The acquisition price was seen as much too high.

November 8	Rumors of a takeover by Vodafone, which would have to divest Orange, or France Telecom, pushed the stock back up to a comparable level.
November 15	Vodafone made a hostile bid to acquire Mannesmann for €103 billion. It offered to exchange 43.7 of its shares for one share of Mannesmann. Vodafone needed only 50 percent plus one share of acceptances to acquire Mannesmann.
	The two major risks to the deal were the potential monopoly situation of the new group and a rejection of the deal by a majority of shareholders of the target.
	Mannesmann's CEO Esser found the price too low and asked the shareholders to reject the bid. Three main shareholders with about 30 percent publicly disapproved of the bid. Mannesmann's supervisory and management boards rejected the bid, arguing that the price was not high enough.
November 18, 1999	Vodafone increased its bid for Mannesmann, offering 53.7 of its shares for 1 share of Mannesmann. Vodafone wanted a 50.1 percent approval for the takeover and if it succeeded, it would divest Orange.
December	German Chancellor Gerhard Schroeder and other political leaders rallied against Vodafone's bid.
December 22	Guy Wyser-Pratte declared that he was fully confident in seeking support from the owners of 5 percent of Mannesmann's shares, the amount needed to call a special shareholder meeting. He wanted Mannesmann to start talking to Vodafone. The goal

of the Extraordinary Meeting was to obtain a vote of "no confidence" against the managing board "Vorstand."

Wyser-Pratte was confident that the deal could be completed on a regulatory basis. Vodafone said it would dispose of Orange, the only potential antitrust problem, if it succeeded in acquiring Mannesmann.

Wyser-Pratte believed that if Esser were not able to create enough shareholder value to compete with Vodafone's offer, he would have to accept the bid under pressure from shareholders. Vodafone could have increased its bid to assure the result of the acceptances to the offer.

December 27   AFL-CIO pressured U.S. ERISA plan managers not to tender their Mannesmann shares to Vodafone. Wyser-Pratte publicly asked the U.S. Secretary of Labor to investigate AFL-CIO's pressure on U.S. ERISA plan managers, thereby freeing said managers to tender to Vodafone and maximize the value of their investment in Mannesmann.

IV. Subsequent Events

February 4, 2000   Mannesmann agreed to an increased offer from Vodafone, in which it would get 49.5 percent of the new group. The new exchange ratio was 58.96.

February 9   The offer became unconditional.

March 1   Wyser-Pratte received its Vodafone shares resulting in an annualized return of 151 percent.

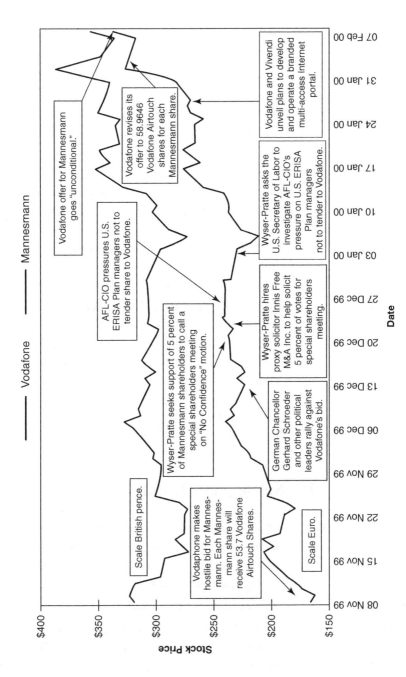

Figure C.20 Mannesmann AG (Germany)

Willamette Industries, Inc.
USA   Defensive

I. Investment Statistics

Capital Invested*		$36.00M
Wyser-Pratte Initial Purchase	November 29, 2000	$49.61
Wyser-Pratte Initiates CG Action	March 19, 2001	$46.40
Wyser-Pratte Ends CG Action	January 22, 2002	$55.12
Wyser-Pratte Sale Date	February 13, 2002	$55.50
Annualized Rate of Return—Period of Corporate Governance Action		26.09%
Ticket In/Ticket Out Return		17.16%

* For all Wyser-Pratte managed accounts invested in this stock.

II. Company Description

Wilamette Industries, Inc. is an integrated forest products company that operates manufacturing facilities in the United States, Europe, and Mexico. The company's principle lines of business are white paper, brown paper, and building materials, which include hardware pulp, fine paper, kraft linerboard, corrugated containers, paper bags, lumber, plywood, and particleboard.

III. Chronology of Events/Investment Rationale/Wyser-Pratte's Role

November 6, 1998   Weyerhaeuser (WY) sent a letter to Willamette (WLL) proposing to acquire all of the outstanding common stock of WLL for $48 per share in cash, a 38 percent

	premium on the close of November 10, 2000 and a 60 percent premium on the average share price for the prior 60 days.
November 11	WLL informed Weyerhaeuser that the Willamette board had met on November 9 and failed to act on Weyerhaeuser's proposal.
November 13	Weyerhaeuser confirmed in the press that it had contacted Willamette with the proposal.
	Weyerhaeuser began a hostile takeover bid and says it intends to field a slate of three board candidates who favor the offer at Willamette's annual board meeting, scheduled for April 17.
	Willamette's board unanimously voted to reject Weyerhaeuser's takeover bid.
December 21, 2000	Weyerhaeuser proposed to nominate four candidates for election to Willamette's board.
	Willamette set the annual meeting for Thursday, June 7, 2001, making shareholders of record as of the close of business on Monday, April, 16, 2001, eligible to vote.
March 16, 2001	Wyser-Pratte Management sent a letter to the president of Willamette expressing its dissatisfaction with the manner in which the board of Willamette handled Weyerhaeuser's offer and vowed to fight Willamette over its "just say no" takeover defense.
May 7	Willamette raised its offer to $50 per share.
May 11	Wyser-Pratte sent a follow-up letter again denouncing Willamette's "just say no" defense.

May 31	Willamette sent a letter to Willamette shareholders asking them to elect Weyerhaeuser nominees at the June 7th annual meeting so that the two companies could begin to negotiate a definitive merger agreement.
June 6	Wyser-Pratte sent a letter to Willamette questioning its valuation models.
June 7	Weyerhaeuser got its slate of three directors elected to the Willamette board.
Sept. 14	Weyerhaeuser extended its offer to buy shares in WLL for the sixth time.
Sept. 28	The founding family of Willamette said it is willing to negotiate a deal with Weyerhaeuser and would seriously consider an offer of $55 per share.
December 13	Weyerhaeuser made its "final" offer for Willamette boosting its cash bid to $55 per share.
December 14	Wyser-Pratte urged Willamette directors to back the new $55 per share bid.
January 3, 2002	Wyser-Pratte Management urged the Willamette directors not to use seemingly "erroneous" synergies as a pretext to do the proposed Georgia Pacific transaction to defeat the Weyerhaeuser offer.
January 4, 2002	Willamette rejected the $55 offer and opted to pursue a transaction with Georgia Pacific involving its building product business. Wyser-Pratte Management announced that it was commencing a class action lawsuit against Willamette's directors for breach of fiduciary duty in connection with their announcement rejecting the $55 tender offer from Weyerhaeuser.

January 8	An Oregon judge granted Wyser-Pratte's request to expedite the case and ruled that Willamette must give shareholders at least 48-hours notice before closing any alternative transactions with Georgia Pacific.
January 10	Wyser-Pratte Management sends a letter to Chubb as the carrier of the D&O coverage for Willamette to inform the company of its concerns that recent actions by Willamette's directors may constitute a breach of their fiduciary duties to shareholders.
	CalPERS, at the urging of Wyser-Pratte Management, called on the board of directors of Willamette to give up its fight with Weyerhaeuser.
January 21	Willamette announces it has accepted a bid from Weyerhaeuser of $55.50 per share.

IV. Subsequent Events

February 2, 2002	97 percent of Willamette is tendered to WY.
March 15	Weyerhaeuser completes the acquisition of Willamette.

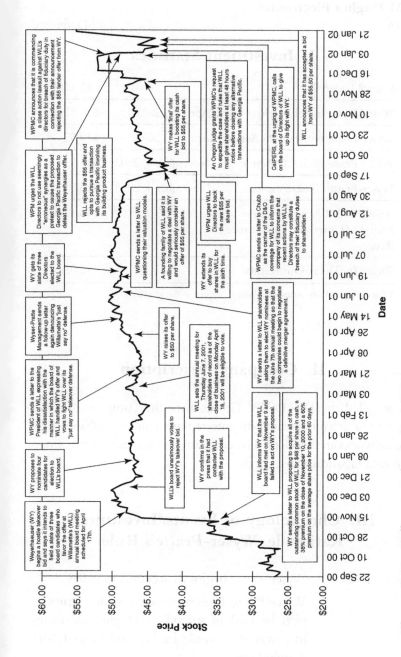

Figure C.21 Willamette Industries, Inc. (USA)

GM Hughes Electronics
USA   Defensive

I. Investment Statistics

Capital Invested*		$5.10M
Wyser-Pratte Initial Purchase	April 11, 2003	$10.52
Wyser-Pratte Initiates CG Action	April 11, 2003	$10.52
Wyser-Pratte Ends CG Action	November 4, 2003	$16.33
Wyser-Pratte Closes Position	November 4, 2003	$16.33
Annualized Rate of Return— Period of Corporate Governance Action		46.12%
Ticket In/Ticket Out Return		42.02%

* For all Wyser-Pratte managed accounts invested in this security.

II. Company Description

Now called the DIRECTV Group, Inc., the company provides digital multichannel television entertainment and broadband satellite networks and services. The company also provides global video and data broadcasting services.

III. Chronology of Events/Investment Rationale/Wyser-Pratte's Role

April 11, 2003   Wyser-Pratte begins to accumulate shares.

Wyser-Pratte takes a proactive stance against a plan by GM to spinoff its Hughes subsidiary in a way that would be harmful to its GMH shareholders.

	Wyser-Pratte seeks legal action, planning to force GMH tracking shareholders to sell a 34 percent interest in Hughes to the News Corp. for $6.6 billion.
April 28	Wyser-Pratte believes that GM would receive superior compensation than planned for GMH holders. Guy Wyser-Pratte says that this would violate GM's own Certificate of Incorporation, which prohibits discrimination between GM and GMH shareholders.
	Wyser-Pratte initiates legal action against General Motors board. Suit alleges that GM directors breached fiduciary duties by approving a transaction favoring GM pension fund over other shareholders in the News Corp. acquisition.
August 22	GM plans to seek shareholder approval for its proposal to spinoff its wholly owned subsidiary, Hughes Electronics Corp.
October 6	GM shareholders give strong approval to spinoff Hughes Electronics.
November 4	Wyser-Pratte closes its position.

IV. Subsequent Events

December 22	GM, Hughes, and News Corporation complete Hughes transactions. Litigation is still pending.

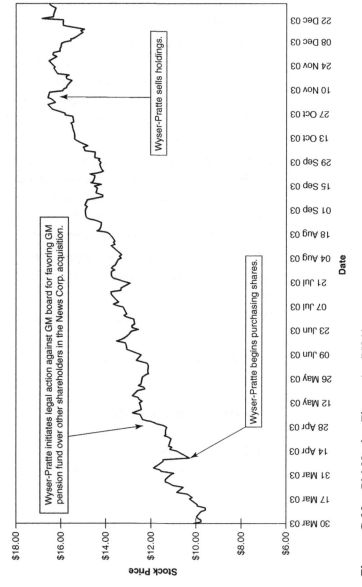

Figure C.22 GM Hughes Electronics (USA)

The following labels appear within the figure:

- Wyser-Pratte sells holdings.
- Wyser-Pratte initiates legal action against GM board for favoring GM pension fund over other shareholders in the News Corp. acquisition.
- Wyser-Pratte begins purchasing shares.

Stock Price axis: $18.00, $16.00, $14.00, $12.00, $10.00, $8.00, $6.00

Date axis: 30 Mar 03, 17 Mar 03, 31 Mar 03, 14 Apr 03, 28 Apr 03, 12 May 03, 26 May 03, 09 Jun 03, 23 Jun 03, 07 Jul 03, 21 Jul 03, 04 Aug 03, 18 Aug 03, 01 Sep 03, 15 Sep 03, 29 Sep 03, 13 Oct 03, 27 Oct 03, 10 Nov 03, 24 Nov 03, 08 Dec 03, 22 Dec 03

Prosodie S.A.
France

I. Investment Statistics

Capital Invested*		$38.70M
Wyser-Pratte Initial Purchase	December 17, 1999	€48.00
Wyser-Pratte Initiates CG Action	March 19, 2004	€22.50
Wyser-Pratte Ends CG Action	March 21, 2007	€25.25
Wyser-Pratte Closes Position	March 26, 2007	€25.25
Annualized Rate of Return—Period of Corporate Governance Action		4.07%
Ticket In/Ticket Out Return		−2.18%

* For all W-P managed accounts invested in this security.

II. Company Description

Prosodie develops and operates telecommunications services and IT solutions that allow customers, clients, partners and/or employees of even the largest public and private organizations to access and exchange information. Prosodie also produces and delivers information to the general public in three activities: (1) weather forecast through the two brands Meteo Consult and La Chaine Meteo (TV channel), (2) horse racing through GENY courses, and (3) exam results through France-examen. These four brands form its PROSODIE Info unit. In North America, Prosodie Interactive, a regional operating unit of Prosodie, provides value-added ASP eCommerce, interactive voice (IVR/CRM), and Web and data solutions for businesses. Prosodie also owns 100 percent of nCryptone, leader in strong authentication solutions (ISO Banking card size) embedding an energy source.

III. Chronology of Events/Investment Rationale/W-P's Role

March 19, 2004	Wyser-Pratte announced a 10.27 percent holding in telecom operator Prosodie SA. After witnessing years of management failing to realize maximum value for Prosodie shareholders, Wyser-Pratte entered the stock.
December 27, 2004	With regards to Prosodie's recent corporate repurchase offer, Wyser-Pratte elected to retain the entirety of it shares, which then amounted to 12.8 percent of the company's capital stock.
January 28, 2005	Guy Wyser-Pratte was appointed administrator of Prosodie by the company. Guy Wyser-Pratte would occupy the position until Prosodie's General Shareholder's Meeting approved the 2006 financial figures.
June 14, 2006	On behalf of Wyser-Pratte and himself, Prosodie director Stephen Pierce stood up at the Prosodie Annual General Meeting and challenged founder, chairman, and CEO Alain Bernard about poor corporate governance at the company.
July 2006	Wyser-Pratte introduced the economic consulting firm Stern Stewart to chairman, and CEO Alain Bernard. Bernard reacted favorably to conducting an EVA review.
October 27, 2006	Prosodie founder, chairman, and CEO Alain Bernard agreed to sell his 46 percent stake in the company to Apax Partners for €20 per share.

October 2006	BT Group plc contacted Wyser-Pratte to express their interest in acquiring Prosodie. BT Group stated that it was "surprised at the announcement that chairman Bernard had sold his shares without fully exploring [their] offer." Additionally, BT stated they had offered €27 per share for Prosodie.
November 2006	At Wyser-Pratte's insistence, Prosodie names an indedendent expert to evaluate the fairness of Apax's bid.
December 1, 2006	Apax Partners plans to offer €23.40 per share to buy the shares of Prosodie it does not already own.
February 5, 2007	Under pressure from Wyser-Pratte, Apax Partners raised their bid to €25.25 per share. Wyser-Pratte stated that it will tender its shares at that level.

IV. Subsequent Events

March 2007	Wyser-Pratte tendered all of its shares to Apax Partners' buyout offer.

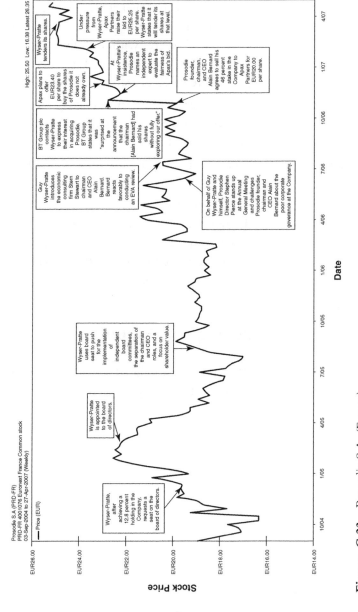

Figure C.23 Prosodie S.A. (France)

Notes

Chapter 1

1. Morgan D. Evans, *Arbitrage in Domestic Securities in the United States* (W. Nyack, 1967).
2. Ibid., p. 14.
3. Ibid. p. 71.
4. "More Brokerage Firms Try the Frenetic, Risky Business of Arbitrage," *The Wall Street Journal*, April 7, 1967, p. 1.
5. "Huge Profits Out of Tiny Margins," *Business Week*, March 28, 1966 p. 114.

Chapter 2

1. "Huge Profits Out of Tiny Margins," *Business Week*, p. 120.
2. IRS Code, SEC 368 a (1) A-F.
3. Reference to technical charts, and knowledge of the probable size of the Arbitrage Community's position, are helpful indications in determining the downside risk.
4. A clue to the magnitude of this potential danger may be found in the monthly "short interest" figures published by both the New York and the American Stock exchanges.

5. The purported reason for the termination of the merger agreement between White Cross Stores and Zale Corporation.

6. Kenneth Lewis Edlow, "The Role of the Arbitrageur in the Investment Field" (Unpublished thesis of the Institute of Investment Banking, 1968), p. 14.

7. New York Stock Exchange, op. cit.

8. Op. cit., Rule #325(b).

9. "Post-Merger Selling Pressure." The Value Line Merger Evaluation Service, May 5, 1969, p. 1.

10. Richard H. Baer and Alan B. Slifka, "Does Arbitrage Create Institutional Opportunities?" *The Institutional Investor*, April 1967, p. 40.

Chapter 3

1. New York Stock Exchange Constitution & Rules, Rule #325(b).

2. Per $10 market value of security, the $3 would be the "haircut" under the 30 percent rule. The remaining $7 ("aggregate indebtedness") would incur a charge of 1/16, or $0,438, and thus 4.38 percent of market value.

3. There is always a technical oversupply situation in any aborted merger, as arbitrageurs do not wish to become investors in the common stock of the Bride.

4. While only roughly 70 percent of this amount represents borrowed funds, an opportunity cost is computed on the remaining 30 percent, which is capital.

5. Taking the ITT common at the price of $58\frac{5}{8}$.

6. Utilization of a "payback" concept implies a constant dividend rate on the common. Thus, a period of increasing dividend rates, such as ITT's, would increase the "payback periods" delineated. Nevertheless the basic assumption provides a common denominator.

7. Taking into account the adjustment for the stock dividend.

8. A fractional share would be sold by the exchange agent.

9. Maximum market value in Warner Lambert common.

10. Maximum market value in Warner Lambert common.

11. The maximum distribution of Frawley.

12. On the same day that the price of Alloys was $19\frac{1}{2}$.

13. Which could presumably have been expected should British balance of payments have improved.

14. The premium on Security Sterling was still 25 percent.

15. New shareholders approved merger, NYSE declared long/sale.

16. Received blotter.

17. Geometric mean of monthly broker loan rate—Dec. 1979 through March 1980.

18. Payable 2/27/81 to holders of record 1/9/81.

19. Payable 3/14/81 to holders of record 2/25/81.

20. Under the alternative net capital requirement the broker/dealer has the option of:

    1. Deducting 15 percent of the market value of the long position plus 30 percent of the market value of the short position that exceeds 25 percent of the long position, or,
    2. Deducting 30 percent of the greater of the market value of the long or short positions.

    In this example, option 2 is preferred. The "haircut" is $1,443 vs. $1,765.50 for option 1.

    The alternative net capital requirement also calls for a reserve requirement of the greater of $100,000 or 4 percent of the aggregate debit items computed in accordance with exhibit A 17 CFR 240. 15L3-3a. This formula is based on customer-related situations. It does not apply to a proprietary risk-arbitrage position. It is assumed for this presentation that the broker's or dealer's customer-related business is large enough to necessitate minimum net capital greater than $100,000.

21. New shareholders approved the merger and the NYSE made a long/sale ruling the transfer of shares were effective 3/9/81.

22. Under the aggregate indebtedness method, brokers and dealers are required to deduct a 30 percent haircut on the greater market value of the long or short risk-arbitrage position. In addition, aggregate indebtedness cannot exceed 1500 percent of net capital as per 17 CFR240. 15c3-1.

23. Ibid.

24. Geometric mean of monthly margin account rate December 1979 through March 1980 the opportunity cost rate would be less than this, but to simplify calculations, the margin rate is used.

25. Margin of 50 percent is required on long and on short Federal requirement.

26. House maintenance margin requirement is 30 percent long + 30 percent on short position.

27. House margin for bonafide arbitrage position is 10 percent on long.

28. For purposes of this offer, the purchaser shall be deemed to have purchased tendered shares when, as, and if the purchaser gives oral or written notice to the depositary of its acceptance of a tender of such shares" (as quoted from prospectus). This date is assumed to be the "Blotter Receive Date" as follows:

Dividends	Ex Date	Stk Record
.40	Jul 10	Jul 16

29. Dividends = ($.65) 100 Shares Record Sept. 10
    ($.65) 38 Shares Record Dec. 14
    ($.21429) 38 Shares Record Jan. 31
    $98

30. The total number of shares issued by Dow was determined by dividing $260,000,000 by the average closing price per share of Dow Common Stock on the New York Stock Exchange Composite Tape for the 20 trading days immediately preceding the merger. There were 23,303,139 shares outstanding as of January 29, 1981. At a March 10, 1981 price of $35\frac{1}{2}$ the terms of the merger come out to 1 share Richardson-Merrell = .31429 shares of Dow Chemical, which is very close to the actual terms of .31158 shares of Dow Chemical.

31. "Haircut" = (.15) ($3900) + (.30) [(1100.5) − (.25) (3900)] = $740.

32. "Haircut" = 30 percent of market value of options underlying
    security
    = (.30)(130)($54.125)
    = $2111

Chapter 4

1. Rules and Regulations, SEC Act of 1934, Rule 10 b. 4, "Short Tendering of Securities."

2. The task was often simplified due to the fact that, barring unusual loyalties, institutions tend to act in a similar fashion in response to cash bids. In one way or another, the consensus on their activity usually seeps out.

3. The SEC was prompted to act by virtue of the fact that in a partial tender by Paul Revere Corp. for Avco Corp., more Avco shares were tendered than there were outstanding.

4. Boiler plate contingency clauses permit withdrawal of offer prior to date shares are purchased or paid for, necessitating application of "haircut" until proceeds are received.

5. Haircut = ($5400 × .15) + .306 [(2538−(.25) (5400)] = $1166 vs. 5400 × .30 = $1600

6. Conditional on 5,400,000 shares being tendered. Consecutive separate tender pools kept latecomers from receiving cash and assured those already in the pool of getting cash.

7. Haircut = (.15) ($1467) + .30 (433)−(.25) (1467)

8. Haircut = (.15) ($1467) + .30 ($898)−(.25) ($1467)

Chapter 5

1. Such a short sale would result in the loss of the $1.50 dividend that would be simultaneously received on the B preferred long via the exchange.

2. IRS Code of 1953, Section 331.

Chapter 6

1. Martin Lipton and Erica H. Steinberger. *Takeovers and Freezeouts* (Law Journal Seminar New York, 1978).

2. *Edgar vs. Mite Corp.*, 14 BNA Securities Regulation and Law Report 1147 (June 25, 1982).

Chapter 7

1. "Broker and Head of Gerber Spar on Offer by Anderson, Clayton," *The New York Times*, August 1, 1977.

2. Alex Taylor, "Broker Challenges Gerber on Takeover," *Detroit Free Press*, July 28, 1977.

3. Priscilla S. Meyer, "Cancelled Poll of McGraw-Hill Holders Signals End to American Express Bid," *The Wall Street Journal*, February 26, 1979.

4. "McGraw-Hill's 'Let Them Eat Cake' Attitude," *Institutional Investor*, June 1979.

5. Richard Phalon, "A Modest Proposal," *Forbes*, April 30, 1979.

6. Jack Etkin, "Shareholders Criticize ERC Board's Action on Merger," *The Kansas City Times*, April 25, 1980.

7. "ERC Corp. Directors, As Expected, Endorse Getty $97-a-Share Bid," *The Wall Street Journal*, June 6, 1980.

8. "Amax Receives Takeover Offer for $4 Billion," *The Wall Street Journal*, March 1981.

9. Priscilla S. Meyer and Theodore Lowen, "Best Interest of Stockholders?" *Forbes*, June 1982.

10. Bryan Burrough, "Houston Natural Gas Chairman Quits; Transco Energy President Is Successor," *The Wall Street Journal*, 1984.

11. Tom Scott, Barbara Shook, "Lay Move to HNG Sparks Top Reshuffling," *Houston Chronicle*, June 7, 1984.

12. "American Takeover Defences: Stand Still, You," *The Economist*, April 30, 1988, p. 79.

13. Michael Siconolfi, "Arbitrage Concern Brought Back to Life by Founder's Son: Wyser-Pratte, Originally Opened in 1929, Returns Despite Lull in Takeovers," *The Wall Street Journal*, February 12, 1991.

14. Diana B. Henriques, "Making a Difference: A Nemesis of Management Strikes Again," *The New York Times*, August 16, 1992.

15. "Why It's Not Smart to Rile Guy Wyser-Pratte," *Institutional Investor*, May 1992.

16. Jeff Cossette, "Rexene, Turn On Your Red Light," *Investor Relations*, August 1997, p. 25.

17. Michael Davis, "Major Shareholder Urges Pennzoil Deal: Resistance to UPR's Offer Questioned," *Houston Chronicle*, November 13, 1997.

18. "Shareholders Gag on Pennzoil's Pill," *USA Today*, December 2, 1997.

19. Peg O'Hara, "A Poison Pill Revolt," Council of Institutional Investors, December 3, 1998, vol. 3, no. 40.

20. Jonathan R. Macey, "Shareholder Rights Will Be Next Battleground," *The National Law Journal*, February 16, 1998, vol. 20, no. 25.

21. Seth Goodchild and Daniel J. Buzzetta, "Shareholder Rights By-Law Amendment," *New York Law Journal*, October 30, 1997, vol. 218, no. 85.

22. "Cet Ancien des Marines Terrorise Nos Patrons," *Capital*, April 2000, p. 22.

Chapter 8

1. Evans, loc. cit., p. 32.

Appendix A

1. Report of the Investment Bankers' Association to the Commissioner of Internal Revenue, October 8, 1963. For a later analysis see D. Gralai and M. I. Schueller, "Pricing of Warrants and the Value of the Firm," *Journal of Finance*, 33 (December 1978) and references cited there.

2. Ibid.

Bibliography

Books, Periodicals, Proxy Statements

Abrams, Alvan, *Arbitrage in Taxes and Securities*, New York, 1957.

Baer, Richard H., and Slifka, Alan B., "Does Arbitrage Create Institutional Opportunities?" *The Institutional Investor*, April, 1967, pp. 24–28.

Bellemore, Douglas H., *Investments: Principle/Practices/Analysis*, 4th Edition, South Western Publishing Company, Cincinnati, 1974.

Edlow, Kenneth Lewis, "The Role of the Arbitrageur in the Investment Field," unpublished thesis, Investment Banking Institute, 1968.

Evans, Morgan D., *Arbitrage in Domestic Securities in the United States*, W. Nyack, 1967.

"A Feast for Arbitrageurs," *Fortune*, February, 1969, pp. 165–166.

"Federal Trade Commission and the Courts," *Topical Law Reports*, Volume 3, Commerce Corporation Clearing House, Chicago, 1975.

Graham, Benjamin and Dodd, David, *Security Analysis*, 4th Edition, McGraw Hill, New York, 1962.

Hieronymus, Thomas A., *Economics of Futures Trading*, 2nd Edition, Commodity Research Bureau, Inc., New York, 1977.

"High Profits out of Tiny Margins," *Business Week*, March 28, 1966, pp. 114–120.

Interpretation Handbook, Regulation and Surveillance, The New York Stock Exchange, Inc., 1976.

Joint Proxy Statement and Prospectus of Pullman Incorporated and Wheelabrator-Frye, Inc., October 9, 1980.

Laws, Margaret, "Risk and Reward—The Arbitrage Game Provides Plenty of Both," *Barrons*, November 30, 1981.

NASD Manual, Commerce Corporation Clearing House, Chicago, 1977.

New York Stock Exchange Guide, Commerce Corporation Clearing House, 1980.

Prospectus of Frawley Enterprises, Inc., March 26, 1970.

Prospectus and Joint Proxy Statement of J. Ray McDermott & Co., Inc. February 22, 1978.

Proxy Statement of

Alloys Unlimited, Inc., May 26, 1970.

Beech-Nut Life Savers, Inc., September 1, 1967.

Bendix Corporation, February 15, 1980.

C.I.T. Financial Corporation, December 17, 1979.

Canada Dry Corporation, June 3, 1968.

City Investing Company, February 17, 1967.

Dart & Craft, Inc., February 19, 1981.

Exxon Corporation, June 21, 1979.

Fluor Corporation, April 6, 1981.

General Electric Corporation, 1976.

Grand Metropolitan Limited, April 18, 1980.

Grand Pacific Enterprises (U.S.) Inc., February 14, 1981.

Kennecott Copper Corporation, November 29, 1977.

Landis Machine Company, March 14, 1968.

New England Nuclear Corporation, February 6, 1981.

Oxford Chemical Corporation, December 2, 1966.

Richardson-Merrell, Inc., February 5, 1981.

Rosario Resources Corporation, December 27, 1979.

St. Joe Minerals Corporation, June 19, 1981.

UTD Corporation, August 20, 1968.

Report of the Investment Bankers Association of America to the Commissioner of Internal Revenue, October 8, 1963.

Securities Credit Transactions: Regulation X, Regulation G, Regulation T, Regulation U, Board of Governors of the Federal Reserve System, June, 1977.

Trade Regulation Reporter, Commerce Corporation Clearing House, Chicago.

Twentieth Century-Fox Film Corporation, 1980 Annual Report.

Welles, Chris "Inside the Arbitrage Game," *Institutional Investor*, August, 1981.

A current source for research and other information on mergers and acquisitions and related issues is *Mergers and Acquisitions: The Journal of Corporate Venture*, published by Information for Industry, Philadelphia, PA. The following citations are of special interest:

Austin, Douglas V., "A Tender Offer Bibliography, 1976–1978," Volume 14, Number 1, Spring 1979.

Austin, Douglas V., "Tender Offer Update: 1978–1979," Volume 15, Number 2, Summer 1980.

Austin, Douglas V., and Mandula, Mark S., "Tender Offer Trends in the 1980's," Volume 16, Number 3, Fall 1981.

Bowers, Thomas L., "Tender Offers: A Guide for the 1980's," Volume 16, Number 2, Summer 1981.

D'Alco, Joseph S., "What Kills the Deal?" Volume 3, March–April 1968.

Friedman, Howard M., "The Validity of State Tender Offer Statutes" Volume 13, Number 1, Spring 1978.

Friedman, Howard M., "The Validity of State Tender Offer Statutes: An Update," Volume 13, Number 3, Fall 1978.

Long, Lynn Thompson, "Director Fiduciaries: Protecting Shareholders' Interests," Volume 14, Number 4, Winter 1980.

Milefsky, Norman R., "The Hybrid Acquisition: A New Tax Concept in Acquisition Planning," Volume 15, Number 3, Fall 1980.

Phalon, Richard, "Tipping the Takeover Balance of Power," Volume 16, Number 4, Winter 1982.

Reilly, Robert F., "Pricing an Acquisition: A Fifteen Step Methodology," Volume 14, Number 2, Summer 1979.

Shay, Scott A., "Setting the Right Premium in an Efficient Market," Volume 16, Number 1, Spring 1981.

"Takeovers: A Survey of Corporate Defense Strategies," Volume 15, Number 1, Spring 1980.

Von Bauer, Eric E., "Meaningful Risk and Return Criteria for Strategic Investment Decisions," Volume 15, Number 4, Winter 1981.

Wallner, Nicholas, "Leveraged Buyouts: A Review of the State of the Art, Part 1," Volume 14, Number 3, Fall 1979.

Index

Printed and bound by CPI Group (UK) Ltd, Croydon, CR0 4YY

09/06/2025

14685912-0001